# ALIGN
## YOUR BUSINESS

How to find your *Windows Of Opportunity*
and claim the Next Level of YOU!

## CANDICE HOZZA

# ALIGN
## YOUR BUSINESS

How to find your *Windows Of Opportunity*
and claim the Next Level of YOU!

## CANDICE HOZZA

Paperback ISBN: 978-0-9993991-9-4
E-book ISBN: 978-1-955811-00-2
LCCN: 2021914251

First paperback edition: September 2021

Written in partnership with Bryna Haynes/WorldChangers Media
Cover photo by Jennifer Alyse / www.jenniferalysephoto.com
Cover design by Curtis Silverwood
Interior layout by WorldChangers Media

Published by WorldChangers Media
PO Box 83, Foster, RI 02825
www.WorldChangers.Media

# People are saying ...

"It's so important for business owners to trust their intuition and embrace the deeper parts of themselves. This book makes it easy and natural. It's light, funny and very human. And at the same time, it's absolutely to the point."

– **Sarah McCrum, author of** *Love Money, Money Loves You*

"WOO Baby! Candy takes the expression of 'seeing the best in people' to a deeper and more appreciative level in *Align Your Business,* and shows us how to tap our inner—and often unrealized—resources. In over thirty years in business, I've 'heard" my intuition, but I didn't know how to truly listen; only in hindsight did I know what the messages truly meant. Candy helps you discover how to use your inner knowing to make the journey not only easier, but more impactful. Candy's distinctions are not your typical business theory; they come from her own experiences and are told conversationally in a way that makes you take pause and reflect on the role your own intuition has placed in your life, both personally and professionally. She takes concepts that I thought were beyond the limits of possibility and brings them home. Take this moment to not only realize your WOO, but to truly listen to Candy as she takes you on an undeniable journey through your own past and future. By the time you turn the last page, you, too, will know how to Align Your Business with your own true 'WOO.'"

– **Steve Linder, Founder of Neuro Strategies International & Strategic Brain**

"What a beautiful combination of woo and practical action! *Align Your Business* helps the reader release money blocks to create more flow, abundance, and joy. If you are ready to monetize your mission and gain clear insights from your intuitive knowing and your personal Akashic Records, look no further! Candy really hit it out of the park on this one. I can't wait to share this valuable book with my clients and community."

– **Amber Dugger, Founder of Profit for Keeps**™

"This book comes at an important time, as more and more business owners are discovering that their heart and soul holds the key to their momentum and impact. Candice has produced a powerful way for entrepreneurs to tap into their fullest gifts and shift spiritual gears no matter what they are going through."

– **Simon Lovell, Entrepreneur.com contributor, creator of the Super High Performance Formula**

"I have always known that my business has its own voice and heartbeat, yet I struggled for years to learn how to truly listen to it. The tools Candice shares in *Align Your Business* have helped remove the barriers and blocks that kept me in a suspended state. Through this work, I'm finding *my* way, and *our* way (me and my business), which are different than the ways I've been conditioned to approach and relate to my business in the past. If you're an entrepreneur, creative, or visionary, Candice's work is the bridge back home to understanding and embracing the spirit of your business; she will show you how to trust that your unique way of tapping into its energy for clarity, direction, and financial abundance."

– **Monica Rodgers, Co-Founder, The Revelation Project**

"*Align Your Business* is an absolute must-read for all business owners. There comes a time for every business owner when they feel out of alignment and uncertain about their mission, purpose, and focus. Having both coached and personally worked with Candice as a client, I know firsthand how powerful her work is—and it's all here in this book. This work will absolutely change your life and business for the better!"

– **Jeannie Spiro, Business Coach**

"Candice's work is a guiding light and force for good in my life and business. This essential book will gently lead you through her healing process and leave you feeling refreshed by her words. It's for anybody who is ready to listen to their intuition and use that as a springboard to leap into their next and most compelling future."

– **Sage Polaris, Copywriter to the Stars and Launch Strategist**

# Dedication

This book is devoted to your inner light.
Let the light that shines in you warm the hearts of others.

# Table of Contents

# Introduction

When I was four years old, my mother brought me to a baby shower.

The other kids stayed home with their babysitters, but I always went everywhere with my parents. They'd waited ten years for the chance to adopt me, and they never left me behind. It was super sweet—but in our small Pennsylvania town, where everyone knew everyone (and their family for three generations back), you really had to be on your best behavior in public.

And so, there we were, in the basement of our local church, and I was bored.

I liked being a "good girl," so when my mom directed me toward one of the hard, wooden folding chairs, I immediately wriggled up into the seat. My feet, in their black patent-leather shoes and white ruffled socks, swung several inches above the floor. The chair dug into the backs of my legs, making my calves tingle. Looking at all the pretty decorations kept me occupied for a while, but I was starting to squirm.

When there was a break in the conversation (and it was safe to interrupt) I finally said to my mom, "I don't see the baby. Where is it?"

"Inside that lady's belly," she said, gesturing at the mother-to-be, who was opening presents on the other side of the room.

I was quite fascinated by the fact that there was a baby living inside another person. What was it like, I wondered, living inside a belly?

Then, I felt a presence—a sweet little girl. I knew that this girl lived inside of the woman who was getting all the presents. And, of course, being a little girl myself, I started to play with her.

My mother noticed nothing until the shower was over. I probably just looked like I was daydreaming. As everyone was packing up, I walked over to the mom-to-be and asked her if I could touch her belly.

"Of course," said the woman.

The moment I laid my hand on her, I felt instantly connected to the life inside her. I could feel that little girl's presence even more clearly than before.

"I love your little girl," I said. "She's going to come tonight so that means I'll get to play with her tomorrow!"

Her reaction wasn't what I had expected. She looked confused, and a bit scared. It was the first "hairy eyeball" look I can remember getting.

Now, this was in the 1960s, when we didn't have the technology to determine a child's sex beforehand. This woman had no idea she was having a girl! Eventually, she found her voice and muttered, "Um … thank you."

As she moved away, my mother—who had no idea what had just transpired—came to get me, and we headed for the car.

The next day, I was sitting on our living room floor, taking Barbie and Ken on a pretend date, when the phone rang. My mom dashed into the kitchen to answer it—we had a pink rotary phone with one of those extra-long cords—and I soon heard her exclaim, "Oh, congratulations! That happened quickly. And it's a girl? How lovely … and Candy said *what?*"

My mom, still holding the phone to her ear, came around the corner. She stared at me, nodding and *um-hmm*-ing while the new grandmother on the other end of the line informed her of what I'd said at the shower yesterday.

I wasn't sure what was wrong with what I'd done … but I had definitely done *something* wrong, because my mom never got that look on her face when she was happy with me.

*I'm never going to do that again*, I promised myself. And I didn't for many years.

At four years old, I thought everyone could feel and sense energy as naturally as I did. But that day, I learned that if you use your intuition and tell people about it, you're going to get that look—the one that says, *that's weird. You're scary.*

I don't blame my mom at all for this moment. She simply had no idea what to do with the information she was receiving. At that time, talk of "paranormal activity" and "sixth senses" was reserved for art films and hippie love-ins. Certainly normal, hard-working families from a Pennsylvania steel town didn't believe in that sort of thing.

Maybe you've had similar experiences—times when you've just known things, heard things, or seen things that others didn't have access to. Maybe, like me, you turned off those "extra" senses as a child in order to manage others' comfort levels.

But here's the thing: your intuition is a gift from the Divine. You can hide it, or turn down the volume, but it never leaves you completely.

***

There have been so many times in my life where I've received messages from the Divine—through angels, signs, visions, even whole otherworldly conversations. The gift that was blossoming inside my four-year-old self was kept in the dark for many years but always reemerged in the moments when I most needed guidance. I'll share many of these amazing stories with you throughout this book.

What's really magical is that, since I decided to "let the cat out of the bag" in my mid-thirties, my intuitive and energetic gifts have become my primary guidance system in every aspect of my life—including my business, where I've guided hundreds of entrepreneurs and leaders to harness their own intuition and inner knowing.

There is so much more available to us as energy beings than what we can assimilate with our five senses. We are multidimensional, complicated, messy incarnations of the Divine, and we are built to receive guidance from that source. It's not weird, or crazy. It's who we are.

Every human being—including you—has access to a realm of information beyond this three-dimensional world. When you learn how to access that body of wisdom and apply it to your business, you will move into a place where you can be more purposeful, discerning, and more empowered than ever before.

To me, goosebumps are one of the ways I know my gifts are working. Every hair on my body will stand up. My skin will get tingly. And I will know that somehow, in some way, I'm in the presence of the Divine—so it's time to listen.

# Who is listening?

I once went to a conference where Deepak Chopra, author of *The Seven Spiritual Laws of Success*, was speaking. As he took the stage, the audience was chattering excitedly.

His first words were, "Who is listening to me?"

The room fell into a guilty hush.

"Who is listening to me?" he asked again. "Is it your ears? Is it your brain that's processing what you're hearing and translating it? Or is it someone else? *Who* is listening?"

The "who" that Dr. Chopra was referring to, of course, was our consciousness. The part of us that is separate from our brains, that can observe our thoughts and actions as they play out. The part of us that our intuition speaks to, and through.

You've likely picked up this book because you're a visionary, creative, or conscious entrepreneur who wants to increase your intuitive capacity in your business. I'm happy to say that you're in the right place.

Heart-centered, mission-driven, purpose-guided … If this is your path, you are already tapped into something greater than just the next shiny product or idea. You want to feel *aligned* in your business—with your mission and offers, but also with your soul. You want to become more of who you truly are, and transform the world while you're doing it.

I find that most heart-centered creators are already using intuition in their business—they're just not doing it with conscious competence. Perhaps this is you, as well. You know that when you lean into your "gut" feelings, you make better choices and create better results. You know that when you get those goosebumps it's time to get out of your head and pay attention.

And, you might be hiding these gifts, as I did for so long. Maybe you've kept them a secret so you don't have to deal with those judgmental "hairy-eyeball" looks. Maybe you're terrified that your clients or customers will think you're too "woo-woo." Maybe you're still carrying around some old ideas that being intuitive makes you less trustworthy, reliable, or competent.

It's time to come out of the "woo closet," my love.

You're not weird. You're not an alien. You are simply a human built to receive the energy of All That Is. The information you receive through your intuition isn't what's keeping you stuck and confused. The fact that you're *not* listening to those messages is the problem.

Intuition is the jet fuel that will take your business from "pretty good" to "OMG!" When you align your business using your own intuitive gifts (whether you're currently aware of them or not), you begin to perceive the WOOs—Windows of Opportunity—that are constantly opening up new possibilities for you. You move out of stuckness, resistance, and fear, and into flow. You learn to trust yourself and the Universe. It's a beautiful way to live.

And yet, too many entrepreneurs and visionaries try to deny their intuition. They make "logical" decisions that look good on paper but don't *feel* aligned. They rely on their intellect, rather than their intuitive intelligence. I can't even count the number of times clients have told me, "My gut feeling said no, but I did it anyway, and now I'm *so far* from where I wanted to be!"

Your business is your vehicle for conscious awakening. It's part of what you came here to do! And so, it deserves more than just your eyes and ears. It deserves more than your analytical mind. It deserves the "who" that is "you"—your consciousness.

When you align your business using your intuitive guidance, you will always know which choice is the highest and best for your business and life. You'll know how to use your gifts in their most powerful capacity and honor your life force as you apply them. You'll know when to say "yes" to an offer or opportunity, and when to say a big, beautiful "no."

In this book, I'll share with you the proven pathway I've created to help you release your blocks around receiving and integrating intuitive guidance, integrating your Soul Values, and uncovering your unique blueprint for wealth. I'll also share how you can access the most powerful storehouse of soul-aligned information available to you: the Akashic Records.

When you're done reading this book, you will get to know and love yourself and your business in a whole new way. You'll have the tools to align with the purpose, path, and profits you were always meant to enjoy. You'll finally understand how to step out of the "apple spin" that's kept you locked into a repetitive cycle of stress and resistance in your business, and how to recognize your misaligned patterns before they become major blocks. You'll learn how to tap into the internal drivers that control your behaviors so you can live in greater alignment with your value system. And, you will learn to read your personal Akashic Records to make consciously aligned decisions in your business every day.

Most of all, this book will give you the insight, framework, and support you need to take your intuition from a "sometimes" thing to your trustworthy inner GPS, and step into the highest and best expression of *you*. That framework is my Align Your Business system.

My wish for you is that, no matter where you are in your life and business, you always know there's a WOO for you.

With love and light,

Candy Hozza
Lancaster, PA
September 2021

# ~ 1 ~

# Hozza Hears a WOO

*I* would never have embraced my path as an intuitive and business owner if it hadn't been for cancer.

After shutting down my intuition as a little girl, it made its way back into my awareness in various ways. I'd taken a parapsychology class in college and had a mind-blowing experience with a medium who channeled my great-grandmother. I'd experienced profound moments of "knowing" around major decisions. At thirty-three, I read a book about how to connect with guides and angels, and began to practice using my intuitive powers again. When my son, Phoenix, was young, I took a course on how to read the Akashic Records—my first introduction to the modality.

One way or another, though, I always went back into hiding. By the time I was in my early thirties, I was communicating with my angels, departed loved ones, and spiritual guides regularly. Eventually, I learned to read my own Akashic Records ... but I never spoke about any of it.

It was like I was in "woo jail." I put myself in a protective box and tried my best to throw away the key.

Part of my reason for hiding my "woo" was my job. I was the Associate Director of the Center for Student Involvement and Leadership (CSIL) at a state university in Pennsylvania. Basically, I handled anything and everything related to events: leadership training, homecoming, speaker visits, fraternity and sorority programming, you name it. I was also in charge of the Freshman Year Experience which was a freshman retention program in the Housing and Residential Programs. I loved the students, and it was challenging work. We had a small budget, and there was never enough time in the day. I regularly ate lunch at my desk while meeting with students.

The home front was also a challenge. My husband traveled often for work, so I was managing the household and my son's schedule on top of my insane workload. My daughter, Carlie, was in college at the time. It felt like it was all on me.

In January of 2013, things started to shift. I took five days off to visit my aunt Clara, who'd been diagnosed with terminal lung cancer four months prior; my boss never actually granted me leave, but I knew I had to see Clara while she still had some good days left. While I was traveling, my tooth started to hurt—but I didn't get it looked at, because the day after I got back from that visit, I had to leave for a work conference in Philadelphia. By the time I got home, the damage was so bad that I had to have the tooth pulled.

From then on, things started to go wrong with my health. I had to have a partial hysterectomy in April. I actually found myself looking forward to the surgery because it would give me a break from the stresses at work. On top of everything, I was going through a rough period with my husband, and we had decided to separate. My son, who was twelve at the time, was living with me; my daughter was already in college.

During this pause, my spiritual guides kept speaking to me about creating a change in my life. "We need you," they would say. "It's time."

"Give me health insurance and a decent income, and I'll think about it," I'd retort.

Eventually, I reconciled with my husband (I'll tell you that story later in the book!), and our family was reunited. I went back to work on August 25, after the summer break period. On August 26, I got the call: I'd just been diagnosed with thyroid cancer. I literally threw back my head and laughed, thinking, "What kind of trick from the Universe is this?"

The doctor wanted me to get surgery immediately. But my bosses had already given me so many issues about time off that I was afraid I'd be fired if I went out on another leave. I put off the surgery until January of 2014.

The thing no one tells you about thyroid cancer is that it gives you a new brain. A brain that doesn't process thoughts, information, or words the same way. A brain that perceives the world differently.

After my surgery, I was thrown into hypothyroid disorder and was exhausted. My body didn't want to accept the new medication. I could barely read a sentence or manage a conversation. My body became so weak that I could not walk across the room or stand for any length of time. Meanwhile, I was still getting resistance from the university even though I had extensive medical documentation proving I wasn't fit to work.

For months, I traveled back and forth from my home in Pennsylvania to the Cancer Treatment Centers of America in Illinois. While there, I would often sit alone in the cafeteria. Since I hadn't lost my hair and I wasn't on an IV, many patients thought I was a caregiver. They would sit with me and tell me about their lives.

I remember one woman who shared that she and her husband had received cancer diagnoses on the same day—breast cancer for her, lung cancer for him. He had passed away just a few weeks before our meeting.

"I have no idea what to do now," she said. "I have no idea where my life goes from here."

In some small way, I knew how she felt.

Between my surgeries, the hormone imbalances, and the general upset of the "c-word" diagnosis, it became clear to me that I could no longer muster the level of mental focus and concentration needed to succeed at my job. My brain literally refused to cooperate. After one year, I had to accept that I couldn't go back to work. Instead, I needed to heal.

And so, I started to put my internal questions out to the Universe. What did I want to do with the rest of my life? How did I want to serve? And, most importantly, what did I truly love doing? If I was going to be called into some sort of "spiritual journey," I sure as heck wanted to create it from a space of happiness, abundance, and ease.

I was terrified about the financial impact of this new direction. But every time I checked in with my intuitive knowing, I felt protected and safe. I knew something was coming, but I had no idea what.

In December 2014, a decision was put before me. The University was changing its health policies. If I retired from my position, I would now be able to keep my health care coverage and pension, even though I was only fifty-four.

My guides had come through with exactly what I'd asked for regarding my health insurance—but my pension was another matter. I was too young to start dipping into it. And so, I received a whopping fifty-eight dollars a month. That amount might cover my Grand Central Bagel habit, but that was about it! Although technically I *was* receiving a pension, as I'd asked, I took this as a lesson to be much more specific with my guides when making a request!

I spent the next year or so recovering my strength. It seemed so decadent to be able to devote time to *me*. Every day, I drove my son to school with a smile on my face and joy in my heart. Although I enjoyed working, it had always been a dream of mine to be home at home with my children. While my son was at school, I went to the gym to swim and work out—another dream fulfilled! Afterward, I'd take myself out for lunch at a local café. And then pretty soon each day I would rinse and repeat. Watching all of the (much older) retirees around me, I wondered if this was truly how I wanted to spend the rest of my days on this planet.

*I'm still young,* I thought. *My life isn't over. I'm not ready for retirement!*

And most importantly, a little voice kept saying, *"You were born for so much more than this."*

Maybe this was the chance I'd been waiting for—the chance to do something I loved, without the sixty-hour workweeks and crushing pressure.

And so, I started to let my "woo" out to play.

# The Golden Threads

I knew I could talk to angels and guides, so I got involved with a local holistic center. Seeing the advertisements for my classes freaked me right the heck out. I knew *I* could read the Akashic Records and receive angel messages for myself, but I had no idea if I could teach anyone else to do it.

The morning of my first workshop, I stopped at my favorite bagel shop, a place I'd been visiting for over twenty-five years on my way to my university job. After placing my order at the counter, I stepped back and waited for them to call my name over the loudspeaker. I was fidgety and nervous as I thought about putting myself out there publicly as a purveyor of "woo."

"Angel?" the shop owner's voice announced. "I've got an everything bagel and a small coffee for Angel."

I looked around and immediately focused on the gentleman behind me. "Is your name Angel?"

"Yes, my mother named me Angel. I've always been blessed by my name."

"I'm leading an angel workshop later today. You're my sign from the Universe."

"And I think *you* are my angel today," he replied.

I felt like the Universe had answered a prayer.

I led my first workshop in a glorified "she-shed" with twelve amazing souls and one very loud box heater on the floor. One person broke into a fit of shaking mid-event and had to leave. (I think he was extremely sensitive to energy, and just opening the Records overwhelmed his system.) Another woman was struggling with a chronic illness and cried the entire time. And then, in my mind's eye, a gentleman appeared and stood right next to an elderly woman. He kept saying, "I want to talk with my wife and it's important." As a novice presenter, I wasn't leaning into my mediumship abilities just yet, so I was a bit shaken. This demanding spirit guy was really throwing my game off.

"I don't believe in you, but I really need you to stop so I can talk to my wife," he told me. "There's a financial investment she's about to make and there are things I need her to know." When I tried to ignore him, he just kept getting louder!

I finally had to interrupt the session to say, "Is there someone here who has a deceased spouse and who is about to make a big financial decision?"

Immediately, the elderly woman next to the spirit gentleman spoke up. "I do."

"Okay, great. We need to speak after the session is over."

Then, I directed the gentleman to sit down behind his wife and be quiet so I could finish the workshop. Finally, he complied.

This was my first experience with tuning into multiple guides while trying to create a positive experience for a group. As sweat trickled down my back, I prayed, "Please don't let me let them down."

That was the first time I saw the Golden Threads.

I intuitively understood that I could invite a golden thread of energy to come forward from each person in the room, and "plug into" the collective energy field of the workshop. When I did this, I could simultaneously sense how each and every person was feeling, and what their blocks and challenges were in the moment. It was so cool!

When the workshop was over, I couldn't wait to do it again.

In the meantime, I started a ninety-day juicing program. As I began sharing this publicly on Facebook, I was contacted by a man named Steve, who invited me to an event he was hosting in Washington State. His work helped me to begin integrating my new "woo" identity and exploring what was really waiting for me on the other side of this "retirement."

When I returned to Pennsylvania, I decided to take a class on public speaking—which made no sense, since at that point I was only speaking at my little workshops. But I felt the call to join, so I stepped into a group of ten CEOs and executives and learned how to speak on stage.

It was full-on intensity. Every stutter and "umm" was amplified. During one session, we were asked to present a sales offer from the stage as if we were in a boardroom full of investors. I didn't even *have* a business, let alone an offer, but my guides said, "Just get up there and start talking."

What came out of my mouth was the first incarnation of the system I'm about to teach you in this book: my map to release your blocks, lean into your values, and strengthen your connection to your spiritual guidance system so you can use intuition as a resource. At the time, I called it the Sacred Soul Map.

It was a little strange to stand in the front of that room and deliver a presentation about a business that didn't exist. But to me, it felt like I was *speaking* it into existence. It was another version of the Golden Threads; I could see, in that moment, how this model could weave together intuition and action to create a literal map to someone's soul purpose and alignment.

When that speaker training was over, I was determined to find a way to launch the business that had just appeared for me. That quest led me to a whole host of adventures and helped me connect to my aligned business coach, Jeannie Spiro (who you'll meet in Chapter 3), at her live event in Rhode Island. At that event, I also met my now-office manager, my customer liaison expert and copywriter, and the publisher of this book. Talk about a Window of Opportunity!

With Jeannie's help, I was able to create a framework to serve women as they connected to their intuition and learned to use it in their daily lives.

At first, I wasn't sure who my ideal client would be. I felt relationships were my mission because I was negotiating a new path in my own long-term marriage. But what I quickly discovered was that my process could help mission-driven women entrepreneurs make critical decisions in their businesses.

I was fascinated by these women. They were passionate, driven, and committed. They would stay up all night, doing what it took to build their businesses and brands. They were powerful visionaries, working toward making real change in the world.

I also noticed that many of them were operating from a place of logical, analytical thinking. They were operating from a value system of hard work and "hustle" energy, and they were getting burned out. It was as if they were pushing a boulder up a hill, always striving but never arriving—and it was costing them their joy, their health, and their long-term potential.

I could see that all it would take was a step to the left—a step into their intuitive wisdom—to let that boulder roll away forever.

As I sat with these women in my intuitive reading sessions, I let my own intuition guide me to facilitate the conversations and energy shifts that would bring them into greater alignment with who they were, and who they came here to be. As I looked into their Akashic Records—a process I'll teach you to do for yourself in this book—I started to see the self-identities and disempowering belief systems that were keeping them stuck. Those inner "blocks" were the boulders they were pushing!

Something else was happening, too. When I opened the records for each heart-centered businesswoman, I would see something that, at first, I didn't quite understand. In my mind's eye, I would see my client transform. Her skin would be glowing, her hair flowing, her eyes bright. It was like an energetic makeover—or one of those magical selfie apps.

My guides would say, "Do you see? *This* is who she really is."

I was seeing her higher self—the fullest expression and potential of her and her unique gifts. The version of her that is always intact. The version of her that is speaking to and guiding her through her intuition—if only she will open her heart and listen.

# Your Business Was Born from Intuition

You had a *feeling* that you wanted to do something, be something, create something. You decided to use your business as your vehicle to bring more love, joy, alignment, abundance, or justice into the world.

Maybe you wouldn't have called this an "intuitive" decision. Maybe, like me, life gave you a huge shove off the path you thought you were going to be walking. Maybe you heard that little voice inside saying, "It's okay, I've got you," even as everything seemed to be falling apart. Maybe you simply noticed that there was a problem in the world that you are uniquely equipped to solve.

However your business got its start, it began with a WOO—a Window of Opportunity—and you jumped right through it.

Goosebumps up, baby!

Yes, your intuition birthed your business. And then, most likely, your brain took over. It made things complicated. It wanted strategies, tasks, and metrics. It wanted things to "work" according to the rules it's been programmed with.

It might feel like you're working toward a mission and serving in a bigger way now, but you're still pushing that boulder up the hill … with your nose. You feel like everything is working against you, not for you. And while you are strong enough to keep going for now, you know this isn't sustainable.

You don't need more time, more clients, or another strategy. You need a way to make decisions that are aligned with the energy and desire of the highest version of you. When you can tap into your intuition to get clear insights in the moment, you open up a new, more expansive container. You shortcut all the hard work and struggle, and replace that energy with aligned action.

The more time you spend pushing that boulder—aka, struggling with your blocks—the more you're missing out on what you're really here to do.

You have an internal GPS that already holds the answers to every question you will ever ask. When you activate it, you take your foot off the energetic brake, clear the roadblocks, and allow flow to happen in your world. Then, you can merge your path and align with that glowing, vibrant higher self who is waiting to express their brilliance through you.

# Finding Your WOO

To create a life and business that's fully aligned with your highest self and soul's mission, I invite you to consider these inner shifts that will support you to find and claim the next level of *you*.

1. Be willing to acknowledge and listen to the nudges you are already receiving from your higher self, Spirit, God, the Universe, Source, angels, guides, or whatever other energy you align with.

2. Be willing to accept that your inner wisdom may not always make sense to your logical mind, but that you will always feel its truth in your body and heart.

3. The most important and most challenging of all: be willing to believe in yourself!

That's it!

You don't need to change who you are in order to become more intuitive. You don't have to become a wide-eyed mystic who lives in a cave and only eats berries picked under a full moon (although if that feels good to you, go for it!). Yes, things in your life and business may change when you unlock the doors to your inner knowing and learn how to access the infinite information available to you in your Akashic Records, but those changes will always move you closer to alignment with your higher self—the version of you who you ultimately came here to be.

Nothing your intuitive guidance tells you will lead you—or your business—to harm. However, it may be intimidating, even scary, to see exactly how big your mission is on this planet!

Every connection with, and piece of guidance from, your intuition is a W-O-O—a *Window Of Opportunity*. It's a choice being offered to you by your soul. You can decide to move through the Window into a greater expression of yourself and your business … or you can choose to stay where you are. Both have different consequences. Neither is wrong.

You don't need to identify as "woo-woo" to find and claim your WOO. Your intuitive gifts are hardwired; they're part of your human body, human energy, and human experience. More importantly, they're part of your soul. How you use them will be unique to you—but never, for a moment, assume that these kinds of gifts are only for other people.

If you've been a "secret woo" for years (like I was before my cancer journey), this is your Window of Opportunity to bring your gifts into the light. You don't have to shout your WOO from the rooftops (or write a book about it), but the more you lean into it, trust it, and acknowledge it, the more magical and serendipitous your experiences will become.

And if you're already a full-blow "double woo-woo" spiritual leader, I know what you'll learn in this book will take you even deeper into your power and alignment, and help you see your creative power and potential in a whole new way through your personal Akashic Records.

## The Gifts of the Akasha

I've mentioned the Akasha several times so far in this book. If you're not familiar with the Akashic Records, you may be wondering what the heck this spiritual "resource library" is all about.

*Akasha* is a Sanskrit word meaning "sky," "space," or "ether." The Akashic Records are a collection of mystical information encoded in a non-physical plane of existence. They are, essentially, a universal filing system—a soul-sourced database connected to Divine Source. They are also an infinite space of wisdom, truth, and possibility. They are also a space of Love, the highest and most powerful energy there is.

Some people describe the Records as a book or a library, but I think that's just their visual cue. You can visualize the Records in any way that feels natural to you. Personally, I sometimes see a white room without windows, no floor, or a ceiling (more on that later). Other times, I see a body surrounded by circles of light, images, and colors, and the spinning wheels of the chakras. I can tell what we are about to work on by which chakra lights up—and when I move my awareness toward it, it reveals an infinite matrix of information that I can convey as a channeler.

When people come to me for an Akashic Records reading, I often tell them, "This is a Google search for your soul, and I am the voice of Siri." As I connect with this database of *you*, you can ask detailed questions and I can channel the response, which includes the highest and best options your soul is revealing to you right now. Then, you can weigh in on the choices with your intuition and decide which feels lightest to you.

Learning to access your personal Records is a key part of my Align Your Business process—the process I will teach you in this book. When you follow the steps I'm going to share later in this book, you can be your own Siri, and use the soul-sourced information in the Records to streamline your decision-making process in your business and life. You will also learn to recognize the clues toward healing that reside in the Akasha, and access the inner "GPS" of your intuition that exists to support you throughout your time here on Earth. This will allow you to cut out the "apple spin" of indecision, break through the blocks that have been holding you back, and come into a place of alignment. From there, you can get grounded, shift what needs shifting, monetize your mission, create balance in your life, and fall in love with your business again.

Before we dive into the Align Your Business Process, there are a few things I would like you to understand. The first is something I call the "Dorothy Effect."

# ~ 2 ~

# You Can Always Go Home

*I*n 2019, I was asked to lead a group session at my friend Bryna Haynes's *Evolution* event. Of course, I said yes, because speaking is one of the best ways for me to connect with the conscious business owners I love to serve.

I spent over thirty hours preparing my talk. I created slides, a playlist, and several fun exercises to engage the audience. Then (as my speaking coach taught me), I rehearsed it every day for two weeks. But as I made the drive from Pennsylvania to the event location in Rhode Island, everything still felt misaligned, and I couldn't for the life of me figure out why.

I knew I wanted to speak about believing in ourselves— because that's the secret sauce that opens those Windows of

Opportunity in our lives—but nothing was coming together, and I was starting to get nervous.

When we got to the hotel, I got in the shower to recover after the long road trip. As the water washed over me, I stopped overthinking my presentation and started feeling into the infinite connection between my spirit and the spirits of the thirty powerful women I'd be leading in our session the following day. I asked, "If I could share a powerful message in six words or less, what would it be?"

As I reached for the shampoo, I started humming a new favorite song—but I couldn't remember the words. Then, a deeper question emerged: "What is the misalignment that is keeping me from accessing this presentation?"

Damn. Sometimes intuition can really get in your face.

With conditioner still on my head, I leaped out of the shower, grabbed my phone, and looked up the lyrics to the song I was humming. One line stood out: *If you want it, you just got to believe.*

If I wanted to help these entrepreneurs at a deep, transformational level, I needed to understand who they were. I knew they were beautiful, heart-driven, and confident. And yet, sometimes, they didn't believe in themselves, or in the power that was already available within them.

I got back in the shower to let this new line of thought percolate (and rinse off the conditioner that was now dripping down my face). Then, I grabbed a towel and opened my suitcase to pick out my clothes for the evening. As I pulled out various outfits, I realized that I had packed a pair of lipstick-red heeled shoes. I'd never worn these shoes, but for some reason I'd tossed them in my suitcase at the last minute.

Then, it hit me. They were my ruby slippers.

*If you want it, you just got to believe.*

I grew up knowing myself to be Candice, or more often, Candy. But the woman who gave birth to me, who gave life to me, named me Dorothy.

And so, while I am Candice, and will be for the rest of my journey on this planet, Dorothy is part of my soul.

Just like the beloved character in the Wizard of Oz, I spent long years following that yellow brick road. I found pieces of my joy along the way. I also got some rude awakenings. But it wasn't until my cancer diagnosis that I finally pulled back the curtain and saw that my old identity had run its course, and the next level of me was being born. Everything that had happened up until now was in service to that upleveling, but if I truly wanted to go home—to the place where my soul had always been leading me—it was time to lean into the power that had always been present within me.

In that moment, I knew I had my talk.

The presentation I delivered at that event was nothing like the one I'd originally planned, but it was one of the most powerful I've ever given. The reminder that "you can always go home" was so needed by this group of powerful creators. That message has since become a core part of my teaching.

Belief, trust, and intuitive magic aren't things that happen outside of us. They don't live in the things we're chasing. They can't be manufactured. They are our ruby slippers, and all we need to do to activate them is to remember that they're there.

If you've been waiting for your own version of the wizard behind the curtain to come along and make things better in your life and business, I have news for you. *You* are the wizard. *You* are the magician. You already have the answers.

As Glinda the Good Witch told Dorothy, "You've always had the power, my dear. You just had to learn it for yourself."

# Your Ticket Home

Every person's intuitive journey is different. As you go through the Align Your Business Process, your unique gifts will begin to surface. You may think of these gifts as your "ruby slippers," as I do—or you might see them as diamond stilettos, angel wings, or a crystal crown. However you visualize your power, one thing is always true: your gifts, if you choose to acknowledge and activate them, will carry you home.

"Home" is not where you are living. It's not a place on the physical Earth plane. It's within you. It *is* you. It's your soul. You carry it with you no matter where you go, and nothing in this life can ever take it from you.

You were created to be a multifaceted energy being. Part of that energy is visible, in the form of your physical body. Part of that energy is invisible, in the form of your thoughts, feelings, breath, personal magnetic field—and, of course, your intuition. The invisible parts are just as much "you" as your arms, legs, toes, or nose. In fact, they're even *more* "you" than your body is, because your energy governs your entire physical experience.

We have all been Dorothy. We've all quested through this strange, illogical world in search of the love, connection, abundance, and joy we want most. But you don't need to go on a quest for your power, because you've had it all along! This book will teach you to look in the right place for that power, and use it to transport yourself home to the fullest expression of yourself—to the place where you can be and receive *all* of who you are, including your "invisible" gifts.

Have you ever searched for your glasses for an hour, only to realize that they were on your head the whole time? Or frantically torn apart your purse for your keys only to find them already in your pocket? Coming home to your natural intuitive power feels like that. It's more remembrance than a discovery. It will feel strange at first because you'll need to get out of your head and into your heart space. You'll need to change your decision-making processes and lean into what is true for *you,* not what appears to be working "out there" in the world for others. And you'll need to trust yourself in a *big* way—maybe like you never have before—and let your intuition lead the way.

# Unwrapping Your Miracles

When I enter the Akashic Records for myself or someone else, I often see myself in a completely white room. This room has no floor, no ceiling, and no walls—but it's still a defined space. It's as bright as a photography studio—almost blindingly bright—and yet, it still feels comforting, expansive, and warm. It is full of the most beautiful gifts you can imagine; big ones, little ones, all shapes and sizes. Every box is wrapped in pristine white paper, and tied with a vivid red velveteen bow.

To me, this is the "between-space"—the realm between Heaven and Earth, where the physical and the spiritual can interact and communicate with a clarity unavailable anywhere else.

Early in my business, I was reading for a client when I was guided into her white room. This had never happened before—I had only ever been shown this space by my own guides when I was doing my spiritual connection practice.

I asked my client if I could approach the boxes. She said I could.

The first one I touched had her name on it. Then, I picked up another. Her name was also on that box! One after another, I went through all the boxes in the lovely white room. They were all for her.

"These are all of her wants and desires," her guides told me. "But she's never asked for them. She's never opened the boxes." There was such a sense of longing within my client. All that we want is there for us. When we ask, we start the process of receiving.

As I've said, I'm Siri for my clients; I just repeat the information I'm given! "These gifts are all for you," I told my client. "And they are all present in this space of possibility. If you believe, they can appear in the world. Once you ask for what you desire, it brings that desire through into your heart—just like opening a gift. Once you open the magic box, your intuition will guide you about how you can fully integrate what you have accessed."

My client burst into tears. She'd been feeling so constrained by the demands of her daily life and business that she'd forgotten how to see the gifts that were always available. This glimpse of possibility felt like a gateway to her new, compelling future.

The first time I saw the white room was in early 1996. For weeks, I kept having the feeling that a baby was nursing my right breast. For a while, I ignored it, but the feeling got stronger and stronger. Finally, I opened my personal Records and entered the white room.

"Is there a baby here?" I asked.

Almost immediately, I saw a child. He had straight blond hair, almond-shaped eyes, a square jaw, and a smile like sunshine.

I knew he was a boy, and every cell in my body knew he was coming to me.

Then, I was diagnosed with abdominal hyperplasia. I would need surgery to prevent the condition from escalating into cancer—and that surgery would render me unable to carry a child. The procedure was scheduled for April 16, 1996.

My doctors were clear that this surgery was necessary and lifesaving. But I was in full belief that my boy was coming to me—and through me. And so, despite the fact that all the experts told me I was making a dangerous choice, I decided to postpone the surgery and focus on the child who was waiting for me to birth him.

It wasn't an easy journey. Many times, I wondered if I'd made the right choice. But then, two years to the day after I was supposed to have surgery, I found out I was pregnant with my son. There was no trace of my hyperplasia.

My doctor told me recently that, in more than three decades of practice, he had never seen anyone heal from this condition and subsequently conceive a child. My story was so unusual that it landed me on TLC's television program, "Baby Story." (If you want to watch that segment, you can find it at www.CandiceHozza. com/media.)

What happened to me was a divine healing—an intervention that came through the Window of Opportunity created by my belief. I believed *so much* that my child would come that my body healed itself to make room for him.

You can bring this same level of belief to bear in your life and business. If you truly believe that you are destined to make a difference, to create an impact, to bring a certain type of healing or wisdom to the world, your belief will open the gateway for miracles.

In your Akashic Records, you have a similar room. Maybe

your possibilities don't come wrapped in white boxes. Maybe they are revealed to you as stars in a galaxy, or as books on a shelf—or even as dragon eggs, as they are for one of my clients. Once you unwrap them by asking for what you want, you will need to hold the belief in what's coming for long enough to let them come through.

Holding a pure belief while the Universe manifests a miracle isn't easy. In fact, it might be the hardest thing you've ever done. It might feel like you're going crazy or denying "reality." But the truth is, your inner knowing is *more* real than what you can see, taste, and touch with your physical senses. It's your direct line to All That Is.

There will be times, as you work with the knowledge and techniques in this book, that your ruby slippers will feel invisible. There will be times when your inner knowing conflicts with your perceived reality. This is normal. It happens to everyone.

When in doubt, *believe*. Your soul knows the way, even if your mind does not.

# The Gift of Your Business

If you haven't already guessed, your business is one of the gifts in your white room.

Your work is a gift to the world, but it's also a gift to *you*. Through your work, you can invite all of the joy, fulfillment, abundance, flow, and impact you desire.

But here's the biggest secret of all. All of the gifts in your white room are for you. In fact, they *are* you.

Yes, *you* are the gift.

(Did you just get goosebumps? I know I did!)

Every unopened box in the between-space is an aspect of you that is waiting to be birthed into the world. Before you came here to this planet, you decided what energies, work, and mission you would explore. But in order to access these gifts, you need to become willing to open those boxes and truly see and experience the energy and divinity of *you* that waits inside.

I always know when someone has unopened "gifts" in their energy field. They feel stuck. They feel like something is off, or something is missing. They might be hiding parts of themselves out of fear, or missing opportunities because they don't know their own inner power or trust their own ability to open their Windows of Opportunity. They feel overwhelmed, unsupported, burned out. They're pushing that boulder with all their might—and yet, nothing is changing, and so burnout, shame, and doubt seep in. They might have issues with their money flows. Maybe there are even health problems at play.

When I was still working at the university, I had multiple unopened gifts in my energy field. There were aspects of myself and my gifts that I refused to even look at, let alone expose to the world. As I've shared, it took numerous health crises to bring me to a place where I was willing to see and embrace the "more" that was waiting for me.

You always have the choice to unwrap your gifts and bring the possibilities of all that you are through into this physical reality. You were meant for more in this lifetime. And that *more* is always available to you, even if you don't feel ready to acknowledge it. It never goes away. It's part of you.

Over the course of this book, we will unwrap the beautiful gifts in your white room through my six-step Align Your Business Process.

## *The Align Your Business Process*

- Release your blocks to create more flow

- Lean into your Soul Values (your core internal drivers)

- Balance your Alignment Wheel and create your Clear Vision

- Align with your Quantum Leap Blueprint for Wealth

- Gain clear insights from your intuitive knowing and your personal Akashic Records

- Monetize your mission with a 12-Month and 90-Day Next Level Plan

It's your choice whether you open your gifts one at a time or all at once. You can go fast or go slow. You can read through the whole book in one sitting, or work with each chapter for a few days or weeks until you feel something shift. Just follow what feels right! What's more important is that you know you have the choice to access these beautiful, powerful, gifted parts of yourself at any time.

Remember, you are the gift. Your business is the vehicle—the box, if you will—through which you deliver the gift of *you* to the world. Bringing all the parts of you into full expression is the most powerful work you will do in this lifetime. Once you are aligned, everything aligns with greater ease and flow.

You have access to the beautiful gifts of your soul at any time—and it's a lot easier to open those boxes once you lean into your intuitive, soul-sourced wisdom. Your white room is the space between Heaven and Earth; your intuition is the door you walk through to get there.

So I invite you, here and now, to accept these truths wholly and truly:

- Everything you need to create your dream life and business is already inside you.

- Your belief is the most powerful creative force in this world.

- You are the gift. Always and forever.

If you can't fully believe these truths yet—and most people can't—give yourself permission to ask, "*What if* these things are already true? *What if* I am already whole and complete? *What if* I am enough, just as I am?" And as we make our way into the next section of this book, engage my words with that childlike openness.

I promise the results will be magical.

# Take a Deep Breath

"Just breathe."

How many times have you heard that expression? But how many times have you actually paused in a moment of decision to do just that?

Breath is one of the simplest and most powerful ways to reconnect to your intuition.

Whenever you need to make a choice and you can't hear the voice of your soul over all the noise in your head, pause, and breathe in. Fill yourself with the life force of your breath.

Breathe in love, grace, and forgiveness of self and others. Follow that breath into your body, into the deep still space of your heart, and ask, "What is aligned with the miracle I'm asking for?"

Then, breathe out any energies that are no longer serving your highest purpose.

I wanted to offer this simple technique now, rather than further along in the book, because it will help you overcome any logic- or experience-based resistance that arises as you read. As you begin to Align Your Business through the power of intuition, there will be moments when your brain will step in and say, "No way. No *way* can that be true. That doesn't sound like all the stuff I've learned/studied/lived through before." Maybe this has already happened in this chapter!

But your mind isn't equipped to have a dialogue with your soul. Only your heart, and your intuition, can do that. And so, when your mind starts to spiral, just breathe.

Breath is *chi. Qi. Prana.* It's an energy resource. When you feel like your thoughts, doubts, or worries are spiraling out of control, take a deep breath, and return to the life that is *now*. That's where your power is. That's where your intuition is. That's where the guidance is. And the window into the *now* is your breath.

It's the simplest of things.

# ~ 3 ~

# Release Your Blocks

B y the time I was thirty-three, I knew that I was stuck in a lack of truth. I felt like something was trapped behind a door inside of me, pounding on it and trying to get out. I had no idea how to deal with this.

More, I desperately wanted to have a baby. My daughter was seven at the time, and I'd been trying for three years to have a second child. I couldn't figure out why nothing was working.

So, I decided to get some help—but not in the usual sense. Rather than get the runaround from one more doctor, nutritionist, or fertility specialist, I booked my first intuitive reading.

My husband wasn't convinced this was a great idea. "You're spending seventy-five dollars on *what?*"

But I had a feeling this was the right thing to do, and rather than ignore that inner nudge as I had so many times before, I decided to follow it.

That reading blew my whole world open.

The reader—a well-known psychic who often worked with the local police department—shared that I had been born in an orphanage in Pittsburgh, not in a hospital as I'd believed. I lived there for three months until I was placed with my parents. It was a closed adoption, which usually means that the likelihood of the child ever connecting with his or her parents is small. I couldn't believe that so much information about me was coming through this woman on the other end of the telephone line.

Then, I blurted out a question that had literally never passed my lips before. "Why was I placed for adoption?"

"Candice," the reader said, her voice growing more serious than it had been during this entire process. "This is honestly one of the most challenging readings I've ever done. I feel that you've come to accept that you were adopted, but I also am being guided to tell you that your birth mother has been wanting to meet you for your entire life. You are the only child she ever had. Giving you up was the hardest thing she has ever had to do."

Thinking of my beautiful seven-year-old daughter, with her blonde hair and sparkling blue-green eyes, I burst into tears. It was so healing to hear that my mother wanted me as much as I had wanted my own daughter. I had always felt a deep sense of rejection when it came to my birth parents. Now, I knew that love had been present there, even though they weren't able to keep me with them.

The reader continued. "If you choose to search, you can find both of your parents, even though yours was a closed adoption.

But it's your choice. If you decide to do so, you will have success finding both of your birth parents."

I put the phone down, sobbing—then immediately picked it up again to call my husband. As I explained what had just occurred, he paused, and said, in a voice completely unlike his own, "Stay there. I'll be right home."

When he arrived, he sat me down on the couch. Looking uncomfortable, he said, "I've been keeping a secret from you for five years."

I was dumbstruck.

"When your father passed away five years ago, I was with your mother when she opened her home safe to get his birth certificate for the final paperwork. She handed me an envelope labeled 'adoption information.' I said to your mom, 'Bette, this isn't the day to open this can of worms. I think we should put this back in the safe until you've had some time to grieve.' But she never brought it up again. And you never seemed to want to know, so ..." He held up his hands, helpless.

It was all coming together. Every year for the past five years, on my birthday, he'd asked me, "Do you want to find your birth mom?" And each time, I responded in the same way. "It's okay. She gave me life, and now I give her hers." I always said it with a sense of peace and completion. I didn't have a "birth story"; I had a "the day we got you" story. I always believed I was okay with that.

Until today, when my reading made my mother real to me, instead of just a dream from the depths of my past.

Still shaking from my husband's revelation, I called my mom—my adoptive mom, the mom of my heart, the one who'd raised me—and told her the whole story.

She paused. I held my breath. "You know what, Candy?" she

said after a moment. "I think I'd like to wait to give you that paperwork. Maybe you can have it after I pass."

"Okay, Mom." I knew that I never, ever wanted to hurt this beautiful woman who'd loved me my whole life. I made the decision not to hurt her, and not to explore this further with her. But I did do some research.

I knew that the place my parents had adopted me from was called Roselia. The full name of the institution was The Roselia Foundling and Maternity Asylum. My mother must have been unwed—which, considering I was born in the 1960s, explains why she would have had to give me up.

I made some phone calls and tracked down the facility that stored the records from Roselia. I talked to a nun named Sister Esther Marie. She said if I sent a notarized letter and documents proving my identity, she could send me some general information. "I want to warn you, though," she said as she took down my contact information, "there aren't a lot of details to be had about our residents. It was a very hard time for the women who came here." I could only imagine.

My birthday was just a few months away. I set an intention to meet my birth mother on or before my birthday. I felt like I was putting my foot into a Window of Opportunity, asking the Universe to align so I could finally connect with the woman who had carried me for nine months. I also asked that this unfold in a way that wouldn't bring any hurt or pain to my adoptive mom, because I could never be okay with that.

That June, my father-in-law got really sick. In August I found out I was pregnant. Then, within just a few weeks, my father-in-law passed away and I lost my baby.

I was devastated. But losing so much in a short time reminded me that I couldn't put off the things that were vital to my heart.

Out of the blue, my mom called me. "Candy, I've been watching Oprah and Maury Povich," she said. "They're doing all these beautiful adoption reunions. And …" she paused and took a breath. "I want that for you."

She retrieved the information for me the next day.

That paperwork, combined with the information I'd received from Sister Esther, revealed that my birth mother's name was Gerri.

My whole life, I'd never known where I came from. I felt like an orange at the grocery store that knew it came from a tree but had never seen one. Now, I was seeing the tree. I hadn't realized it would mean so much to me.

I had uncles named Richard and Robert. I had grandparents named Anthony and Mary.

And I had a name. My birth name. Dorothy Marie Ronczka.

I picked up the phone and called Information (which, if you're too young to remember, was kind of like the Google of the telephone world, only it was a real person looking up your information). The operator gave me two numbers. I dialed the first one. A woman answered.

"Hi," I chirped, shaking so hard I could barely speak. "I'm a friend of Gerri's. Is she available?"

"Oh?" Clearly, I sounded suspicious.

"I'm an old friend of the family. I'm looking for Gerri. Her parents are Anthony and Mary."

"I'll have someone from the family call you back," the woman replied. And hung up.

My husband, seated on the other side of the table, raised his eyebrows. "You'd better think about what the heck you're going to say if they actually call you back."

My hand was still on the phone. I wasn't about to give up so easily.

Then, the phone rang. I answered, and heard a sweet voice say, "I'm Gerri. I'm looking for Candy."

I thought my heart would stop. "You're my mother!" I gasped. We both started to cry.

When she could speak again, my birth mother said, "I just want to tell you that I love you. I always have, and I always will." She sniffed. "I've waited my entire life to tell you that."

We talked for endless hours. She asked, softly and politely, if she could meet me. Of course, I agreed.

Three days later, I picked her up at the airport. I bought her yellow roses. She was carrying a Barney toy for my daughter. She cradled my head. I put my hand on her womb—my orange tree, the place I came from.

I spent the whole weekend with my mother. We listened to music from when she was a teenager. We went shopping. We drank gin and tonics. We had a pajama party, and I painted her nails red. On Sunday, when she was supposed to leave, a snowstorm canceled her flight, so we got an extra day.

When I brought her back to the airport, we sat for a while watching the planes land and take off. I kept glancing at her. She was only fifty-one, but somehow she looked older and more careworn than my adopted mom, who was fifteen years her senior.

"Candy," she said, "I want to tell you something. On my father's death bed, he looked at me and said, 'Gerri, I'm so sorry I didn't fight for you to keep your baby. I know how much you always wanted children.'"

"I think he helped us meet," I said. I believe that when spirits pass, they can send us energies and attributes. I think this was my grandfather's gift—a way to help us both fully heal in this lifetime.

"Tell me about your health," I said. "I don't know anyone who has had both a kidney and pancreas transplanted. What's the prognosis? I mean, I just found you!"

Just then, Gerri's flight was called. She never did answer the question.

I walked her to the door of the plane, which you could still do in those days. And then I sat and watched as her plane took off. Watched it grow smaller and smaller in the distance, until it was nothing but a speck in the winter sky.

We talked almost every day that week. Then, Saturday came, and she didn't call. Sunday, too, passed without a word.

On Monday—one week to the day since I'd watched her fly away—I got a call from a woman named Sybill, a dairy farmer who owned the property adjacent to Gerri's. "Candy, are you sitting down?" she asked.

I was immediately confused. "What's happening?"

"I'm with your mother. I can see that her nails are painted red. She told me you did that for her."

"Yes," I whispered.

"Candy, your mother is gone. She's passed away."

Later, sitting in a silent room, I asked, "Why would God bring us together, only to tear us apart? How could this be right?"

But time, I realized, hadn't been the gift of our journey.

I'd only known Gerri for thirteen days—but those thirteen days had healed me. Knowing that my parents had wanted me—and that they had chosen to give me up out of love and a desire for me to have a good life—was beautiful. My parents, Bette and

Bill, had wanted a child of their own but couldn't get pregnant. Gerri, through me, gave them the gift they prayed for.

For years, Gerri had longed to hold me in her arms, and she'd gotten her wish. And, I realized, I had also gotten mine.

If I hadn't realized that there was a "block" in my life, a place inside me where something bigger and more beautiful was trying to come out, I might never have found my birth mother. I would have kept on going with that unsettling feeling gnawing at me from the inside—maybe for years, maybe for the rest of my life. But because I followed my intuitive guidance, I was able to land within myself in a new way. The release of my block brought grief, yes—but also peace, and a sense of acceptance. I wasn't broken. I hadn't been thrown away. I had been loved from the beginning. For the first time in my life, I felt a sense of total belonging. It was a foundation I'd never known I was lacking.

# Your "Blocks" Are Gifts from the Universe

I had no idea what I was saying yes to when I booked that first session with the intuitive reader. It was so against my normal way of being at that time. I'd always known I had a special connection to what was "beyond," and that there was more to life than what I could see and understand—but the threat of "hairy eyeballs" and judgments from others meant I rarely spoke about what I sensed. This time, I chose to trust the feeling inside me that said, "go this way"—and the results were profound.

I know you have those moments, too. Your intuition isn't always a roar; some days, it's more like a whisper. Sometimes, when there's a block to be released, it can sound like you're hearing a voice on the other side of a thick, heavy door. You can't quite make out what it is saying, but you know it's talking to you.

Saying yes to my intuition around my adoption journey led me to connect with the Universe in a whole new way. From that point on, I was far more open to the Windows of Opportunity that opened into my life—up to and including receiving messages from guides, angels, ascended masters, and loved ones now dwelling on the other side of the Veil. The more I embraced my WOO, the more magical and aligned my life became. I received my beautiful son. I navigated my cancer journey. And, eventually, I birthed my business.

All because I walked through that first WOO.

When you're truly ready to seek out the most aligned path for yourself and your business, you will be called to heal what feels broken inside you. Where your fear lives, your truth lives too. And when you open those Windows of Opportunity, you will be led to the place where your truth can finally emerge and be free.

For me, that started with healing the wound of my adoption. But leaning into my WOO also required a huge shift in my identity. I didn't see myself as one of those crazy hippie cat ladies who gazed at crystal skulls and wore nothing but tie-dyed sarongs. I wasn't going to braid my underarm hair or trade my glitzy heels for leather sandals. And yet, at the time, I thought that was a requirement for someone who talked to invisible energies and operated from "feeling" rather than logic. It just didn't feel like my personal identity.

It took time to realize that, no matter how "woo-woo" I became, I could still be me. In fact, I could be more me than ever before. I did have to give up some stuff—like powering through life when my inner knowing is screaming at me to stop—but those things were hurting me anyway. Never, in all my evolutionary journey, have I been asked to give up any part of who I truly am.

When we come here (to this Earth, in this incarnation), our highest and best self chooses our body, our situation, and our mission. This mission is born from our hearts, and no one and nothing can take it away from us or lessen its power.

Along the way, we get injured. We get hurt. We feel pain. And these pains create patterns or attitudes that help us navigate and survive the pain.

None of us are broken, but our blocks often steer us away from the path we chose before we came here. When we work to release those blocks and clear the path, we can find our way back to the road of our soul and align with our mission and truth.

Some of us have been walking around with our blocks for so long that we can't even see them. But when we pay attention, we can *feel* them. They feel like our darkest corners, our shameful secrets. Our biggest fears. The unhelpful patterns we repeat around money and relationships.

When my business was just beginning to take shape, I asked my guides, "How can I help my clients align with their heart-centered missions, exponential growth, and their own deepest truth?"

Their answer? "Help them lean into the fear."

If you've been feeling "blocked," there's a reason. Chances are, the core of that reason is fear. Fear of changing. Fear of letting go. Fear of being judged. Fear of not being good enough. That fear feels like a mountain in the middle of your path to success, fulfillment, and purpose. It makes you want to run away and hide. But if you have the courage to get closer, to really look at what's lurking there, you'll see that the mountain is a shadow, cast by something much less overwhelming. The "block" is almost never as big or scary as you imagined. And if you can get close enough to touch and feel it, you will be close enough to shift it.

When you lean into the fear enough to see it for what it is— the "mountain" that is really a shadow—and gain clear insight from your intuition, you will pierce the veil of fear and find the clarity you need to take your next step forward. Whatever it is you're afraid of, your soul is asking you to address it so that you can get to the next level of *you*. That job you don't want to quit, the new venture you don't want to start … they're just indicators.

So, ask yourself, "Why am I afraid? What is *really* scaring me?" Asking higher and better questions will send out a vibrational message to the Universe to seek an aligned action. Asking what you *do* want, rather than focusing on what you don't, will help you release the fear block and get back into movement, ease, and flow.

## Your Block Isn't in Your Business

So many people come to me wanting help to solve their business problems. But your "business problems" are never actually in your business. They're in the parts of your energy field that overlap with your business.

Let me explain.

Your business has its own energy field. You created it, but it's separate from you. It is its own entity, and it has its own energy container. Pretty cool, right?

Know what else is cool? Your business doesn't have fear. It doesn't have stuckness. It doesn't have confusion. It is simply waiting for you to own your truth and step into who you are so you can be in alignment with it, and with your true mission.

So, if you feel like your business isn't working for you, the more likely challenge is that it's not working *with* you, because you are experiencing a block in your energy field that is disrupting the flow in the space where you and your business overlap.

Everyone experiences their blocks in unique ways. However, there are four common types of blocks I see over and over again in my clients. They are:

1. Birthing Blocks

2. Personal Energy Blocks

3. Identity Blocks

4. Past Life Blocks

Chances are, if you feel stuck in your business, you're running up against one of these blocks. Let's explore them one by one.

## *Birthing Block*

This block is all about divine timing. There's something that is trying to come through you, but it hasn't fully formed yet.

Just as you wouldn't say to a perfectly-formed rosebud, "You're not opening fast enough for me!" you can't unwrap the gift of your current idea, program, product, or income stream until it's ready. Your idea has multiple moving parts, and it needs to be revealed slowly so you can prepare for all that birthing it will require. Sometimes, this will even require you to create multiple iterations of a program or offering before you land in the space you had been intended to occupy all along.

You'll know you have a Birthing Block if you have a business that's functioning and sustaining itself, and you're moving, doing, and contributing—but you're still feeling impatient. You want to move forward with that new idea that's hanging out in the wings (like your book, your podcast, or your new course), but every time you try to push the start button, something gets in the way.

Instead of letting your impatience overwhelm you, lean into the frustration. Is this thing you're creating worth the wait? If so, trust that, like the beautiful rose, it will unfold in its own time— and when it does, you'll be ready.

## *Personal Energy Block*

A Personal Energy Block happens when your habits, schedule, activities, or relationships are in conflict with your highest and best energy.

Maybe you've been telling yourself that you want to work less for years, but you're still logging sixty hours a week (plus being a mother and/or partner, caring for your house, volunteering, etc.). Maybe you're not honoring your body, your mental health, or your time boundaries. Maybe you're putting energy into tasks that your team should be taking on.

When a Personal Energy Block is present, your business may be thriving, but you are not. The energy around your business feels heavy to you. You might feel depleted, exhausted, frustrated, and angry. You might even be wondering why you keep doing this work you once loved.

The solution isn't to quit on your business. Instead, ask, "What do I need, and how can I give that to myself, every single day?" This might mean creating new habits around food and exercise, honoring your time boundaries, shortening your workday, or something else entirely—but trust me, this one is all about *you*.

## *Identity Block*

This third type of block is one I've been seeing a lot of lately. The Great Pandemic of 2020 brought a lot of things to the forefront for people, including many misalignments that needed to be healed in order for our planet to move forward.

This block is all about transition and heading into your next phase of personal growth and development. You are no longer who you were, and your old life and business model doesn't feel like it fits any longer. You may be experiencing a slowdown in your business, or maybe the valve has shut off completely. You may feel like you're struggling to get traction in anything you implement. Nothing you try feels completely right or aligned.

The reason your business feels like it no longer fits is that you've outgrown it. You are ready to level up—to take your next steps into the expression of what you came here to do. But first, you have to let go of what is no longer serving you in your life. You don't have to change who you are at a core level—you are simply integrating the next level of you. You will pack what is needed for the journey, and release what is not. In order to do that, however, you will need to do a deep dive into your values, your desires, and your business model (all of which I'll support you to explore in this book!). Once you lean into who you really are and what you really want, I promise, your business will start to move!

## *Past Life Block*

If you've worked with and ruled out all of the block types above, and you're still running into resistance, it's possible that you have a karmic or past life block in your energy field. If this is the case, you'll know it because your block makes no logical sense and because you can't identify an issue in this lifetime that might be tied to your challenge.

While it's possible to break through a past life block on your own using the tools I give you in this book—along with breathwork, meditation, and other modalities—I usually encourage people to ask for help with blocks of this nature, because it can be hard to see the scope and depth of them clearly on our own. Dissolving past life blocks is actually a huge part of what I do with clients!

If you feel you might have a past life or karmic block in your energy field, the first step is to ask your spiritual guides for support or insight. You'll learn a full process for doing this in Chapter 7—but for now, just practice breathing in love, grace, and forgiveness of yourself and others, and breathing out all of the energies that no longer serve you.

***

Chances are, you recognized your block in one or more of the descriptions above. This is great! Now you know where to put your focus and where to lean into the Windows of Opportunity that will begin to come your way now that you have become aware of the issue.

No matter what kind of block you're dealing with, releasing it will be an inside job. I help my clients and course students identify the nature of their blocks, and give them information about how those blocks can be moved—but in the end, it's always up to them. The same goes for you. No one can do this for you, but I promise, if you follow the guidance in this book and do the practices I will teach you in the upcoming chapters, you will begin to see and feel a profound shift.

If you're still not sure where your block is or where to begin, look for pockets of resistance. Ask for one clear insight, and act upon it. Follow the nudges of your soul. I had no idea that I had a major energy block around my adoption … but once I put my feet on the path, the magic unfolded, and my life (and business) were forever changed. The same will be true for you.

Your healing journey starts when you say yes to the WOO. Your angels, spiritual guides, and other invisible allies will always give you the information you need to move forward … if only you are open to listening. You are always being guided. You are always held, loved, and protected. And your business—that beautiful engine for positive change—is there to support you as well!

I think of releasing blocks like wiping off old makeup. By revealing where your energy may be stuck or stagnating, you've just washed your face. You now have a clean slate to start applying a better, more glowing foundation for your life and business. This doesn't mean that your block has to be completely resolved, only that you've cleared the fog away so you can see what's actually there.

Goosebumps up, my love! Let's get started.

# ~ 4 ~

# Your Soul Values

W ell, Candy, I'm not really 'woo.' I'm maybe half a woo."

Those were the words my beloved business coach, mentor, and friend Jeannie Spiro said to me when I suggested that we work together to introduce more intuitive wisdom into her coaching business.

"Other than you," she continued, "I've only worked with one other person in the spiritual space."

"Really?" I asked. "Are you okay with that?"

At that point, Jeannie had been my coach for several months. But when I asked her if I could gift her a session so she could understand what I actually did for my clients—and help me shape my offers accordingly—she hesitated.

Jeannie's intuition was the pink elephant in the room. She was highly empathic and perceptive, and this sensitivity informed her logical, strategic coaching methods. But she wasn't bringing these energetic superpowers to the forefront with her clients—and, of course, her guides couldn't wait to open those floodgates.

Jeannie shared with me later, "That first reading was hard for me. I wasn't sure what to do with the information. But it was *so* good, because it gave me a taste of what was possible for me if I opened up to that side of myself. I was still so trapped in my corporate space, my corporate mindset, and my corporate body. After our reading, I wanted more of what I glimpsed in this new space."

Soon, Jeannie started to look more closely at the direction in which she was taking her business. Our session was a Window of Opportunity, and despite being only "half a woo," she stepped right through and into something bigger than she could have anticipated.

Her inner wisdom started poking at her around the time of her annual live event. "I recognized that I didn't want to be working in the same way anymore," she said. "I was beginning to get more familiar with these feelings that came up in my body around my business, and something didn't feel right. I was at the point in my business where I had a lot to lose by showing up out of alignment. I needed to tune into the path that felt right for me—and I needed intuitive guidance, not just strategy, to keep growing in that direction."

What Jeannie discovered was that the way she was building

her business was out of alignment with her Soul Values—the things she desired at the deepest level for her life. She wanted freedom, flow, and heart-centered connection, but her business model had her locked into overworking and hustling. "I didn't want to see it," she told me, "but there it was. I felt it. I saw it, and I needed to step in and stop it."

The more we continued our work together to align her business, the more Jeannie was able to clear the barriers between her and the ease, flow, and comfort she wanted. She was able to evolve her business model to serve in a way that centered her heart, not just her head—and that aligned with what she wanted for her own life.

"I was working from a masculine space of 'hustle and grind' for such a long time," she said. "That's all I knew. That's what I was good at. I left corporate, but I brought the same energy into my business and repeated those same patterns over and over, even when they didn't serve me. I was working nights. I was working weekends. I was killing myself, all because I wanted to maintain this high standard of service. It took time to pull all of that apart, but the results have been incredible for both me and my clients. I'm making more, working less, and actually enjoying my life again."

We aren't often given permission in our culture to make business decisions according to what our soul is calling for. We are told to follow this program, implement that strategy, and duplicate others' "success habits." But if we really want to live as we were meant to live on this planet, and make the difference we came here to make, we need to pause, and ask—

"What is right for *me*?"

# Your B.S. Story

When we align our business with the things that matter most to us in life—what I call our Soul Values—we are not only setting ourselves up for success. We are raising the energetic *experience* of business to another level of consciousness.

The conversation about "values" is everywhere in the business space, but I think the approach is misaligned. We're told that values are the things we will fight for. The things we'll die for. The things we'll go to war for.

But the truth is, your soul doesn't want you to die for your values. It wants you to *live* for them. To live by them, and as them—to embody them.

What makes us go to war for our values is the same thing that makes us choose against them: our Belief System story—a.k.a., our B.S. story. Our soul wants one thing, but our conditioning says another. Our soul wants peace, but our B.S. story says we can't have it until *those* people are out of the way. Our soul wants freedom, but our B.S. story says we need to work harder to make more money. Our soul wants us to lead our clients intuitively, but our B.S. story says, "People will laugh you off the stage."

Until you decide to throw out the old B.S. story in favor of a new one, your Soul Values will stay buried.

Learning what your Soul Values are, and what they are asking of you, is one of the most valuable things you can do for yourself and your business. Your B.S. story is a result of conditioning; once you align with your Soul Values, you can recondition your behaviors and patterns to align with what you desire, not what you're fighting against.

If you feel blocked in any way, if you're uncertain, if you're confused, if you feel defeated ... chances are there's a misalignment between how you are operating in your business and what your soul truly desires. Remember, your business (in its energy form) doesn't know fear, stuckness, or confusion—so it will flow along whatever pathway you provide. If that pathway is misaligned with, or in opposition to, your Soul Values, you will experience "blocks" in your business until that discrepancy is resolved. Your soul wouldn't have it any other way.

As we explored in Chapter 3, it all comes down to fear. Our B.S. stories are born out of fear, and fear keeps them alive. But when we lean closer, and see that the fear is just a shadow cast by our story, we can begin to shift that belief and come into greater alignment.

As Jeannie told me, "I see a lot of people working really, really hard in their businesses, and I think, 'That used to be me!' So many women are grinding away, struggling to grow—but what if it can be really simple and easy instead? Releasing the grind and growing into a beautiful, amazing, aligned space is actually possible. It's not unrealistic. But it is a process of awakening."

The other day, I was watching a storm roll in over my hometown in Pennsylvania. The wind was whipping, and there was this bird gliding on the air in front of the storm. He was having the best time—gliding, diving, circling back around, and doing it again. Through it all, he barely had to flap his wings; the wind just carried him.

When you're in alignment with your Soul Values, your life and work will feel like that. Even on difficult days, you will feel the wind carrying you up, and over, and beyond. You'll want to jump for joy because your clients are so amazing. You'll have room for presence and grace in your work. And you'll feel supported in the choices you make because your Soul Values will tell you what is aligned, and what is not—even when the outcome is still unclear.

# Decide from Your Soul

I once worked with a husband-and-wife team who we'll call John and Yvette.

John had a particular strategy that he used to help people release energetic blocks. He was strategically building this work with the intention of allowing him and Yvette to step away from their successful work in the insurance field and concentrate on the healing work. (They had already sold another brick-and-mortar business for over a million dollars, so they knew what they were doing in this realm.) At first glance, it looked like everything was coming together.

However, when I got on my video call with them. I took one look at their faces and knew something was wrong. Despite the fact that they were financially secure and knew how to build their new business to match their vision, they still didn't feel good about moving forward. There was still something that needed to shift in order to bring things into alignment.

"You don't have to build a mountain," I told them. "You just need to shift enough for the flow to begin."

As we continued the session, it became clear that, although John and Yvette wanted to do this business together, their Soul Values weren't aligned in this area. Their guides had messages for each of them. John was to focus on serving his new clients, while Yvette approached three new people to offer their unique clarity formula and sell them into the upcoming beta program.

A week or so later, Yvette asked if we could meet.

"I wanted to tell you what happened," she said excitedly. "The first person who I thought was an easy yes for this gave me such a hard time that I was almost in tears. I thought this was going to be so simple to articulate and sell, but she just didn't get it! Then, I went to the next person on my list, and it was the same thing. The third person was even worse."

I nodded, wondering where all of this was going. It hardly seemed like something Yvette would be excited about.

"What I realized," she continued, "is that I don't want to build this business at all. I'm nearly sixty. I don't want to start over again at this point. I don't want to convince people about the value of this work. My guides told me to talk to these three people—and when I did, it was so clear! I want to keep working in insurance, not struggle with this new business. I make great money, and I can provide stability for us as John does his work in this other realm."

Yvette's Soul Values—vitality, security, and abundance—weren't aligned with the energy of John's new business. She realized that she was happier where she was. Because she was willing to listen to her inner guidance, she saw this clearly. John, on the other hand, was fully aligned with his new venture, and went on to achieve mastery in his clearing work and create a successful new business in that space.

We were each put on this planet for a special, unique reason. There is no one right answer. There is no one way to do things.

There is only the way that is aligned with your Soul Values at this moment—the way which will be revealed as you lean into this awareness and your own inner wisdom.

Most people don't pivot away from their B.S. story and move into alignment with their Soul Values until they come to a place where the suffering is greater than their fear of change. For Yvette, the small suffering of experiencing rejection from three people she thought would be "easy yeses" to her new business was enough for her to say, "I don't want this." For Jeannie, it took the experience of utter exhaustion and frustration that came from years of overworking.

For me, as I've shared, it took cancer and early retirement to bring me to a place where I could finally start to hear what my soul wanted from me.

Pain, in any form, is a clue that something needs to change. It's a message from your soul. You can ignore it for a while, maybe even with great success—but ignoring it won't make it go away. It will just keep growing until you can't ignore it anymore.

If you pay attention to the pain when it's small, as Yvette did, you can prevent it from becoming catastrophic. One way to do this is to identify and connect with your Soul Values. Just starting this process can bring you great freedom, joy, and understanding around your internal drivers and the choices that have brought you this far in your life and business.

# Soul Values Training

Your Soul Values are your touchstone for alignment.

You might have many values, but you only have three to five top Soul Values, and these are the most important to clarify if you want to bring your business and your personal energy into alignment.

As human beings, we make somewhere around 35,000 decisions a day. As business owners and entrepreneurs, we make even more than that! What we base those decisions on will determine whether we end up aligned and soaring like the bird in the storm, or pushing that familiar boulder up the hill with our nose.

If our B.S. story is the primary basis and metric for our decisions, we will end up blocked, frustrated, and far away from where we originally intended to go. It's like getting on a bus and saying, "Take me to Florida!"—but the bus driver only knows how to get to Los Angeles, so that's where he goes.

On the other hand, if we make decisions—even small ones—according to our Soul Values, we will feel much more ease and flow. Each time we make a choice, we will be reminded of who we are, who we have chosen to become, and why we are here on this planet. Instead of yelling at the driver that he's going the wrong way, we can relax and enjoy the journey—and, at the same time, set free all the people, things, habits, and experiences that belong to the old route so they don't have to come with us to this new destination.

To tune into your Soul Values, the first step is to get a glimpse of what your soul actually desires. Set a timer for twenty minutes—no more, no less. For those twenty minutes, free-write about what you really desire for your life. If there were no limitations, no "shoulds," and no obstacles, what would you really want? If you could spend one day doing anything you wanted, anywhere in the world, what would you be doing (and with whom)?

This process will help you clearly see your top values. Feel free to dream as big as you can—and don't stop writing until that timer goes off, even if you feel like you're repeating yourself.

In my experience, the best information will come through you in the final three to five minutes of this exercise. After the time is up, go back and read what you've written. You may notice that certain words come up over and over again, and that they evoke a sense of resonance or alignment for you. These may be words like Love, Romance, Magic, Flow, Freedom, Achievement, Fame, Wealth, Connection, Independence, Compassion, Fun, Service … or something else entirely. What matters is that the words have meaning to you.

On a separate sheet of paper, write down all of these words in a list format. Then, rate each of those words on a scale of one to seven—with seven being "I'll die if I don't have this!" and one being "I care about it, but it's not vital." Remember, this isn't a shopping list. This isn't about which ideas or values you "should" identify with, or what the people around you identify with. Let your soul wisdom lead the way.

You can also clarify your Soul Values with statements like:

- "When I have _____, I feel peace and harmony with myself and the world around me."

- "If _____ was missing from my life, I would be totally miserable."

Insert each word from your list, say the statement aloud, and feel into the energy. (If you use a pendulum or know how to use muscle testing, you can apply those practices here!) Take note of the answers that arise, and the degree of feeling you experience in the "yes" or "no."

When you're done with the above exercises, you should have

a list of three to five words that represent powerful, meaningful energies in your life. This is a snapshot of who you are on the deepest level. These are your Soul Values.

Write each of your top values on its own index card. Then, post the cards somewhere you will see them every day—on your office door, your car's dashboard, or your bathroom mirror. (The more places, the better!) Consult them every time you need to make a decision. Ask questions like, "Is this choice in alignment with my value of _____?" Keep your values in sight until you know them by heart and are comfortable making decisions that honor them.

You can further refine your Soul Values by comparing them against each other. For example, "If I could choose Freedom or Romance, but not both, I would choose …" This will help you rank your Soul Values in order so that you can prioritize your highest values in your decision-making.

I know this series of exercises seems simple, but I promise you, it will be profound. You will begin to see all the places your soul is calling you to go—and all the ways in which you are choosing against your values in your daily life and business. More, you'll be able to lean into the fears that are keeping you stuck, and start to release them one by one.

# The Fear, the Block, and the Flow

Your soul only wants the highest and best for you.

In other words, it wants nothing more than for you to live in alignment with your own divine nature as expressed through your Soul Values.

Your fears aren't part of your divine nature. Just as the energy of your business doesn't know fear, injury, or lack, your highest self is always in flow. Instead, your fears are part of your B.S. story—your old belief system. And if they're driving your bus to Los Angeles instead of following your directions to Florida, it's your job to stop that bus and get off.

So many times, I see that my client's Soul Values run counter to their B.S. story. Jeannie wanted to experience flow, freedom, and ease in her business, which was why she left corporate to become an entrepreneur—but her B.S. story about hustle and hard work followed her into her new life, and it manifested as a Personal Energy block (exhaustion and overwhelm). Only when she got clear on her Soul Values could she begin to pay attention to her inner wisdom, shift that block, and align her business with her true gifts of intuition, flow, and empathy.

Yvette, on the other hand, had an Identity Block. The person she was trying to "be" in her new business with John wasn't aligned with her Soul Values of vitality, security, and abundance. Her soul wanted her to keep growing where she was because there was more for her to do there—for herself, her clients, and the world.

When the WOOs open, your soul is sending you a message.

When they don't open, that's also a message.

If you are experiencing any kind of block or resistance right now, the first place to look is your Soul Values. Are the strategies you think you "should" be using in your life and business out of alignment with your Soul Values? Where can you stop doing what works for others, and do what works for you instead?

Once you are clear on your values, you will start to make decisions differently in every area of your life. You will start to open those Windows of Opportunity and let the voice of your intuition guide you. You'll open the way to receive a clear vision for what you want, where you're going, and where you refuse to go ever again.

Do you have goosebumps yet?

Me, too.

Let's move forward.

# ~ 5 ~

# Your Clear Vision

After working with me in my Totally WOO program, my client Monica wrote about her experience creating a clear vision using the tools I'm about to share with you in this chapter.

After identifying and beginning to work with her blocks, and getting clear on her Soul Values, Monica knew something in her life was imbalanced. "This work revealed where I really needed to be spending my time and energy," she said. "In order for me to make a shift, I had to ask, 'What kind of structure do I require to fulfill the things that are asking for my attention?'"

One of the things on Monica's mind has been her goal to write and publish a book. "Writing a book is a longtime dream, and yet, the business of my everyday life has kept me from carving out the time necessary to truly immerse myself in my passion and honor the visionary inside me who has something important to say. The revelation I have had by using Candy's tools allowed me to form a plan to take the time I needed over a 90-day period to write my book. It also gave me an opportunity to assess what areas of my life need to stay balanced while I take that time. I was able to have conversations with my family, friends, and team, all of whom agreed to support me and keep my business on track while I endeavor to make my dream come true.

"So, this summer, I'll be taking time each day to walk, meditate, connect with Spirit, and receive the messages I know need to come through me to write my book. All the while, the other areas of my life will be tended to by my support network.

Monica concluded, "Candy's tools for alignment are so powerful—not only to make things happen but to see what additional support is needed for us to accomplish our dreams."

As you'll learn in this chapter, creating the life and business you desire is all about creating balance and getting support in the right places. Now that we've done the work to lean into your blocks and get clear on your values, it's time to figure out what you actually want. Or, more accurately, what your soul and higher self want for you.

Your Soul Values are your new lens for decision-making— which means that the things you thought you wanted, or the things you thought you had to get in a certain way, may no longer be applicable. From now on, you will be asking different, better questions, like, "Is this aligned with my Soul Values?" "Am I doing it this way because I want to, or because I feel like I have to?"

In order to get out of stuck energy and into flow, you need

to know where you're going. You need a clear vision to help you make aligned decisions. That's what Monica was able to do around her writing dream. Once she decided to follow her soul's guidance, everything else was able to come together in her favor. She saw what was needed to create and maintain balance as she undertook this journey, and was able to plan for something that, just a few months before, she would have said was impossible.

You may be asking at this point, "Being 'in flow' sounds nice, but why does it matter?"

As a heart-centered entrepreneur, flow is everything. Flow is where the money is. Flow is where the joy is. Flow is where the ease is. And flow is where your mission meets the Universe to create a ripple of positive impact.

When you don't have a clear vision and are making decisions that are not aligned with what your soul is calling for, you will run into struggle, which is the opposite of flow. You will go back to pushing that boulder when you could be running downhill toward what you desire most.

The work we will do to create a clear vision in this chapter is not actually about your business. It's about your life—specifically, what kind of life you want to live, and what will bring you joy, balance, and fulfillment. More, it's about who you will need to become to have what your soul and highest self so deeply desire for you.

Max De Pree, the author of *Leadership is an Art*, wrote, "We cannot become what we want to be by remaining what we are." Creating a clear vision is about identifying what you desire most in your life and business. To get to where you want to go, you first need to create a picture of your new, compelling future, and then create a strategy to bridge the gap from there to here.

# The Alignment Wheel

To help you create a detailed vision for alignment in your business and personal energy field, I've created the Alignment Wheel.

The Alignment Wheel has eight categories that I like to call "heart cups." Each of them represents a distinct energetic area of your life. When your cups are full, the Wheel can turn smoothly. When they are out of balance, you're in for a bumpy ride.

You may have seen "life wheels" before; this is based on that core concept. However, I use the Alignment Wheel slightly differently than most people. Instead of simply striving for balance, we will transpose your Soul Values onto the eight "heart cups" to figure out how much of your energy is spent in each category, and how aligned your experience in that categories is with your Soul Values.

With the insight you'll gain from the Wheel, you will create a clear vision and 90-Day Alignment Plan for your life that you can then apply to your business through your Quantum Blueprint for Wealth.

Let's explore each category one by one.

### *Health & Vitality*

In order to do our work in the world, we need to be healthy. If our vitality is low, so is our creative output, our cash flow, and our ability to give. Everything we create is connected to our energy. And although our business has its own energy, we are still intimately connected to it, and our personal energy (or lack of it) has a huge impact on the overall vitality of our business.

Vitality isn't just about physical health, although that's a big part of it. It's about joy, freedom, and lack of stress. It's about our

# THE ALIGNMENT WHEEL

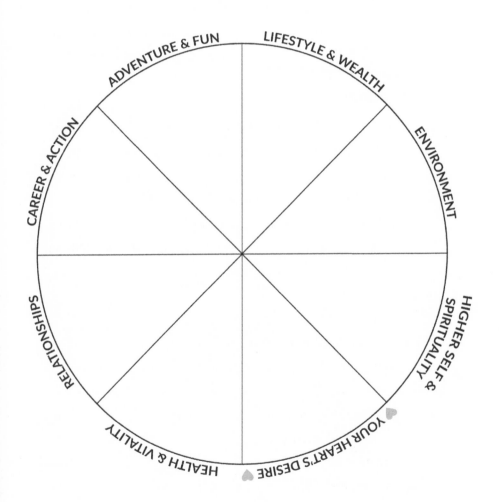

mental health, our spiritual health, and our overall energy level.

Where are you today in terms of your personal vitality? Do you have daily aches and pains? Do you have sleep issues? Do you move your body regularly? Do you eat well? Do you have other issues sapping your energy? Do you feel content, even joyful, most days—or do you feel sluggish, angry, resentful, depressed, or anxious? All of these are indicators of your vitality.

## Relationships

Everything we do in life is in some way connected to a relationship. We have partners, children, family, friends, colleagues, clients, acquaintances ... and nearly everything we do in life revolves around or relies upon one or more of those connections.

So, where are you in your relationships? Are they aligned with what you want for your life? Do they nourish you? Do you nourish them? Do they energize or drain you?

## Career & Action

I put career and action together because they require a lot of the same things from you. However, what I've noticed after working with hundreds of clients is that many of the things that they do in their business aren't action, but "busy work." This creates misalignments and energy leaks.

Action is what moves you forward in work and life. Busy work, on the other hand, keeps the wheels spinning but doesn't necessarily get you anywhere. If we want to be effective in action, we need to learn the difference between the two and spend our time on the things that move us forward, not the things that keep us stuck. So, ask yourself: Are my daily actions moving me closer to where I want to be, both personally and in my business?

## Adventure & Fun

It's necessary to have some fun and laughter in your life. Do the things that feel like a stretch (and that leave you wondering why you hadn't done them sooner)!

Adventure doesn't have to be travel or thrill-seeking. It could simply be hanging out with the right people, or being spontaneous when you otherwise tend to be a planner. For example, I had a great girlfriend who loved to pop into my life with no forewarning. She had no conventional parameters. When she was in town, you might as well put your day on hold, because there was going to be a lot of drama. She was hilarious, spontaneous, and always insisted on VIP treatment. At the end of a whirlwind day with her I knew I would expand and see life differently.

So just take a moment and think of how adventure and fun currently show up in your life. How important are they to you? Do you want more of them?

## Lifestyle & Wealth

My first iteration of the Alignment Wheel had this section labeled "finances." But "finance" isn't juicy. In fact, most people don't even want to talk about it! So, I renamed this section of the wheel "Lifestyle and Wealth" to represent the vast space of abundance we want to occupy.

I once had a friend come to stay with me. She gave me the best compliment. "You have such an amazing lifestyle."

I was confused, so she explained, "You have so many gifts in your life. You fly for free. You get to go to really exotic and cool places. You have access to some of the most amazing people and events. You are living the dream."

When I created my business after my bout with cancer, I envisioned a life where I could enjoy all the gifts I'd been given. And regardless of the scale of "dollars in, dollars out" in my life, I always feel wealthy and free to make the choices that serve me.

So, in terms of lifestyle and wealth, are you where you want to be? Recognize that your lifestyle goals will be uniquely your own. There is no benchmark for "wealth." It's a mental state. This is about identifying the life you want to live and figuring out what it will take to get you there.

## *Environment*

We often underestimate how much we are influenced by our environment. What's happening around us can either enhance our energy or deplete it.

The most obvious piece of environment is where you live. If you have a place to land each night that's safe and comfortable, that's pretty great—but is it a place that actually meets your standards? Do you feel like the most abundant, creative, and vital version of yourself in that space?

Environment can also encompass the little things—like what your desk, bedroom, and refrigerator look like. Do you feel more creative, focused, and productive when things are neat as a pin, or lovingly messy? Do you love your home when it's clean and tidy, but feel stressed out whenever you look around at the piles of things to be put away?

## *Higher Self & Spirituality*

For me, the Akashic Records are a major presence in my life. Without a dedicated spiritual practice and continual growth of my intuitive gifts, I can't do my best work for my clients.

What spiritual practices are in alignment for you? Do you meditate? Do you do yoga? Do you have a daily prayer practice, or do you find God/Spirit/Source through communing with nature? What fills you up and helps you feel connected to your heart, soul, spirit, higher self, and intuition? Consider making those practices a key part of your daily life.

Ask yourself: "How present are my higher self and my spiritual practices in my daily life? Am I nourishing these aspects of me, or ignoring them?"

### *Your Heart's Desire*

This last piece of the Alignment Wheel is reserved for what matters most to you.

Maybe it's art, music, or writing. Maybe it's teaching or mentoring. Maybe it's restoring antique furniture. For Monica (whose story I shared at the beginning of this chapter), it was writing her book. Whatever this last piece is, are you making space for it in your life?

## How does the Wheel Roll?

Now that you understand all eight "heart cups" in the Alignment Wheel, take a moment to actually write down, on a scale of 1 to 100, how full those cups are for you today.

You can do this analytically, by picking a percentage—as in, "My Lifestyle and Wealth cup is 88 percent full"—or, you can pick up your crayons or colored pens and intuitively color in each "cup" to the level you feel you're experiencing. Either way, when you're finished, you should have an accurate picture of where you are spending your life force energy.

Please don't judge what you see in this iteration of your Alignment Wheel. Remember, all of this is in service to your clear vision. Instead, grab the list of Soul Values you created in Chapter 4, and let's move into the next stage of creating your vision.

# Values & The Alignment Wheel

The cool thing about the Alignment Wheel is that it shows you not only where you need more balance in your life, but also how closely your current energy use is aligned with your Soul Values.

If you haven't already, put your Soul Values in order, starting with the most important. We will then look at each of the "heart cups" on the Alignment Wheel through the lens of your Soul Values to see if your energy expenditures are aligned with what your soul wants for you, or if they should be adjusted.

The best way to experience this is through an example, so I'll share one here.

### My personal top five values are:

- Vitality
- Connection to Higher Self
- Mastery & Excellence
- Romance & Magic
- Environment

However, when I plotted out my Alignment Wheel in March of 2020, it looked like this:

As you can see, my Career & Action cup was overflowing at

100 percent. (If I'm being honest, it was more like 110 percent because I was giving energy there to the point of depletion.) My Higher Self & Spirituality cup was fairly full at 80 percent, but Environment (which is a cup but also a Soul Value for me) was only at around 72 percent. And my Health & Vitality cup was half-empty at 55 percent!

When I did that version of my Alignment Wheel, I had just come off of a big launch. I'd been working at full capacity for weeks, and all the things I had been doing to support myself in other areas—boxing lessons for exercise, healthy organic foods, good sleep—had fallen by the wayside, which was affecting

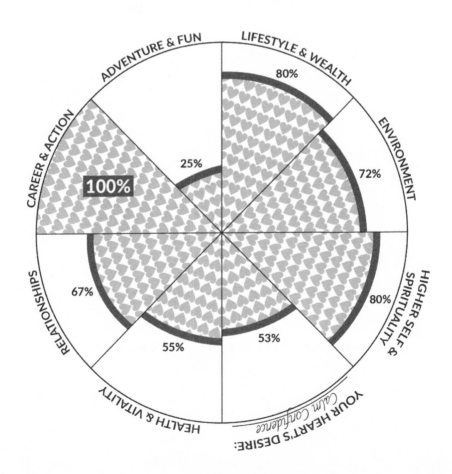

my vitality. By the end of the day, I was so tired that I didn't even want to meditate, so my Higher Self & Spirituality cup was being slowly depleted. And my relationships were sitting around 67 percent because I felt like I lacked the energy to nourish them properly.

If you compare my Alignment Wheel to the list of my Soul Values, it's easy to see where things weren't working. I was putting my life force energy into areas that weren't aligned with my top values!

Knowing this, it was easy to sit down and create a clear vision for the next ninety days in my life. To regain my balance and help my Alignment Wheel "roll" smoothly, I would:

- Spend time in meditation daily

- Nourish my body with good food, good rest, and good care

- Restructure aspects of my business that were taking too much of my energy

- Ask for help when I needed it

- Clean up any clutter in my environment that was causing mental distraction

- Prioritize time with my partner, family, and friends to nurture my important relationships, and pay attention to the magic when we were together

- Recognize where my drive to pursue Mastery & Excellence was overtaking my highest Soul Values of Vitality and Connection to Higher Self

That last piece was key for me. I knew that Mastery & Excellence was a high Soul Value for me, but when I stopped to feel into it, Vitality clearly came first. My natural tendency was to work myself into the ground in pursuit of excellence, but my soul wanted flow, not struggle.

Often, we will find that one of our Soul Values conflicts with another. In those situations, your top Soul Value will come first.

Your Soul Values are the key qualities of who your soul wants you to become—who you need to become if you want to create what you desire. When you put your Soul Values on top of the Alignment Wheel, the path forward becomes clear.

At some point in the next week, I want you to do the exercises in this chapter for yourself. Create your Alignment Wheel and compare your results to your Soul Values. What needs to shift to create more flow, ease, and balance in your life force energy? Where do you want to spend your time going forward?

# Your Clear Vision and 90-Day Alignment Plan

So, where might you want to spend a little more of your life force energy in the next 90 days?

You might look at your Alignment Wheel and see a few places where you can tweak your daily routines and business goals to better support you. Or, you might look at it and think, "I need to change *everything!*" Either way is okay! What matters is that you have accurate information about how and where your energy is being spent. Now, you can create a clear vision and 90-Day Alignment Plan to move into greater balance and ease in your life and business.

Whatever your Wheel reveals, I would encourage you to create your 90-Day Alignment Plan with the intention to balance your Heart Cups as much as possible. How full do you want each of your "heart cups" to be? What changes can you commit to that will facilitate those shifts? Who do you need to be *today* to have more joy, balance, and flow in your life?

I want you to think about this as establishing *ways of being,* rather than numerical or action-oriented goals. You can do this by asking, "Who do I need to be *right now* in order to fill my 'heart cups' to the level I've envisioned and create what I desire?"

## Here's how your "goals" might look through this lens.

- "I commit to being a person who takes care of her body with nourishing, vitamin-rich foods." (Health & Vitality)

- "I commit to being a person who moves her body often and with joy." (Health & Vitality)

- "I commit to being a person who is present for her family and prioritizes connection time with those I love." (Relationships)

- "I commit to being a person who asks for help in my business so I can reclaim my energy and serve on the highest level." (Career & Action)

- "I commit to being a person who has a beautiful relationship with money." (Lifestyle & Wealth)

- "I commit to being a person who deals with clutter daily." (Environment)

- "I commit to being a person who is willing to let go and have fun, enjoy life, and live in gratitude." (Adventure & Fun)

- "I commit to being a person who connects to her higher self daily in meditation." (Higher Self & Spirituality)

It's much more important to understand who you need to *be* every day to accomplish your goals than it is to know all the details of how, when, and where you will take action. If you are being the kind of person who embodies your Soul Values, your actions will automatically shift to align with your goals for filling those "heart cups."

Next, write more about the next level of you—the "you" who you are committing to embody. Who is she? What does she look like? Feel like? Act like?

Write down some of the qualities that come to mind, as well as activities that are natural and fun for this version of you. For example, you might write statements like:

- *I am now glowing, full of energy, and comfortable in my body.*

- *I am relaxed and at ease.*

- *I have unlimited abundance at my fingertips.*

- *I meet challenges with full trust in myself.*

- *I proceed with calm, confidence, and ease as I help and empower myself and others.*

- *I love freely and without reservation.*

- *I laugh a lot.*

Get as detailed as you like as you envision this version of you. Notice how your vision of yourself is fully supported by the commitments you've made in your goal-setting.

Now that you have an idea of the new ways of being you'd like to incorporate, you might want to narrow down some of the specific actions you can take to embody the energy you've identified. For example, if your vision of yourself is "glowing and full of energy," write down some things that this version of you does on a daily basis to maintain that glow, such as remembering daily supplements, regular workouts, eating organic foods, drinking lemon water each morning, etc. These things will become the daily action steps and to-do lists that support your embodiment. You can even put them in your calendar to make sure you remember!

# Becoming More of Who You're Meant to Be

The core of this process is to help you become who you are meant to be, so you can have the life—and business—you are meant to have. The more you embody the change you want to be, the more movement you'll start to see in your life.

Embodiment is about feminine energy. It's not forced, it's flowing. So, get curious. Have fun with it. Stay in the now.

Once you decide who you are going to be, make a plan to fill those "heart cups" in your Alignment Wheel over the next 90 days. Record a video of yourself speaking to yourself as the 90-days-in-the-future version of you. Whatever it takes to get you into the energy of evolution.

You may be asking, "Yes, Candy, but when do we get to my business? Especially to that 'Lifestyle and Abundance' part?" The answer can be found in the next step of our process—mapping your Quantum Leap Blueprint for Wealth!

Goosebumps up! Let's turn the page.

# ~ 6 ~

# Your Quantum Leap
# Blueprint for Wealth

When I speak at events, I often do an exercise I call "The Golden Envelope."

I hand out these envelopes to everyone in the audience and invite them to write themselves a check for whatever amount of money they'd like to manifest. In the "memo" field, they write how they created or earned it. Then, I instruct them to put the check in the golden envelope and mail it to themselves— quite literally sending the request out into the Universe. Once they receive it back, they open the envelope, put the check in their wallet, and keep it there in plain view until the money manifests.

I have many stories about magical manifestation using this technique. In an interview with Oprah Winfrey, Jim Carrey shared his story of using a similar exercise at the start of his acting career. One day, he wrote himself a check for $10 million and put it in his wallet. The memo field read, "For acting services rendered." Just a few years later, he was paid $10 million for his role in his breakout movie, *Dumb and Dumber*.

But the most amazing story I have about the Golden Envelope technique comes from someone who had never seen me speak on stage or heard Jim Carrey's story. Instead, Danielle found me on Facebook. After listening to me describe the technique in a video, she decided to try it for herself.

Danielle and her husband were living paycheck to paycheck. One of their cars was held together by duct tape and prayers. They were struggling to pay their bills. Danielle literally had nothing to lose when she wrote her check for $1 million and put it in her mailbox. "I placed my hands on either side of the mailbox and imagined the money I'd requested coming to me," she said.

Once the check returned to her a few days later, she placed it in her pink flamingo wallet and went about her life. The thing was, she really believed that she could manifest this money. After all, others had done it—why not her?

About six months later, her husband, a sales representative, made the largest sale in the history of his company—a $25 million deal. Guess what his commission was? $1.5 million. He and Danielle also got a bonus trip to the South Pacific and a bunch of other perks. Danielle felt so blessed, and so abundant, that she started giving money away. Recently, she started a nonprofit to empower marginalized women and children with housing, healthcare, and education services.

The key to Danielle's success was her belief that she would manifest the money—that she deserved it, and that it would come to her because she had asked. She was aligned with the vibration of receiving, and the Universe responded in kind. Her Quantum Leap Blueprint for Wealth was to receive and flow money through her generous heart, and she tapped into it with jaw-dropping results.

## Making the Quantum Leap

Your Quantum Leap Blueprint for Wealth isn't a to-do list. It's not a "do this, don't do that" kind of blueprint. It's literally mapped onto your soul. And when you align with it, you will attract wealth in exactly the right proportion to power the mission, lifestyle, and business that you've chosen.

Many of the blocks my private clients experience appear, on the surface, to be around wealth. They want it, but they aren't receiving it. Or, they *are* receiving it, but at the expense of their joy, relationships, or life force energy.

But the truth is, their blocks aren't about money and wealth at all. They're about self-worth. What they're really asking is: "Am I worthy of the abundance I desire? If I receive abundance without working myself to the bone, am I 'taking' it or being unethical? Do I actually *need* the wealth I'm dreaming about?"

Once we release the energy blocks around self-worth, the money often comes pouring in. One of my clients once joked with me, "Candy, can we put the block back? I can't hire enough people to serve all of my amazing new clients!" Another got her first $1 million contract after twenty-plus years of frustration and slow growth in her business.

Over and over, I've seen transformations like these occur, almost overnight. I kept asking myself and my guides, "What is the blueprint for this? What is the one piece that will help people do this for themselves?"

The answer didn't come in my daily meditations. In fact, I was getting frustrated at my lack of clarity. Then one day, while puttering around in my garden, I noticed that the sunflowers I'd planted earlier that summer were in bloom. I took a picture of them with my phone's camera—and, low and behold, I saw it ... The Flower of Life.

## THE FLOWER OF LIFE

Now, I had something to take to my guides. I started asking better questions, like, "How does this Flower of Life influence wealth consciousness?"

After doing more research, I realized that everything on this planet—from sunflowers to human beings—*is naturally progressing toward something,* just as the Flower of Life spirals out from its center in an ever-expanding matrix. Once you release your energy blocks, get clear on what you are *progressing toward* using your Soul Values, and create a clear vision to get there, you can press the "start" button on the natural creation spiral of the Flower of Life and expand into your most aligned expression.

You already have a Blueprint for Wealth inside you. Everyone on this planet came here with a mission, and that mission always included you being fully supported by the Universe, God/Spirit/ Source, and your guides. Your job isn't to force that Flower of Life to bloom on your behalf. It is to align your energy so that what blooms is *exactly* what you need to do your best work in the world.

Your Blueprint for Wealth is already within you, but the Quantum Leap comes from alignment and intention. When you have the pieces in place, release your blocks, identify and align with your Soul Values, and manage your life force energy in support of those values, you are putting the building blocks in place to support a rapid unfolding of that Flower of Life energy. This is the space where miracles happen.

Now, please understand: Your Blueprint for Wealth will be there regardless of whether you do this "prep work." It doesn't have an expiration date; it's never too late to bring it to light. But until you align your conscious energy with it and open the door to that Quantum Leap, it will remain dormant, like a seed waiting for spring. When you're not aligned, you will work harder to create and receive abundance, and may feel like you need to sacrifice in other areas of your life to make the money you desire.

So many high-performing women I meet struggle with this alignment piece. They have so much at stake. They've built thriving businesses despite their blocks and misalignments. They're proud of how much they've struggled to push their boulder up the hill. And they're afraid that, if they let go and step into this new, more graceful alignment, that the boulder will come rolling down the slope and flatten everything they've worked for.

The truth is, nothing that is vibrationally aligned with our highest and best good will ever be damaged or destroyed by us stepping into our Quantum Leap unfolding. We don't need to sacrifice what we've built in order to invite something better. Remember, our business doesn't know fear or lack; when we become aligned, our business will inevitably shift into more flow and abundance, not less. New Windows of Opportunity will open the moment you understand that you can choose to receive everything your heart desires, and more.

That's what happened to Danielle. She chose to step away from the boulder of fear, poverty, and misalignment she was pushing and align her whole family with the vibration of wealth. Her Quantum Leap Blueprint for Wealth didn't ask her to work harder, or do more, or learn a new skill. It didn't even ask her to create the funds directly. It simply asked that she *receive*, so she could be fully supported in the empowerment work she came to this planet to do.

## The Money Shift

"I want to make more money."

I hear these words from ninety percent of my clients.

"Great," I usually reply. "But *how* do you want to make that money? *How* do you want to attract your ideal lifestyle and wealth? What are you willing to do—and what do you want to stop doing?"

Chances are, you know how to make money. You're likely already doing so in your business. But if you have all the pieces in place, why are you not hitting your goals?

There are patterns within each of us that push us away from our natural Blueprint for Wealth. They are usually rooted in fear, uncertainty, doubt, and wounding. We are doing business through the energy of our injured selves and default values, not our highest selves and Soul Values.

When I coach people through this process, the first thing we look at is their current identity. Are they aligned with the identity of a hugely profitable business owner? Just like we created intention statements in Chapter 5, you can create wealth identity statements—aka beliefs—to support the new version of you who is aligned with your clear vision.

Choose a new belief about money that aligns with your 90-Day Alignment Plan and clear vision.

Here are some sample beliefs to get you started.

- I am financially free.

- I naturally attract money and financial opportunities.

- I have all the money I need to make a huge difference in this world.

- Money flows to me with ease.

Once you have a belief to work with, remember a time when the new belief you want to cultivate was actually true for you. (Or, imagine how you will feel when this belief is your "new normal.") What emotions do you associate with this belief? Write them down.

Here are some possibilities based on the examples above.

- Confident, empowered, excited.
- Magical, aligned with purpose, at ease.
- Empowered, strong, being a leader, making an impact.
- Relief, excitement, peace, joy. Feeling like, "That was easy!"

Finally, you'll take the new belief and combine it with your desired emotions to create an "I am" statement, like the following.

- Everything I need is inside me now. Opportunities are available to me at all times.

- I am a money magnet! I am energized and confident. I am walking my own path with purpose.

- I am an empowered leader. I am fully supported to bring my positive messages and teachings to the world.

- I am a co-creator with money. I am worthy of abundance. I am powerfully aligned to create the wealth I desire.

The real statement of who you are is "I AM." When you use these statements, you're conditioning your mind and body to align with your new, compelling future. Evolving to the next level of you is part of that process.

Use these affirmations daily for at least twenty-seven days until you feel that your identity is aligned with the affirmation. When you do this, you're conditioning yourself into new behaviors that will support you as you step into the next level of you and your business. On the days when you're really struggling—when you feel uncertain, and when your fears come up—those are the best times to use the affirmations, because they will help you come back into alignment. (Need a little extra guidance? Get my morning affirmations at www.CandiceHozza.com/BookResources.)

## Your Aligned Earnings Calculator

Many of my clients—even those who are great with money—can't clearly state how much wealth they *actually* want to manifest. They often feel misaligned with their earnings. They fall back on arbitrary numbers, like "A hundred thousand dollars. A million dollars. Ten million dollars." But we have to realize that, in our Quantum Leap Blueprint for Wealth, we are not the only ones receiving.

Do you have a team? A family? A cause? They're receiving through your Blueprint. So are your clients, your vendors, and everyone else in your orbit. When you think about it, the amount you want to create may not actually be aligned with the compelling future you're calling in. In fact, you're probably thinking too small.

Take my client Kate, for example. When we started working together, she was making $32,000 a month. Today, three years later, she's making $128,000 a month from her two businesses. Talk about a clear vision and energy alignment! But, let's be clear: not all of this wealth is ending up in her personal checking account. In order to run her businesses with ease and flow, she needs a skilled team, which means she needs to pay salaries. To deal with her extended work hours, she's hired a nanny to help with childcare and household chores. She no longer runs unnecessary errands; she pays for deliveries instead. She bought a bigger house last year so her kids can run around while she works. All of these things cost money. Kate's take-home pay is still substantial, but to create what she wanted for herself, she needed to think much, much bigger when it came to her business—and she chose to do it in alignment with her Soul Values of family, nurturing, and quality time.

To help people conceptualize this more easily, I created the Aligned Earnings Calculator (shown at right). This calculator is based on the percentages Amber Dugger shares in her groundbreaking work around money and wealth. It's a basic outline that you can adapt to your own life and business to understand the level of abundance with which you want to align.

As you can see, when you want to earn $100,000 personally, you are actually aligning with a much larger number in your business. When you allow your mind to expand around this, you will step into resonance with greater money flow.

Another client set her intention to make $500,000 in the first quarter of 2021. She's on track to do it because she did the work: she released her blocks, discovered her Soul Values, and created a clear vision to align with her Blueprint for Wealth. Every quarter, she revisits this work and creates a new, more aligned plan. Every quarter, she creates exactly what she specifies. It brings me great joy to see entrepreneurial moms be able to abundantly support their families.

If numbers don't get you excited, you can also create quarterly blueprints for how many people you want to serve.

# THE ALIGNED EARNINGS CALCULATOR

| $100,000 | 5% | Profit | $5,000 |
|---|---|---|---|
| | 49% | Owners | $49,000 |
| | 20% | Taxes | $20,000 |
| | 25% | Business Account | $25,000 |
| | 1% | Charity | $1,000 |

| $250,000 | 5% | Profit | $12,500 |
|---|---|---|---|
| | 49% | Owners | $122,500 |
| | 20% | Taxes | $50,000 |
| | 25% | Business Account | $62,500 |
| | 1% | Charity | $2,500 |

| $350,000 | 5% | Profit | $17,500 |
|---|---|---|---|
| | 49% | Owners | $171,500 |
| | 20% | Taxes | $70,000 |
| | 25% | Business Account | $87,000 |
| | 1% | Charity | $3,500 |

| $500,000 | 5% | Profit | $25,000 |
|---|---|---|---|
| | 47% | Owners | $235,000 |
| | 20% | Taxes | $100,000 |
| | 25% | Business Account | $125,000 |
| | 3% | Charity | $15,000 |

| $800,000 | 5% | Profit | $40,000 |
|---|---|---|---|
| | 47% | Owners | $376,000 |
| | 20% | Taxes | $160,000 |
| | 25% | Business Account | $300,000 |
| | 3% | Charity | $24,000 |

| $1,000,000 | 5% | Profit | $50,000 |
|---|---|---|---|
| | 45% | Owners | $450,000 |
| | 20% | Taxes | $200,000 |
| | 25% | Business Account | $250,000 |
| | 5% | Charity | $50,000 |

I often create a wall chart with a certain number of blank squares. These squares represent the people I am attracting to my programs. As each new person comes into a program, I add their name to a square. This allows me to celebrate the people who said yes to my programs and the very real contribution I'm making. At the same time, I know that those squares add up to my Aligned Earnings for that quarter!

# Sending It Out to the Universe

So, now that you have your affirmations, your Aligned Earnings numbers, and your 90-Day Alignment Plan from Chapter 5, what do you do with it all?

You send it out to the Universe, of course!

When you're ready to create something new for your life and business, you need clarity first. (Hint, that's what we've been doing up to this point in our work!) Once you know what you desire, and what needs to shift for you to be able to live into that desire, it's time to let the Universe know what's up by activating the energy around your new identity.

You can do this by mailing yourself a check using the Golden Envelope technique, as Danielle did. This exercise is a great way to put your "ask" out there in a simple, clear way.

You can also put all of your affirmations, alignment wheel, etc. on your altar, and cover them with a printout of the Seed of Life or Flower of Life. Some of my students use various crystals and gemstones at each point on the Seed to further activate the energy. Every time they sit at their altar, they can feel the energy of their new identity expanding!

If you have a favorite technique for flowing energy through your desires, go ahead and use that too! It's less about the actual process and more about the practice, attention, and intention. You want to be super clear with the Universe right now—but also with yourself. The more you can be in that energy of who you're becoming, the easier it will be to stay in alignment!

# ~ 7 ~

# Accessing Your Akashic Records

Before my cancer diagnosis, I was in a really disempowered state. I had separated from my husband after twenty-five years of marriage and was living in an apartment with my son (my daughter was already in college). I was still working for the university, which was exhausting. My income was limited. But the biggest thing on my mind was a question:

"Who am I now? What's my identity?" I used to be married; now I was single. I used to have money flow; now I was struggling. Everything felt upside-down.

I hired a coach and worked with her for six months. When our contract was complete, I felt much clearer and more grounded, but the question of identity was still unresolved.

"I don't think you need strategy right now," my coach told me. "I think you need spiritual healing. I'd love to introduce you to a friend of mine who reads the Akashic Records."

By this point, I was already communicating regularly with my angels and guides, but I didn't have any experience with the Records. I decided to give it a try.

Immediately, I knew this modality was different.

During our first appointment, I found myself saying to the reader, "I want to remember who I am and develop at a soul level." She asked permission to open my records—which I loved because I'd had sessions with readers who didn't ask, and it always felt a bit like they were peeking at me around the shower curtain! Then, we were both transported into a brand-new space, where we were simultaneously receiving information about what was next for me and where I needed to focus.

I had my eyes closed the whole time, so when the reader asked for permission to open my Records, I thought it was an invitation for *me* to open them—and I dropped right into that space of infinite possibility. I was seeing the same truths the reader was communicating—the same writing on the wall. Her being there with me gave me confidence, but I was fully present in those moments to my own truth.

I had multiple sessions with that reader. And as I got clear insights, and experienced the soul-deep healing that is another gift of the Akasha, my life started to evolve.

I had been learning about real estate before my separation; after getting more clarity, I started a business in real estate and property management. Aches and pains that had been with me since my thirties started to heal and disappear. My parenting started to change. I started to feel good again, in my body and soul. I started to love myself fully. My new life no longer felt so impossible, or so scary.

Fast-forward to 2014. After nearly four years of separation, I decided I was ready for a new partner. I was back on my feet, and clear about what I wanted in life and love. On Christmas night, after my son had left to be with my daughter in New York City, I ended up having dinner with my ex. We talked until well past midnight. He wanted to get back together. He felt that our time apart had helped him realize how important I was to him, and how much he wanted our family to be together. He asked me to meet him the following day for a romantic date.

I said no.

For over two hours, I held my ground. Finally, discouraged, he said goodnight and started pulling on his coat. I walked him through the kitchen to the door.

Suddenly, I looked up. There was a crack in my ceiling. Soft, golden light was filtering through, as though from the room upstairs. And yet, I knew there was no physical crack in the plaster.

I was being so stubborn in that moment. I so was fixated on our past relationship, and the pain it had brought me, that I couldn't see anything beyond that. My angels and guides were practically screaming at me to see something … but to be sure I wasn't imagining this, I did a quick internal check.

First, I would have noticed long before today if a huge crack had appeared in my kitchen ceiling, so I figured this wasn't actually structural damage.

Second, the light coming through was incredibly bright—so

bright that it should have hurt my eyes. It didn't.

Third, Tim hadn't noticed a thing.

Checklist complete. Either I was losing my mind, or this was a message from my guides. But why would beings of superior intelligence care about my non-marriage?

Then, I heard a deep, male voice speak in my ear. "He's the best thing that you've had going, and this choice is right. Say yes!"

Time seemed to stop. I knew this was a moment of decision. As I hesitated, the crack started to close. The light dimmed. I felt a pressure inside me; I had seconds to choose. Would I say yes to one date?

I blurted, "Yes!"

As I spoke, the crack above me fully closed.

"What?" Tim asked. "I'm confused."

"I'm agreeing to the date you're proposing for tomorrow. *Yes.*"

He smiled—and sealed the deal with a kiss that shocked me. I felt a sense of safety wash over me. He felt like home.

And so, we went on a date. It was the most magical day I'd had since we'd met nearly thirty years before. We had both become new people, capable of having a new relationship. We ended up reconciling our marriage just months before my cancer diagnosis. As you know, my job at the university ended shortly after that. I had to put my real estate business on hold while I healed. I don't know how I would have managed without my husband's support, and that of our kids and extended family.

Throughout this book, I've been preparing you to make a transition of your own—to the next level of *you*. You know something has changed, and something needs to change, to bring you into alignment in your life and business. You've identified your blocks, claimed your values, and gotten clarity with the Alignment Wheel. You've tuned into your Quantum Leap Blueprint for Wealth. And now, you will learn to open your Akashic Records to access the clear insights that will power your next phase of personal and business growth.

At some point as you were reading—or even before you picked up this book—you probably had an "uh-oh" moment—a moment when you realized that it's no longer aligned for you to follow the straightforward A-to-B path you were previously on. Life is going to be different.

When things shift in our lives, the first thing that can happen is that we fall into pain. When I first moved out of the home I'd shared with my husband for more than two decades, I cried every day. I loved being a family. I loved being a wife and a mother. But we couldn't seem to work it out.

I wanted a different life. I wanted a partner with whom I could connect and share my heartfelt feelings, and who could express his feelings in return. I didn't want to keep choosing the old pain—but I was struggling to get a foothold, and the more I fought my new reality, the further away from what I wanted I seemed to fall.

To transition from the point of pain to your next compelling future in life and business, you'll want to follow the process I've laid out for you in this book: clearing blocks, clarifying values, understanding your Alignment Wheel, creating your Blueprint for Wealth. Learning to access and read your own Records is the next step on that staircase—the one that will, more than any other, get you out of the hole of pain, confusion, and fear, and empower you to step into the version of you who is waiting to be known.

# Your Soul Knows the Path

When I first started reading the Records, it was only for myself. I didn't feel confident enough to read them for others. I felt it was a huge responsibility to channel information from someone's energy field and articulate it into language. I also didn't want to disempower them by asking them to rely on me for access to this knowledge. I had found my own ruby slippers; I didn't want to step into the role of the wizard behind the curtain.

I felt like, when I accessed someone's Records, I was seeing and sharing something they didn't have access to. I thought, "I don't want people to be dependent on me to channel their answers." That didn't feel right at all.

It wasn't until I saw the profound shifts unfolding in my life that I saw how this could empower others—particularly women—to create their own identities after periods of change. I realized that anyone can read their own Records because *the Records are part of them.* There is no separation. The Records are literally the place where your soul can transmit truth directly to you.

After spending more than 3,000 hours in the Akashic Records with my clients over the last several years, this has proven to be true. In session, I am a channel and a conduit—but just as I became present to my Records when that reader first opened them, my clients also step into their own knowing with me as a guide. The more comfortable they get in this space of possibility, the more empowered they feel to access it themselves whenever they need guidance in life and business.

Every day, we routinely decide what to eat, what to wear, what route to take to the grocery store, how to have a difficult conversation with a loved one, how to change unhelpful habits, and how to plan for the future. As business owners, we make even more decisions than that—many of them vitally important to creating our desired reality. When you think about it, it's easy to see why we're tempted to give up in exhaustion when it comes to changing our ways of being in the world! The wonderful thing about learning to read your Records is this: *The answers are all there.* When your conscious mind is unsure, your soul knows the path.

Remember, your soul and higher self know no injury, limitations, lack, or fear. When you allow yourself to receive guidance in the space of your Records, you bridge the gap between your current self and who you are becoming. You literally blend the two to create an aligned platform on which you can claim the next level of your identity in life and business.

## Aligning with the WOO

I once listened to James Cameron, the famous director, talk about opportunity. He described it as a Universal bank vault. When you send out your desires and intentions, the Universe aligns to them. Gears start turning, mechanisms start clicking ... and all of a sudden, there's a moment of connection—a split second where everything is aligned and the door opens.

In that moment, we have a choice. We can step through the door that has been opened for us—or we can stay where we are. Our job isn't to create the opening; it's to recognize it when it happens, and leap.

Everything we have experienced and learned has prepared us to step into the next evolution of ourselves. When we release a block in our energy field or have a clear insight about our life or work, the Universal gears start turning. The mechanism starts clicking. And then, there's a split second where that Window of Opportunity—the WOO—opens up, and we are called to make a choice: step through, and receive what's on the other side, or stay in our current state for a little longer.

I often think of our higher self and our conscious self as being on two separate, parallel elevators. The elevator for the higher self can only go up—but the elevator for your conscious self, the one that has been injured by life and experience, can go up and down. Only in the moments where the two elevators are aligned at the same vibrational frequency will you hear that quiet, "Ding, ding!" and feel the doors slide open. Suddenly, you will have the opportunity to step from one elevator to the other and ascend to the next level of your journey. This is the essence of a WOO.

But here's the thing: our conscious, logical mind doesn't always recognize the WOO when it comes. Sometimes, we're confused. "Is this my stop? I'm not sure." Other times, we're so distracted by our current reality that we don't see the doors opening. Or, we're so focused on getting to the floor we *think* we're supposed to get to that we don't see the WOO for the opportunity it is.

Just like that bank vault, your WOOs don't stay open forever. Sometimes, they're only available for a split second—the space of one decision, one thought, one "Yes!"

Your intuition always knows when a Window of Opportunity is opening in your life and business. Your higher self will always guide you in the direction of your expansion—*if* you make the space to listen.

This is why it's so important, at this stage, to learn to access your Akashic Records. All of the information you need to see, recognize, and step into your WOO is there. It's been there for you since the moment you were born, because it's *inside* you.

I'm often asked, "But if the Records hold all the answers, why don't you teach this first?"

Because you weren't ready then. But you are now.

If you don't know where your blocks lie, what your highest Soul Values are, and where you want to go, you won't align as quickly in the space of the Records. More importantly, you won't know which questions to ask to get the highest and best information in this moment. You might have a fabulous WOO ready to open for you—but you won't see it if you're looking in the wrong direction.

When people jump right into the space of intuition and opening their Records, they get caught up in thoughts like, "Am I doing this right?" and "Can I trust the information I'm getting?" Or, they get caught up in questions or explorations that don't align with their Soul Values and the true expression of who they want to be in the world.

Inside the space of your Records—behind the door of the vault—is an ocean of information, possibility, and promise. But if you go in without direction, it will be like trying to search for your keys in the Pacific Ocean. Understanding your Soul Values, and having clear insights before you enter the space, helps you narrow the search area to something the size of a swimming pool. This makes it much more likely that you will get helpful answers—answers that will help you recognize your next WOO.

# Finding Your "Clair"

If I taught you to "see," and you're not a seer, you would think you weren't intuitive.

All of us have one or more mechanisms for receiving information from our higher self, our soul, and the Divine. But these don't always look like the "psychic" or "paranormal" abilities we've seen on television or in movies.

When I enter my own Records or the Records of my clients, I often "see" the information. I receive visions, colors, shapes, or even full scenes. This makes sense, as I'm a very visual person. But not everyone processes intuitive information that way. In fact, there are many ways to receive information from your intuition and higher self. In my world, these different ways of sensing "beyond" our physical world are sometimes called "the Clairs."

Knowing your Clair (or Clairs) is important when it comes to accessing your Akashic Records because this will help you assimilate information as it's revealed to you. While a few people might literally see a library of "records" and read their soul's words from a scroll, that's not the norm! More often, you'll receive information according to your natural, instinctive way of processing.

Here are the five most common "Clairs." See if you recognize yourself in any of these!

If you're not sure which "Clair" you're working with, or if you want to learn more about how you already access your intuition in your business, take the Intuitive Business Superpower Quiz at www.CandiceHozza.com/superpower.

## *Clairvoyance ("clear seeing")*

You are highly visual and often receive information through pictures, visions, colors, symbols, or patterns. You may experience vivid or prophetic dreams, or have the ability to see auras or spiritual presences.

When learning, you prefer diagrams, sketches, slides, and info-graphics to words on a page. Color is key in your life, and wearing certain colors may influence your mood and energy. You are very tuned in to the appearance of your surroundings, and the "look" of your environment is very important. Vision boards can be a helpful tool for you when working with your Soul Values and your Alignment Wheel.

Sometimes, without visual cues, you get lost, especially when it comes to complicated thoughts and information. When you're anxious, you might feel pressure behind your eyes, or visualize negative outcomes like you're watching a disaster movie.

If you're a clairvoyant person, you can use visual prompts and clues to help guide you into the space of your Akashic Records. Pay attention to your visual sense; you may need to close your eyes to get a clear "picture," or you may get more information with your eyes open. At times, you may not understand what you see; be patient.

## Claircognizance ("clear knowing")

I refer to this as "knowingness." Claircognizant people just … know things. They might not understand why or how they know, or when the information came to them—it's just *there* in their heads, and they're certain of it.

If you are claircognizant, you're likely a high performer and super intelligent. While you may have been shy as a child, you crave leadership in adulthood. You have a good work ethic, high stamina, and laser-like focus, so you don't dilute your energy or get distracted easily. You're not overly emotional or sensitive, and actually may not consider yourself intuitive at all. When you're searching for answers, it may take a little longer to tap into the information. However, when you embrace your superpower, you are the most accurate of all readers, because there's no confusion, only clarity.

The biggest challenge for claircognizant people is that they ignore their "knowingness" when it doesn't fit their expected paradigm. So, you may notice that you want to override your internal certainty when it doesn't line up with your expectations. You may also tend to ignore signals from your body, particularly with regard to rest, and are likely to burn out through overworking.

If you're a claircognizant person, accessing your Records will look more like asking powerful questions and then waiting for the "knowingness" to set in. You may not receive signs or visual cues, get "gut feelings," or hear spiritual guidance like other Clairs, so you need to pay close attention to the truth that settles into your consciousness. When you know, you *know*—trust yourself, and act on the divine insight that you're receiving.

## Clairaudience ("clear hearing")

When God/Spirit/Source and the Universe speak, you hear it.

Words and sound are incredibly powerful for you. You're a naturally fluid speaker, and communication is a top asset for you in life and business. Music might be a big part of your life, particularly as a tool to guide or enhance your moods. You play conversations like audio recordings in your head before you make decisions, and often use audio notes to record your thoughts rather than a pen and paper.

Sometimes, you may feel overwhelmed by all the chatter in your head. You may also struggle with poor inner dialogue, self-criticism, and overcoming old, negative stories. When conflict arises, you may decide in advance exactly what others are going to say and how they are going to show up, which colors your expectations and can lead to repetitive patterns in your relationships.

If you are a clairaudient person, you can connect with your Records through music, sound, and breathwork. However, be sure to create some silent time each day where you can be in deep listening, so you don't miss any whispers from the Universe!

## Clairsentience ("clear feeling")

While claircognizant people "just know" things, clairsentient or kinesthetic people "just feel" things.

If you are a clairsentient person, you might be inclined to work with your hands. You process information best while in motion—standing, walking, dancing, or simply fidgeting. When all the pieces of a project come together, you can "feel" the completion in your body.

Touch and physical movement are very important to you. You're probably a serial hugger! Movement, massage, hot baths, and other physical self-care is highly important to your well-being. You are deeply empathic and can often feel the emotions of others in your body, so regular cleansing and energy clearing is vital.

As a highly physical person, you may have challenges around language; you may speak slowly and feel the need to choose your words carefully. You may be easily distracted by physical sensations or discomforts—such as itchy clothing or uncomfortable chairs. When you get into an agitated state, it's important to care for your body first. Physical modalities like massage, Rolfing, yoga, or Tai Chi will almost always be more effective at balancing your energy than more sedentary practices like meditation.

If you're a clairsentient person, you will likely receive information from your Akashic Records in the form of physical sensations. Tingling, tightness, washes of heat or cold, or simple "gut feelings" are all possible. When you receive clear sensations, you may need to do a little digging to find out what they mean—but trust your body and its feelings. It will always tell you the truth.

## Other Clairs (Clairgustance/"clear tasting" and/or Clairalience/ "clear smelling")

Other senses besides sight and hearing can help you receive messages from your soul and the Universe. Sometimes, you might receive a clear, distinctive taste without putting anything in your mouth. You might smell a particular scent that you associate with a departed loved one or another important entity. (I once was overpowered by the scent of roses in a church. As it turned out, there was a woman there who had the stigmata—the wounds of Christ. Often, when she would meditate or pray, the Blessed Mother would come; when this happened, the smell of roses would fill the room, even when there were no roses present.)

## The Clear Channel

Some people are what I call "Clear Channels"—meaning, they use all of the Clairs, sometimes all at the same time!

If you're a Clear Channel, you may receive information in cascades. For example, if you're trying to make a big decision, you may get a kinesthetic "gut feeling" (clairsentience). If that doesn't clarify things, you may receive a vision, dream, or visual sign (clairvoyance). If you're still in the dark, you might hear words spoken in your ear (clairaudience). When you can tap into all of the "Clair" modalities, chances are, something is going to land, so you're more likely to recognize those WOO moments!

Being a clear channel is fabulous—and sometimes confusing!

When you have so much information coming at you from all directions, it can be hard to parse it all. However, if you can lean into your intuition and let yourself process what you are receiving in the moment, you will feel highly protected and guided, and be able to operate in a state of flow.

As a Clear Channel, you need beauty and space around you so you don't get overloaded. Since many people and spirits are attracted to you, you'll need to implement strong boundaries and learn to manage your energy properly or you will get overstimulated and lose focus. Your brain is like a browser with hundreds of windows open all the time! Keeping you in your "lane" in business will take a village—but since your intuition is so strong, you will attract the best people for the growth and expansion of your business.

If you are a Clear Channel, you will receive information from your Akashic Records in various ways, often unpredictably, so keep an open mind. Stay present in each moment, and let information come to you without judgment. Most of all, trust what you are seeing, hearing, feeling, sensing, and knowing.

## Unlocking the Mystery

Now that you have a better understanding of how you might be inclined to receive information from your soul, the Divine, and your Akashic Records, it's time to open the vault and read your own Records for the first time!

Even if you've had a professional Akashic Record reading in the past, your experience of reading your own Records will be unique. Before you begin, take a moment to release any judgments or preconceived notions that you might be carrying around what this experience will be like for you, and what you may or may not learn.

While you can connect with your Records at any time, in just a few minutes (in fact, later in this chapter I'll share how to make it a daily practice!), the first time you do it, I recommend setting aside at least twenty to thirty minutes so that you can relax into the process. Like any practice, the more you do it, the easier it will get!

# HOW TO ACCESS YOUR AKASHIC RECORDS

## *Before you begin ...*

- Purchase a journal with a saying or image that has meaning for you. This journal will be dedicated solely to the insights you receive in the Records. You could also get a special pen that helps you feel more connected while you're writing.

- Create an opening prayer that you will say each time you open the records. (Keep it short as you will be saying it three times!) Or, feel free to use this example:

  *Dear Angels, Guides, and Record Keepers, I am open to receive the gifts and information that you have in store for me today.*

- Create a prayer of thanks to use when you close the records, such as:

  *Dear Angels, Guides, and Record Keepers, thank you for your divine guidance today.*

## *When you're ready to access your records ...*

1. *Find a quiet space* where you feel safe and won't be interrupted.

2. *Open yourself to trust in this process.* Take a few deep breaths and release any negative thoughts or fears that might be swirling in your mind.

3. *Do your favorite grounding exercise* (or use the grounding meditation I've created for you at www. CandiceHozza.com/BookResources.)

4. *Say your opening prayer three times* to set the sacred space.

5. *Write or speak an intention for your reading.* For example, you could say, "I'd like more information about this pattern that keeps coming up in my business," or "What's the best program for me to be marketing right now?" This intention is for the whole reading and will guide the questions you ask once your Records are open. In other words, intention condenses that wide ocean into a swimming pool.

6. *Create a ritual.* Use any movement, sound, music, breathwork, prayers, or other tools that will help you drop into a calm, open state. I also recommend candles, crystals, and symbols that align with your intention and support a clear energy field. Essential oils like frankincense, patchouli, lavender, and ylang-ylang are also wonderful for attuning the energy to a higher vibration.

7. *Come into a meditative state.* Depending on your primary Clair, this could look like sitting in a meditative position, swaying or dancing with your eyes closed, lying on your back in Śavāsana, or something else entirely. Let your intuition guide you into the place where you feel most receptive and open, and where you don't feel distracted.

8. *Ask a clear question that aligns with your intention.* Make sure that you structure it in a way that allows you to receive a clear answer! For example, for kinesthetic/clairsentient people, yes or no questions are always best, since the answers can be felt in the body. For clairaudient or claircognizant people, the questions can be slightly more complex—but they should still be targeted and not open-ended. For clairvoyant people, asking the Records to *show* you the highest and best outcome may be helpful. If you don't have a specific intention, you can still connect with the Records! Just ask powerful questions like, "What am I here to learn today?" or "What is my soul's intention in this moment?" or "What does my higher self want me to know right now?"

9. *Receive the answers you've asked for.* (Pay attention to your Clair!)

10. *Verify the answers you receive.* If for any reason you feel unclear about the information you've received, you can ask for clarification. One of my favorite ways to

do this is to ask for a sign. Pay attention to universal numbers (like 333 or 11:11) or other numbers that are significant to you, as well as scents or tastes associated with a departed loved one, or specific animals or plants that have special meaning in your life. When you see one or more of them, treat it as confirmation that you're on the right track. If you're familiar with the practice of muscle testing, you can also use that to verify information in the moment.

11. *Close the Records.* Thank your soul, higher self, guides, angels, and any other beings that have offered their assistance, and deliberately close your Records. You may visualize this as shutting the door on the bank vault, dimming a light switch in a special room, hugging your spirit guides and saying, "See you next time!" or any other closing ritual that speaks to you. When you're done with your gratitudes, say your closing prayer three times. This step is very important. While you're not shutting off your intention, closing your records will slow down the flow of information when you're not in an optimally receptive state.

Congratulations! You've just read your Akashic Records.

Yes, you really did.

Pretty amazing, right?

# Your Daily WOO

Intuition is like a muscle. The more you use it, the more adept you will become. That's why, especially when you first start accessing your Akashic Records for business and life guidance, daily practice is vital.

While it's always nice to do the full ritual I described above, that may not be practical for you on a daily basis. Once you are comfortable stepping into the space of your Records, you can shortcut the process. At the beginning or end of your day, take five minutes to set an intention and ask a question, knowing that the answer will be made available for you exactly at the time you need it. You can also ask questions like, "Dear angels and guides, do you have a message for me today?" What's important isn't the subject matter, but the fact that you are making the connection. This helps to align you to the vibrational frequency of your highest self and create opportunities for those "elevators" to meet and create WOO moments.

Each day, when you open your Records, record the time and date at the top of your journal page. After a week or two, make space to go back and re-read what you've written each day. As you accumulate months and years of experiences in the Records, use your journals to track what you've learned and how far you've come.

The more time you spend in the space of your Records, the more direction you will get. You will start to pick up on cues from your spiritual guides and higher self. For example, a friend of mine lost her father a few years ago. Every time she thought of her dad, she got a funny feeling in her stomach. She thought it was just the "gut punch" of grief—and so she'd start crying, and her emotional vibration would drop into the space of sadness, which isn't receptive. Then, one day during a reading, her father joined us, and let her know that the "wiggly" feeling in her belly was him trying to reach her. Now, when she experiences that feeling, she knows it's her dad "ringing the doorbell." Immediately, she feels lighter and happier, because she feels his presence. She doesn't have to go deep into her Records to get guidance and support; all she has to do is stay present to that feeling.

Pay special attention to any repeating words, symbols, or feelings in your notes, and also to anomalies like misspelled words, abbreviations you wouldn't normally use, odd or unusual word choices, etc. When these types of things show up in your journaling, you'll know that your higher self, not your everyday self, is leading on the dance floor. The less you impose your own thoughts and conversation onto your experience in the Records, the more open to Universal wisdom you will become.

One more note: Your guides, angels, and Akashic record-keepers are here to serve you and help you unwrap those beautiful gifts from your white room. However, when you first connect to your Records, it's important to let your guides know that you will be doing this at a specific time each day (for example, every morning at 9:00 a.m.). Otherwise, once that door is open and they know you're ready to communicate, they may start communicating with you at other times—like in the middle of the night! Some of your guides have never been human so, while they're excited to do their job of communicating with you, they don't understand that you also need sleep! Just let them know when you are available and ask that they keep their messages to that time frame.

The more you practice, the more aligned and supported you will feel. Most of all, you'll trust your intuition and start to rely on it to make decisions in your life and business. Before you know it, you'll have WOOs popping up all over!

# The Akashic Records Can Heal

There is another layer to working with the Akashic Records that is important to share. The Records are a space of healing.

I didn't know it at the time, but when I began to work in my Records, I was healing at a level beyond that of my conscious mind and physical body. I was releasing generations—even millennia—of challenging energy and unhelpful paradigms. The weight of my old ways of being fell away, and I was given a chance to start anew.

The Records hold the key to your healing in many areas, including: vows (i.e., poverty, martyrdom, chastity, etc.), past life interference, implants, subliminal programs, hooks, energy cords, genetic imprinting, and cultural/trans-generational/societal/archetypal imprinting.

While the scope of this book doesn't encompass healing through the Akasha, it's important to know that deep energetic shifts are possible through this modality. When you are in your own Records, you may be given information about one or more of these areas of healing that need to be addressed before you can fully embody the energy of your new identity. However, it's my recommendation that you always do this deeper healing work with a trained practitioner and guide. We all have subconscious "blind spots," and need someone to mirror to us the disharmony of our deep patterns in order for us to see them clearly and allow them to release and be healed.

\*\*\*

Now, it's time to put everything you've learned so far in this book together to align your business with the next level of *you*.

Are you ready to dive in? Let's go.

# ~ 8 ~

# Your Next Level Plan

A couple of years ago, I was convinced I had finally "made it" in my business.

In the last month, I'd added twenty-six new clients to my Align Your Business program. The cash I'd collected in that thirty days was equal to my entire year's salary at the university. I had achieved a long-term goal of creating a successful business as a spiritual business strategist, using my intuition and the modality of the Akashic Records.

And yet, something was off. I had met my goal, but I had also hit a ceiling.

I wasn't feeling aligned. In fact, I was exhausted. My business was built around speaking and events, which meant I was traveling a lot, plus working with individual clients five days a week. If I was this tapped-out now, I wondered, how I could ever reach the next milestone in my business?

I didn't have an answer.

A few weeks after these thoughts started to arise, I was scheduled to attend three back-to-back events. These events, I reasoned, would fill my business to capacity for the next three months—at which point, I'd need to book another couple of speaking engagements. Tired as I was, I found myself less excited than usual to take the stage.

Then, at the first event, I listened to one of the other speakers. Her question got me thinking.

"Do you know what you're actually exchanging when a client hires you?" she asked.

Of course, my immediate thought was, *"Time. I'm giving my time."* Someone else in the audience piped up with the same answer.

The speaker shook her head. "No. It's not time. What you're exchanging is life force energy."

In that moment, I realized what was misaligned in my business. I had a plan to support my clients in the highest and best way possible and had mapped the income I would generate as a result. I had set myself up for success. But I hadn't planned for the amount of life that success would cost me. I hadn't factored in how much of my time, energy, and attention I would be giving to each client through my current programs.

No wonder I was exhausted!

When I reverse-engineered my offers, I realized two things. First, my pricing wasn't aligned. I was trying to do too much for too little, and the scales weren't balanced. Second, I wasn't giving myself enough space to recover energetically between client sessions and readings. I simply wasn't refilling the amount of energy I was putting out.

More, in my current model, I was only facilitating a shift for one person at a time. I wanted to make the biggest impact I could with every moment of time and life force energy I was spending. My current model wasn't allowing me to make my biggest impact. It wasn't serving me—but it also wasn't serving my clients.

This was, quite possibly, the most important piece of information I had received about my business to date. I had released my blocks. I was clear on my Soul Values. I had decided how I wanted to live, and I knew how much money I needed to make to live that way. I was using my intuition and tapping the resource of my Records to make decisions and follow my soul's path. But I was missing one key factor—the understanding of energy exchange, and how to plan not just for an income, but for a *life*.

Somewhere along the way, I'd gotten distracted by the mechanics of my business. Because I was looking in the wrong direction, I missed the elevator—and ended up in a place that wasn't comfortable. It felt a bit like that moment when, in a strange hotel, you get off on the wrong floor, and instead of waltzing into the spa, you end up in the laundry room.

Now that I knew what was going on, though, I could begin to look for the WOOs—opportunities to shift the way I was working to make it sustainable.

So many entrepreneurs I meet run into this issue, even after they've done the mindset and spiritual work we've explored in this book. There seems to be a disconnect for most of us between business and life; we rarely think of them as one and the same. But the truth is that the highest and best expression of *any* business or work path is the one that supports your most joyful and fulfilling lifestyle.

In this chapter, we'll create a 12-Month Next Level Plan that will actually get you where you want to go. You'll be layering all the breakthroughs, lessons, and expansions from your work throughout this book on top of one another to build a solid foundation and keep you aligned with the thriving business you want and the gorgeous life you deserve.

# Your Next Level Plan

As you know by now, stepping into the next level of you isn't just about intention. It's a powerful combination of intention and intuitive guidance with planning and action!

I encourage my clients to create a Next Level Plan for every calendar year, as well as a plan for every 90 days. In this section, we'll walk through the entire planning process together.

I encourage you to create your 12-Month Plan first, no matter what time of year you're reading this book, and then revise it again at the end of your calendar year (whenever that occurs). Then, at the beginning of each quarter, you can revisit your current 12-Month Next Level Plan and craft your current 90-Day Next Level Plan easily and seamlessly using the same process.

To get the most out of this practice, set a date with yourself. Allow about two hours (or even a whole day) for this work. Optimally, you'll want to do your 12-Month Next Level Plan about six weeks before the end of the calendar year, and your 90-Day Next Level Plans about fifteen days before the end of each quarter, so you always know what your next steps are.

*When you're ready to begin your planning session, gather the following:*

- Your notes and journal entries on your Soul Values, Alignment Wheel, and your notes from working with the Aligned Earnings Calculator.

- Your notes and journal entries from your recent Akashic Records reading sessions.

- Any crystals, oracle cards, pendulums, or other spiritual tools you like to use when you are visioning.

- Essential oils, candles, incense, music, or other sensory tools that help you connect energetically to your Records.

- Water, tea, or another beverage to keep you hydrated and focused.

You are about to access your Records and dive into a flow-based session to vision and plan your next twelve months in business. Be sure that you won't be distracted or interrupted as you go through this process.

## VISION YOUR NEXT TWELVE MONTHS

First, we'll create a vision for how you will be creating your life and business for the next year.

This process is simple; it goes like this.

1. Set an intention

2. Open your Akashic Records

3. Review your clear insights

4. Create your vision

5. Ask for additional guidance

6. Close your Records and offer your gratitude

Are you ready? Here we go.

## Step 1: Set an intention

For this step, simply create an intention for how you would like to be guided and supported in this visioning process. What energy would like to prioritize? (For example, do you want to feel easeful? Excited? Fired-up? Abundant?) What would you like to learn or be shown while in your Records? What would you like the overall outcome of your visioning to be? (Clarity, direction, balance, ease, etc.) Create an intention statement and write it down so you can use it when opening your Records in Step 2.

## Step 2: Open your Akashic Records

Using the process you learned in Chapter 7, and the intention statement you just created in Step 1, open your Akashic Records and allow the energy and voice of your soul to begin to flow through you. Use any tools you prefer to enhance your connection to your intuition. Open fully to your inner wisdom and set aside any expectations or judgments about what this process will entail for you.

## Step 3: Review your clear insights

Before you start to create your vision for the next twelve months, take a moment to look back at all of your notes, exercises, and journaling around your Soul Values, Alignment Wheel, and Quantum Leap Blueprint for Wealth. What is your highest Soul Value? What areas of your life do you want to focus on to create more balance, flow, and ease? What are your Aligned Earnings for this year (or for the next 90 days)?

Allow the clear insights you've gained thus far to sink in. You will want this information fresh in your consciousness before you begin to envision the next-level expression of your life and business.

## Step 4: Create your vision

Spend at least thirty minutes writing your vision for the next level of you! With your Soul Values, Alignment Wheel, and Quantum Leap Blueprint fresh in your mind, journal about what it will look and feel like to step into this next level of you—the you where you're making money in accordance with your Aligned Earnings, serving the clients you desire to serve, honoring your Alignment Wheel, and living according to your highest Soul Values?

Be very clear in this stage about how much money you will make in the next twelve months and where you will ideally spend your life force energy. Then, apply the lens of your Soul Values to determine how much life force energy and time you want to put into earning that money. This part is super important—and the part many people forget when they're planning for the future!

Most of all, write about everything you desire like it's already happened! Use "I AM" statements instead of "I will be," "I wish," or even, "I believe."

Finally, don't shrink your vision to what you think is possible. If you want to make $500,000 in the next twelve months in your business while only working twenty hours a week, set that as your vision and intention! We'll crunch the numbers later in this chapter to find out exactly how you can easefully bring this vision to life.

## Step 5: Ask for additional guidance

When you're clear on your vision and are done journaling, ask your spirit guides, angels, and protectors for any additional information that will help you create your vision. Pull an oracle card, do some automatic writing, or use whatever tool feels most comfortable for you to receive this guidance. Then, if necessary, integrate this guidance into your new twelve-month vision.

## Step 6: Close your Records and offer your gratitude.

Following the process we used in Chapter 7, close your Akashic Records. Offer your gratitude to your guides, angels, ascended masters, and any other beings of light and love that assisted you in gaining this clarity and creating the path toward the next level of you. Say your closing prayer three times to close the space.

Remember, it's important to close your records so that you can reclaim your energy from the spiritual realm and come back to your normal state of consciousness. It's also important to limit the time you spend in the space of your Records—especially at first. It takes a lot of energy to hold that high vibration. So, in the beginning, spend no more than an hour with your Records open, and take time for deep rest and nourishment to keep your energy at an optimal level.

Over the next few weeks and months, you can return to your Records at any time for additional clarity and insight on your 12-Month Plan. Trust that things are unfolding perfectly for you in every moment, and give your attention only to your big vision and your next step!

# CREATE YOUR 12-MONTH ACTION PLAN

Now that you have a clear vision of what you desire, let's get down to the numbers.

In order to create your Aligned Earnings income goal, honor your life force energy, and create your most amazing impact, what programs, products, or services will you need to sell in your business? And, if you have multiple offers, how many of each will you need to maintain your energetic balance and create your life vision while still meeting your earning goals?

Here's a simple formula you can apply to unlock these numbers. For each program, fill out the following. Revise and tweak until you find a balance that feels intuitively right to you.

- Program/Product/Service
- Capacity/units available
- Price for each
- Number to sell
- Price x Number Sold = Annual Income from this offer

Notice that the numbers you come up with may be different than what you were imagining. If you've been selling online classes for $49 each, you will have to make some significant changes to bring in $100,000 in the next twelve months (and remember, as you saw in the Aligned Income Calculator, your take-home income will be a percentage of that overall goal). Or, maybe you're already closer to your vision than you imagined, and simply need to adjust the ratio of sales amongst your programs.

Now that you know how many of each of your offers, products, or services you need to sell to create your Aligned

Income, let's look at how much of your *life force*—your time, energy, and effort—will be required to create each of these income streams. How much time and attention will it take you each week, and each day, to deliver at that level? Is your life force energy expenditure for each offer equal to the amount of abundance you're receiving for it?

Here's a simple formula you can apply to each of your offers to see exactly what's happening in this energy/money exchange.

- Program/Product/Service:

- Number you intend to sell

- Amount of time/energy per offer sold

- Amount of energy per offer sold x intended sales = life force expenditure. (You can calculate energy in terms of your personal time, attention, and client results.)

Often, at this stage in my own planning, I have some major tweaking to do. I once deleted an entire mid-level program because this simple exercise showed me that the program was actually costing me money to host, and wasn't helping me make my biggest impact.

This is where many people tend to start making compromises. They think, "I really don't like doing those particular activities to deliver this product, and they take more time and energy than I'm comfortable with … but I'll do them if I have to in order to make the money I want." This is how we end up burned out, stressed out, and out of love with our businesses. We end up stuck on the hamster wheel because we're too tired to find creative alternatives to the things that are burning us out. So, refuse to cut corners.

# MY 12-MONTH NEXT-LEVEL PLAN

Year: _____    Annual Income Goal: $_____

**Entry Program:** _____

| | | | | | | | | | | | |
|---|---|---|---|---|---|---|---|---|---|---|---|
| Jan | Feb | Mar | Apr | May | Jun | Jul | Aug | Sep | Oct | Nov | Dec |

Price each $_____ x # Annual Sales _____ = Annual Income $_____

**Small Program:** _____

| | | | | | | | | | | | |
|---|---|---|---|---|---|---|---|---|---|---|---|
| Jan | Feb | Mar | Apr | May | Jun | Jul | Aug | Sep | Oct | Nov | Dec |

Price each $_____ x # Annual Sales _____ = Annual Income $_____

**Medium Program:** _____

| | | | | | | | | | | | |
|---|---|---|---|---|---|---|---|---|---|---|---|
| Jan | Feb | Mar | Apr | May | Jun | Jul | Aug | Sep | Oct | Nov | Dec |

Price each $_____ x # Annual Sales _____ = Annual Income $_____

**Large Program:** _____

| | | | | | | | | | | | |
|---|---|---|---|---|---|---|---|---|---|---|---|
| Jan | Feb | Mar | Apr | May | Jun | Jul | Aug | Sep | Oct | Nov | Dec |

Price each $_____ x # Annual Sales _____ = Annual Income $_____

**Top Tier:** _____

| | | | | | | | | | | | |
|---|---|---|---|---|---|---|---|---|---|---|---|
| Jan | Feb | Mar | Apr | May | Jun | Jul | Aug | Sep | Oct | Nov | Dec |

Price each $_____ x # Annual Sales _____ = Annual Income $_____

**Exclusive:** _____

| | | | | | | | | | | | |
|---|---|---|---|---|---|---|---|---|---|---|---|
| Jan | Feb | Mar | Apr | May | Jun | Jul | Aug | Sep | Oct | Nov | Dec |

Price each $_____ x # Annual Sales _____ = Annual Income $_____

Creating alignment between your offers and your energy is one of the most powerful parts of the process because it allows you to get creative in how you reach your goals.

Be sure to stay in your intuitive flow space as much as possible during this reflection. If for any reason your life force energy expenditures don't feel aligned with the income plan you created, or with the scale of impact you desire to make through your work, go back and revise until it feels good. Don't be afraid to backtrack and adjust—but don't get caught in perfectionism either. The only way to know if your plan will work is to take action on it. Remember, you are stepping into the next level of you and your business, so the way you used to do things may no longer be in alignment with who you are now.

If you would like additional information at any point in this process, you can open your records again, call upon your guides, ask questions, pull an oracle card, or use another intuitive practice to gain more clarity. When in doubt, always allow your intuitive guidance to take the lead.

I personally like to do this process over three or four days, even an entire week. Sometimes it locks in more quickly than that—but sometimes, you need to give things time to percolate. Once I have a clear insight into my most aligned path for the next twelve months, I am ready to move on to the goal-setting and action steps.

### *To create an action plan, ask yourself these questions:*

- What do I need to do every quarter, month, and week to create the Aligned Earnings I envision?

- How can I do those tasks with ease within the energetic boundaries I've set around energy expenditure?

- How can I do this work in a way that creates the biggest and most amazing possible outcomes for me, my clients, and the world?

- What do I need to focus on to use my energy most wisely?

- What do I need to delegate to make this plan work seamlessly?

- What will I release to honor my vision, impact, and life force energy?

As you ask these questions, you may get instructions from your intuition or spiritual guides in multiple ways. Pay attention to the feelings in your body and your unique "Clair." Your action steps might revolve around getting X number of clients in X number of weeks to fill your offers—or, they might revolve around daily meditation, salt baths, or exercise! It all depends on your intentions, your Alignment Wheel, and your Soul Values. Try to let your intuition guide you—even if the guidance feels more playful or "easy" than what you've been used to doing.

The final step in this process is to add all of your action steps to your planner, online calendar, or team schedule! After all, these are directions straight from the Records and your soul. Even if they feel illogical, you will know and feel when they are aligned; trust them.

Once you have your 12-Month Plan mapped out, go back and make a more detailed plan for the next 90 days as mentioned at the beginning of this section. Concentrate on the actions and feelings that will create not just the income you desire, but the life you dream of! Then, revisit your plan at least once a quarter, and preferably once a month, so you can update it as your vision evolves.

# Aligning to Your New Identity

I'm so thrilled for you. You are about to fully step into the next level of you and your business.

You are now primed and ready to see, open, and access those beautiful Windows of Opportunity that are becoming available for you. The plan you've created in this chapter will help you keep your eye on those elevator doors and feel empowered to say "Yes!" when they open wide.

Remember, you always have a choice about who you are and who you are becoming. Your intuition and soul offer clear insight and guidance ... but ultimately, the choice is up to you.

Lean into your guidance. Trust yourself, your guides, and your Records. And get ready to expand beyond your wildest dreams.

# ~ *9* ~

# Claiming the Next Level of YOU

I hardly recognize the person I was before my cancer journey set me on the path to claiming the power of my intuitive gifts in my life and business. My "woo-woo," once kept under cover, is now the biggest part of my work and the fullest expression of my calling on this planet.

Just recently, I had an experience where I got some amazing feedback from participants in my "Totally WOO" program, including one woman who is very special to me.

My client, Sage Polaris, a Conscious Launch Strategist and copy coach, decided in January of 2020 to set a big financial goal for her business. However, she was also clear that she wanted to achieve those results with the ease, comfort, and joy she's established as the benchmark in her life. So, she used the Align Your Business Process to release blocks, reaffirm her Soul Values, and create a 12-Month Next Level Plan to receive greater abundance in alignment with those values.

At the end of the first quarter, she used the 90-Day Next Level Plan process to look back over the first quarter to see how things had gone and where she needed to focus next.

"I want to smooth out my Alignment Wheel," Sage told our group. "There are definitely some spikes of energy going into my business, and those are taking a lot of my attention and life force energy. My health is in a good place, as is my adventure cup, but I feel some lower points around my home, spirituality, family, and relationships.

"I'm excited for the next ninety days. They feel like a breath of relief for me. Instead of having big spikes and dips, the next quarter is going to be about creating spaciousness and serving the people who came into my world in the first quarter of the year. Using this process as a touchstone, I was able to get clear on my next steps for everything I want to build in my life."

Being an entrepreneur can be exciting, fulfilling, and empowering. It can also, at times, feel like a lonely mission. There's a lot of responsibility and moving parts—especially when you're in the middle of massive growth—and it can be a challenge to figure out the highest and best ways to serve your clients while still maintaining your energy and Soul Values.

One of the things I love about Sage is that she's always ready and willing to face those challenges head-on and make quantum leaps into the next level of who she is. She knows that she will have to show up differently to meet her money goals without creating imbalances in the rest of her life—and she is tackling that process of shifting her identity with full trust. As she told us, "My theme for this year is, 'Wherever I land is a good place.'" Talk about being fully guided by soul and mission!

# Getting to the Next Level of You

In this book, I've taken you through a system of upleveling that I call the Align Your Business Process. Together, we've:

1. Identified and released your blocks

2. Connected to your Soul Values

3. Worked with your Alignment Wheel and created your Clear Vision and 90-Day Alignment Plan

4. Worked with your Quantum Leap Blueprint for Wealth

5. Learned how to read your own Akashic Records

6. Created your 12-Month and 90-Day Next Level Plans to align your income goals with your life force energy, your desire for impact, and your best, next-level life

But once you've done the work to get to the next level, what happens?

Alignment isn't a one-and-done practice. Even when you step through a Window of Opportunity from one elevator to another, you're still in a growth process. There are always higher levels of *you* to access.

Growth happens in steps. We come into a new version of ourselves through deliberate work, intuitive guidance, and experience. But as time goes on, you will begin to see the next level of your compelling future emerging on the horizon. When that happens, you'll experience one of two things.

One, you will encounter a block. You're going along, happy in your comfort zone—and then, suddenly, things in your life and business stop working as well as they once did. Maybe the level of life force energy you thought you could sustain has changed, and you're feeling tired and burned out again. Maybe your Aligned Earnings goals have expanded, and what once felt like a good financial target isn't actually providing the flow you desire. Maybe life circumstances have forced you to change how you're operating on a day-to-day basis, temporarily or permanently.

When this happens, your energetic vibration will drop as you descend into the pain and discomfort of the block. You may find yourself "regressing" to unhelpful mindsets and behaviors. You might simply feel stuck. Regardless of how it looks, this circumstance is telling you it's time to pause, release the blocks, and revisit the steps of the process we've outlined in this book to break through to the next level that awaits you.

The second thing you might experience is that a WOO opens in front of you. You may not understand why you should step through, but you do, because you trust your intuition when it whispers, "It's time." You see the WOO because you have done the work consistently: aligning with your values, using your Aligned Earnings calculations, accessing your Records, and creating your 12-Month and 90-Day Next Level Plans. When that elevator door opens, you step through, even if you have no idea what's on the other side. Suddenly, you take a powerful leap out of your current state of being and into a new paradigm.

In this case, your WOO is inviting you to undertake a quantum leap to access the next level of you. If you're paying attention, you can literally leap over the block, the challenge, and the pain. This isn't to say that challenging things won't happen—only that you won't experience them the same way.

Take my client, Cindy, who had been diligently using the Align Your Business Process I've provided in this book to stay aligned with her Soul Values and connected to her Akashic Records. One day, out of the blue, she received a message from her guides that she needed to sell one of her two restaurants. She had no idea why this would be, since both were doing amazingly well, but she listened because she had gotten used to trusting her intuitive guidance. Then, the Department of Transportation contacted her with an offer to buy the property adjoining the restaurant (which she owned), and a family offered to buy the restaurant itself. Her business partners, surprisingly, agreed to the sales. They, too, felt it was time to sell the restaurant, but didn't quite understand why.

That was in January of 2020. Three months later, the global pandemic closed down service businesses across the country.

Carrying two restaurants through the lockdowns would likely have bankrupted Cindy. But thanks to the sale of the second restaurant and neighboring property, she was able to carry her remaining business and staff through the spring and summer. It wasn't easy, but when things started to open up again, her business once again began to thrive.

When we follow the WOO, we don't always get to know what might have been. We step forward in deep trust—in ourselves, in our intuitive guidance, in our guides, and in the Universe. Sometimes, as happened for Cindy, we may have no idea why we are being asked to take a certain action until events unfold—but when we listen, we realize that the Universe is always aligning for our highest good.

# Rinse and Repeat

Once you start living with guidance from your Records and your intuition, you'll start to become more sensitive to energetic shifts in your business. When something feels "off" or just "not quite right"—or, conversely, when you start to get a sense of excitement like something big is just around the corner—you will know it's time to revisit the Align Your Business Process. Check to make sure that your Soul Values are still feeling aligned, and that they're in the correct order of priority (as they tend to shift every few years or when significant life changes occur). Do the Alignment Wheel exercises and see where you're spending your energy. Make sure your income targets and the actions you're taking to support them are still aligned with your Quantum Leap Blueprint for Wealth. Check in with your Records and ask for guidance. Any time that you get that feeling of "something's shifting" is a perfect time to go back and do this work again.

What you will notice is that, with practice, you will begin to do some of these things automatically. You'll get quicker at identifying misalignments or blocks in your energy field, and get back on track more easily. You'll instinctively revisit your Soul Values when it comes time to make big decisions. You'll realize sooner when you're neglecting one or more of your Heart Cups on the Alignment Wheel. The whole process will speed up and become more aligned with the ease and flow that is available to you *now*.

Today, I know that the moment I feel myself heading into that "apple spin" in my business, I need to go back to the drawing board. Sometimes, only a small tweak is needed to correct the energy and get me back on track. Sometimes, I need to completely rework my offers, hire a new team member, or stop offering something that's not honoring my energy. Other times, I need to shift something in order to be in alignment with the highest good of my clients. I'm not afraid of these changes anymore. I still get stuck in the swirl of indecision—but I don't stay there. Especially now that my business is growing, I'm coming up against challenges I haven't faced yet as an entrepreneur. Every time that spin starts, I lean more into my intuition—and yet, at the same time, I am also more decisive, clear, and action-oriented than ever before. I know that the next level of me is always waiting on the other side of a WOO.

The same is true for all of my clients, and it's true for you as well. You are *becoming*. You are learning. You are evolving.

You are finding your WOO, every single day.

## Woo-Liciously You!

We all came here to this planet with a purpose. You've heard that before, I'm sure—and it's true. But it's sometimes hard to reconcile that purpose and mission with your desire to *also* have a full, fulfilling, beautiful life.

Your work—your business—is ultimately a vehicle for you to become more of who you already are. That is its highest purpose. Yes, you are in service to the world—and you are also in service to *you*.

You have the infinite resource of the Akashic Records within you to guide your path. As we learned in Chapter 2, you can always go "home"—to yourself, to your divine nature, and to your beautiful, magical, divine soul. You can do anything. You can create anything. You have your inner GPS at the ready! When you are fully tapped into your intuition, life becomes your playmate.

So, goosebumps up, my love.

Take a deep breath, and let it out.

It's time to step into the next level of you. The world, and your soul, are waiting.

# Resources

To download worksheets, graphics, audio meditations,
and other materials to support your work with this book,
visit www.CandiceHozza.com/BookResources.

# Acknowledgments

I pass the golden threads to you—my clients and readers of this book. May you always know that you are supported on the other side in all aspects of your journey. It's my intention that you can now lean into your intuition and watch your magical WOO moments open in your life and business. I gently and lovingly pass the WOO to you as you Align Your Business and step up to the next level of *you*. Thank you for coming on this journey with me.

\*\*\*

First and foremost, I would like to thank my clients and colleagues who believe in me and trust my work. It is my greatest pleasure and honor to channel your messages. It's a joy to witness the transformation as you receive your clear insights, and to see and hear the infinite wisdom inside you. You are amazing, brave, and powerful leaders, and will be the Windows of Opportunity for so many others to come.

Immense gratitude to all the people who have supported my WOO moments. I would like to thank you all in the divine order that my magical WOO moments occurred. They have given me the highest and best opportunities that shaped my life forever.

Gerri, my birth mother: thank you for giving me some really great genes, and for sharing me with a family that was praying for a child. I know you carried me in your heart for thirty-three years until we met. Thank you for an amazing thirteen days of getting to know you, and for telling me you loved me right away; those words healed my heart. Thank you for making the decision to love me from afar, and opening the WOO that delivered me to Bette and Bill.

Bette Chapman and Bill Chapman: the mom and dad who raised me, and the ones I hold today and forever in my heart as my parents. Thank you for wanting me so much, and for taking such loving care of me. Thank you for teaching me what unconditional love means. Thank you for the love and protection I felt when I was in your arms, and for a wonderful home and family to grow up with. I know you will both greet me when I go to the other side. You opened a WOO to Aunt Lennie, Uncle Ralph, Susie, Bob, Matty, and Cyndi.

Aunt Lennie Miller: my sun and moon since I was born. My best friend, aunt, and mother for twenty-five years, you offered me a home after my parents transitioned to the other side. You taught me how to laugh, how to love, and that being silly and enjoying every moment is the highest and best. You taught me to be a free spirit, a storyteller. Thank you for the endless days sitting on your porch and talking about life. I love you to the moon and back. Thank you for opening a WOO to Uncle Ralph.

Uncle Ralph Miller, the best man in my life for so many years, and my father figure after my dad passed: thank you for loving me, and for the pool that became a hangout spot for all of our family and friends. It was great fun for all of the nieces and nephews to be a family. Thank you for our family evenings of "porch sitting" and old fashion conversing. Thank you for always having time for us kids.

Susie and Bob—my cousin and her significant partner: thank you for opening your home to me, for loving and supporting me, and for opening a WOO to your son, Matty.

Matty: thank you for your unconditional love, and for teaching me a new way of understanding life's purpose with laughter and love. You have been a teacher to us all.

Cyndi, aka Sissy, my sister, the jewelry savant who can always pick out the best sparkly gems for us all: I have loved your sense of humor since you were little. Your giggles while watching Benny Hill were the sweetest. Thank you for being so much like our mom, and carrying her sweet, selfless, compassionate heart as well as our treasured family memories. Thank you for sharing your three grandbabies with me—even after Khalil embedded the "Baby Shark" song in my head.

Uncle Jack Chapman: thank you for inviting me to breakfast the very last time we knew we would see each other, and for telling me to write this book as others needed to hear the story of Gerri and our meeting.

Steve Linder: thank you for helping me over the past sixteen years to gain new perspectives when mine needed some polishing, and for believing in me when I didn't fully believe in myself "in the past." Thank you for noticing when I was creating my new identity and supporting my juicing journey. Thank you for being my speaking coach, and for holding space for me while my new business was formed during this process. Thank you for reminding me to always practice (and practice, and practice) before my speaking gigs. Saying yes to my work with you opened my WOO to Priscilla, Summer, and Simon.

Priscilla Stephan: thank you for introducing me to the Akashic Records and for the endless hours of unfolding the akasha together as we grew in its wisdom. Thank you for your love, friendship, and support.

Summer Rose: thank you for your friendship, for being a "forever birthday card" friend, and for being the best environmental energizer. You not only clean and organize, but also infuse your "Summer-nesses" into any space you are clearing.

Simon Lovell: thank you for your course right at the beginning of the pandemic. Your work helped me stay balanced and focused while learning how the gift of meditation can expand who we are. Thank you for helping me develop my first "real" website and my Intuitive Business Podcast. Sending love to you and Buddha Bear! You opened my WOO with Jennifer and Jodi.

Jennifer Alyse: thank you for the awesome photoshoot in Maui that resulted in the cover photos for this book. What a great day of fun, laughter, and the best pineapple we've ever eaten!

Jodi Vaugh: thank you for making me feel beautiful, and so, *so* nurtured for my photoshoot from the inside out. Thank you for our playdates with the whales. Love you to the stars and beyond.

Curtis Silverwood: our WOO opened over ten years ago! Thank you for always having my back in business. You can take what's in my mind and channel a design, audio, or video even better than I was hoping for. Thank you for your constant willingness to take my crazy-ass ideas and plate them to make them look like gold. Thank you even more for your love, support, and willingness to learn and grow with me.

Tina Ko: you are a quiet and strong leader, even if you don't want to be called a "leader." Your shoulders feel strong and comfortable to lean into. You're my "breakfast friend" and sounding board for all things business. Thank you for your advice, and for supporting my next-level journey before I knew I was on it.

Nicole Lewis Keeber: thank you for being an incredible friend and for sharing my life journey. Thank you for showing me how to lean softly into my business so that I could create a sustainable business model. You opened my WOO to Marybeth and Jeannie.

Marybeth Eyler: thank you for stepping in when my business felt a bit misaligned. You created support for launches, click buttons, and my Kartra dreams. Thank you for the long drives to Rhode Island (where you heard the "long version" of many of the stories in this book). Thank you for sharing Scott, and for the lovely friendship that has formed as the four of us explore Lancaster together and listen to Scott's lovely singing voice.

Jeannie Spiro: as I write this, I am crying tears of joy. Thank you for being an outstanding coach and for teaching me how to "close" the stage. I still remember calling you after my first speaking gig, as I looked at my long list of potential new clients, to say, "Jeannie ... I have a business!" I will always treasure the words, "So that you can ..." We often joke that we are living in parallel universes; thank you for helping me get my message out into my universe, and to support myself the way I desire and deserve. You opened my WOO to Angela, Bryna, Sage, and Sunshine.

Angela Todd, my friend and customer liaison: your ears have heard and captured every word that has ever been spoken in my business. Thank you for your kindness and patience. Thank you for treating my lovely clients with such TLC. Thank you for your feedback and brilliant mind, and for turning my channeled messages into clear and concise words. You opened my WOO for my business!

Bryna Haynes: talk about golden threads! Bryna has taken twenty-five years of significant WOOs that shaped my life and business and woven the stories together to create the book you now hold. As I write this, I feel so many emotions. Thank you, Bryna, for being my "book doula"; you applied your brilliance to help me fulfill my dream of becoming an author and birth my little WOO baby into reality. "Thank you" seems like a small thing to say (and I'm excited to see how you edit this later)!

Kind, gentle Sage Polaris: you are a breath of fresh air each time we connect. You always feel like you are just off a vacation as you are in such a flow! I admire you as a business leader. You held space for me on my first ever live launch and created brilliant copy that honors my feelings and words. Thank you again for your love and support.

Sunshine Beeson: you are as your name suggests! Thank you for being my roommate, sister, friend, and co-creator of laughter and health. Thank you for caring so deeply for others, for creating magical moments in Narnia, and for sharing your twin grandbabies.

***

Carlie and Phoenix, my two beautiful children: you have been my greatest joy in life, and also my greatest teachers. Thank you for coming to this earth and choosing me to be your mom. It is my greatest honor. Carlie, you taught me to think about food in a different way—to honor the spirits of animals through a vegetarian path, by saving numerous worms from our driveway, and by educating me that you don't have to buy a brand-new puppy because the best dogs are already waiting for homes. You are the best fur-baby mama ever! Thank you as well for being such an incredibly light-hearted and enthusiastic creative, and for being willing to apply that creativity as a copywriter on my team. Phoenix, thank you for helping me to develop a "forever love" for Star Wars, Legos, Guardians of the Galaxy, and baseball. You have always surprised me—and not just because of your favorite pastime, which involves sneaking up on me every day. You're such an awesome young man. Your perseverance and determination are amazing, and your huge heart is revealed in different ways every day—from helping your team (way to go LCHS Baseball!) to taking another kid to school for a whole year while his sister was sick. I am so excited for all the other surprises you'll show me in this life.

My husband, Tim: thank you for our two beautiful children and for our forty-year journey (with, as you say, an asterisk). We have very different personalities, but you are always my "other half"; when we come together, we make a great whole. Thank you for supporting me through the creation of this business, and for the advice you've given me, even when it seemed like I wasn't always listening.

My beautiful clients: although my work with you is sacred and confidential, many of you have given me permission to share your stories of transformation and healing. Your names have been changed to protect your privacy, but you know who you are. Thank you for your infinite contribution to this book.

And finally, to everyone else who has contributed to my life journey, my Align Your Business process, and the opening of my WOOs: you are too many to name, but please know that I carry you in my heart and I am sending waves of gratitude to you in this, and every, moment. Thank you.

# About the Author

Candice "Candy" Hozza, B.S., MEd, is a spiritual strategist, business intuitive, and speaker. As the founder of the Totally WOO Program and host of the Intuitive Business Podcast, she helps people align their businesses using the Akashic Records. To date, she has supported leaders and visionaries around the world for over 3,000 total hours in the Akashic Records.

Candy grew up in a small steel mill town in western Pennsylvania, where she earned a B.S. in Mental Health Counseling from Gannon University. She earned her Master's in Education from Millersville University, where she would spend the next thirty years supporting emerging leaders in the Student Affairs department. She also has more than fifteen years of experience as a Neurolinguistic Strategist.

Now that she's officially out of the "Woo Closet," Candy is stepping through her own Windows of Opportunity and using her intuitive gifts to support clients through all phases of the Align Your Business Process. She lives with her son, Phoenix; her husband, Tim; her dogs, Abby and Jules; and Dembe the Badass Cat in Lancaster, Pennsylvania.

Learn more about Candy at www.CandiceHozza.com.

# About the Publisher

Founded in 2021 by Bryna Haynes, WorldChangers Media is a boutique publishing company focused on Ideas for Impact.

We know that great books can change lives, topple outdated paradigms, and build movements. Our commitment is to deliver superior-quality transformational nonfiction by, and for, the next generation of thought leaders, conscious entrepreneurs, creatives, healers, and industry disruptors.

Ready to write and publish your thought leadership book with us? Learn more at www.WorldChangers.Media.

Made in the USA
Coppell, TX
15 September 2021

# CREATIVITY:

*Progress and Potential*

# CREATIVITY:

## Progress and Potential

*Edited by*

# CALVIN W. TAYLOR

McGRAW-HILL BOOK COMPANY

*New York*

*San Francisco*

*Toronto*

*London*

CREATIVITY: *Progress and Potential*

62951

*To Dorothy, Craig,*
*Steve, and Nan*

# CONTRIBUTORS

*Hubert E. Brogden*

U.S. Army Personnel Research Office
Washington, D.C.

*John L. Holland*

National Merit Scholarship Corporation
Evanston, Illinois

*J. H. McPherson*

Dow Chemical Company
Midland, Michigan

*Thomas B. Sprecher*

Western Electric Company, Inc.
Princeton, New Jersey

*Calvin W. Taylor*

University of Utah
Salt Lake City, Utah

*E. Paul Torrance*

University of Minnesota
Minneapolis, Minnesota

# PREFACE

The broad aim of this book is twofold: to summarize our current knowledge about creativity and to indicate some of the most promising research leads and urgent research needs. Currently the literature on creativity is scattered throughout a great variety of sources, including unpublished materials. There is no single, integrated, critical review to which the researcher, educator, or layman can turn for a useful, succinct overview. The present volume is intended to fill a portion of this need.

Another purpose of this book is to stimulate the thinking of researchers, educators, politicians, and laymen. The authors hope that the report will lead to more knowledgeable decisions and actions, thus fostering new research, theorizing, and evaluating. Although public interest in creativity has increased enormously, considerable additional support to research is needed in order to provide greater understanding of the nature of creative talent and a better basis for shaping the programs now being developed to foster creativity. This report is intended to provide some guidelines and to suggest possible directions in which support is needed in research on creativity.

Education is treated at some length in order to provide coverage of the research knowledge at each important level from preschool to higher education. All the chapters have been revised by all six authors, and highly selected senior consultants have reviewed the book as a whole. A comprehensive list of several hundred references utilized and assembled in the preparation of this book is presented at the end of the volume.

I want to acknowledge my appreciation to the National Science Foundation for support of this effort to take stock of the knowledge gained from research about creativity. Especially, I want to acknowledge the ideas, guidance, and encouragement of Robert Cain, the monitor on the project, and of Thomas Mills and Milton Levine, also of the National Science Foundation, in seeing the need and value of such a report.

In effect, this was the fourth national research conference in the University of Utah series. Each of the first three conferences, held in 1955, 1957, and 1959, included nearly twenty carefully selected researchers whose work provided the framework and substance of the conferences. Each participant reported on his latest research project, and rather full discussion periods followed each report. For each conference approximately 1,000 copies of the complete reports and discussion were reproduced by the University of Utah Press in multilith form, essentially verbatim. When these conference reports were out of print, thirty papers selected from the three reports were published by John Wiley & Sons, in a single volume entitled *Scientific Creativity: Its Recognition and Development*. Frank Barron assisted me in editing and producing this book.

After the first three large conferences, it seemed wise to produce a stocktaking report with the help of a small group selected from the most active researchers in the field. This fourth University of Utah creativity conference involved a small work group, with participants working in pairs both before and after a three-day summer conference in June of 1961. The emphasis now was on summarizing research findings in creativity and on indicating promising leads and urgent needs for research. In other words, this small conference differed from the previous ones in that it did *not* involve the report and discussion of the latest research of the participants, but turned its attention on all research findings to date. The University of Utah Press graciously gave us permission to quote from the three complete reports of the first three Utah creativity conferences.

I want to thank the five writers who cooperated with me in producing this book, for their extended and extensive work on this project. We divided the field of creativity into three parts, with two persons working on each part. After this, pairs of us met several times and exchanged plans and ideas for the book.

After the whole group met in Chicago, the copies of the resulting draft of the manuscript were sent to three senior reviewers, Frank Barron, J. P. Guilford, and Anne Roe, who made many helpful suggestions. They saw and pointed out our editorial blind spots in coverage of the field, in emphasis, and in estimating research needs. Each of the six authors then worked on another revision of his own chapter to handle the suggestions of these senior reviewers. A total of at least three complete revisions were made after the first draft of the manuscript was put together at the small conference in Chicago. A further review occurred at a meeting of five of the six writers one year after that initial conference. A final rewriting has just been completed, with the help of Lynda Clemmons, whose versatility and editorial skill have proved really valuable. In other words, work on the manuscript for the present book, including additions and revisions, continued from 1960 well into 1963.

The authors want to thank Madge Nickell and others in the University of Utah research laboratory who helped on the manuscript, especially Chandler Cook for his assembling and polishing of the final, lengthy bibliography, most of the items of which were provided by Thomas Sprecher and Paul Torrance. Frank Williams and Connie Tramell helped on the index. Others who deserve recognition for their work in typing the successive revisions and the final manuscript include Connie Tramell, Marianne Cram, Ruesha Snow, Roberta Reid, Karen Rynio, and Sally Meik.

*Calvin W. Taylor*

# CONTENTS

chapter **1**

# INTRODUCTION

*Calvin W. Taylor*

UNIVERSITY OF UTAH

CURRENTLY THERE IS competition for the very minds of men. Among those factors which will determine the outcome of that competition, creativity is one of the most important. Both the quantity and the depth of creativity in the various areas of knowledge and in different nations will be significant. Because creative acts affect enormously not only scientific progress, but society in general, those nations who learn best how to identify, develop, and encourage the creative potential in their people may find themselves in very advantageous positions. As few as three or four highly creative minds can make a crucial difference—many of our present means of travel, communication, and production can be traced back to the creative thinking of a relatively small number of people.

Although creativity has been a topic of some interest throughout man's history, until very recently the scientific method has not been focused upon it to any great extent. In the six or seven decades before 1950, only a trickle of research articles on creativity appeared in the scientific literature. Since 1955, however, increasing interest and activity have opened many avenues of research, as indicated by the lengthy list of references at the end of this book.

Creativity at its highest level has probably been as important as any human quality in changing history and in reshaping the world.

At a meeting at Randolph Macon on creativity, Eliseo Vivas stated that societies cannot be easily and radically changed by the human will according to plan; rather it is the creativity with which the members of a society are endowed that accounts for the internal dynamism of a society. Man's current degree of enlightenment, particularly in certain fields, as well as his vast production of material goods, can be traced in large part to the creative performances of individuals during the course of history—to man's striving to improve his knowledge, to conquer the unknown, and to create new ideas and new, more useful things.

Since 1950, those willing to recognize the true situation have known that our nation has been faced with manpower problems. Even so long ago, it could be seen that we lacked sheer quantity of available manpower in comparison with our potential international competition. Considering manpower needs in only the basic and applied sciences, it was apparent that we were becoming outnumbered in high-quality personnel in sciences and engineering. Another feature of this situation was that the scientists in the competing nations represented a large youth movement—a great many students and recent graduates and a comparatively young faculty. In other words, the long-range scientific effort of these other nations was strengthened by the long careers ahead of a large percentage of their scientists.

If we are to survive in international competition, our most promising solution to this vital manpower problem is for this nation to encourage and support the identification and development of various types of important personnel. One such type is the highly creative person, for even a few such persons in science can keep our scientific movement vigorously in front—recall the World War II race for the development of the atomic bomb. The creative scientist can also vastly improve upon current thinking and practices and materials.

Since creativity can underlie progress in any field of activity, the current awakening of interest and the recent burst of research on creativity promise new developments on many fronts. There is great potential for long-term gains from comparatively small investments of funds and manpower, centered on the problem of identifying and nurturing creative talent. In the future, our nation cannot depend on sheer quantity of manpower, but must strive to find high-quality personnel, especially creative persons, to deal with its vital problems. In fact, an approach utilizing *sheer quantity* of men and facilities can be unduly expensive, so much so that we would probably find on careful analysis that we *cannot afford* such wasteful and inefficient approaches. Since scientists are basic to scientific progress, there may be no potentially greater payoff per unit of expenditure than from continuing to investigate the nature of creative talent and creative performance, preferably more energetically than in the last few years.

An examination of the current national picture in science reveals that many billions of dollars are being spent each year for scientific research and development, not including the additional amounts expended for the education and development of the next generation of scientists. In view of the vital importance of scientific progress and our current vast expenditures in science, it seems obvious that at least a small percentage of such funds should be spent for research on how to identify, develop, and encourage those who will be most fruitful, and especially those who will be most creative in science. Yet it is doubtful whether more than 0.002 per cent of the nation's research and development budget is being spent for this purpose. Could this relatively minute expenditure be termed adequate provision in such a vitally important field?

Our conviction is that the crux of the entire scientific research undertaking is the scientist. It is the scientist, first and foremost, upon whom we depend to push forward the frontiers of science. To obtain the fruits of scientific research, we are dependent *in every instance upon scientists*. When money is spent on research facilities, the scientist is being surrounded with these facilities in an attempt to increase *his* chances of being fruitful.

An Air Force scientist, one of the 166 studied at Cambridge Research Center (C. W. Taylor, Smith, & Ghiselin, 1963), had an interesting idea about the relation between degree of scientific ability and amount of facilities needed in solving scientific problems. He contended that, for a given problem of a certain level of difficulty, the higher the degree of a scientist's ability, the fewer facilities he would need to solve it; or, stated conversely, the lower the degree of ability, the more facilities needed. Furthermore, he felt that, when ability is below a certain level, no matter what facilities are available, the scientist in question will be unable to obtain a solution on his own. It might be added that creative individuals can often accomplish much more at much less expense than other people. Creative and inventive men can do without much expensive equipment that may be required by men with less talent.

Conant has expressed a similar opinion when he said that ten second-rate men are no substitute for one first-rate man in science. He remarked further that it is useless to place second-rate men on a first-rate problem even if one is under pressure for a solution, because second-rate men often do more harm than good on such a problem.

On the other hand, there is some evidence (C. W. Taylor, Smith, & Ghiselin, 1963) that the number of activities for which a person is responsible in a scientific research organization may increase considerably as he moves upward to positions of greater responsibility. A scientist who is promoted within this type of organizational system tends to be involved in more and more activities until, at the higher levels, he is engaged in so many that he is rarely free to concentrate on any one. In other words, the inexperienced scientist whose present and future value is largely unknown is the man who is at present freed to concentrate. Additional equipment and facilities may be required to bolster the attempts of these less experienced scientists who are in the center of the actual research effort.

A more serious problem is the fact that subjecting the more experienced and presumably more successful scientists (those who have been promoted to higher levels in scientific organizations) to so many diverse demands prevents the sustained attention and long, deep concentration necessary for truly profound and creative scientific contributions. Surely those scientists who have proved themselves to be of exceptional caliber deserve as much freedom to do their work as those who are still unproved.

The organizational problems that affect creativity are highlighted in an anecdote about the famous Dutch scientist Jacobus van't Hoff, who won the first Nobel prize in chemistry. We are told that during his graduate years he did two pieces of research. One of them was orthodox and routine, and he apparently wisely chose it to satisfy the requirements for his doctorate. The second was a brilliant work which he did on his own. The latter piece of research, which was less hampered by faculty requirements and influence, launched him on the road to eminence.

Another story pertains to a relatively young mathematician who, according to knowledgeable persons in the academic world, has a number of important mathematical contributions in his notebook. As a result of his experiences in attempting to publish his material, he has decided to publish only one article a year. In that way he feels he can conserve energy, which he would otherwise waste in fights with editors who are not receptive to his new ideas. Yet, as time passes, various individuals have arrived at many of his unpublished conclusions, and each of these men has then "scooped him" by publishing a single article.

Boards of judges are often unable to identify potentially creative proposals or even creative final products; they tend to be less hesitant in passing favorable judgment on orthodox proposals or products that only inch ahead, ignoring others that might result in great strides of progress.

These examples illustrate the importance of identifying creative individuals, of identifying proposals for research projects that will be creative, and of identifying products that are creative.

Some explicit statements should be made concerning what is included and what is not included in the concept of creativity. Some sample definitions from the Utah conference series may be cited. Ghiselin proposes that the *measure of a creative product be the extent to which it restructures our universe of understanding*. Lacklen, of the Space Agency, uses *the extent of the area of science that the contribution underlies*: the more creative the contribution, the wider its effects. Sprecher is interested in the novelty and the value of scientists' ideas, and in their work habits as well; he is also concerned about differences in opportunity to be creative in different work situations. The working definition of creativity used by Stein is that a process is creative when it results in *a novel work that is accepted as tenable or useful or satisfying by a group at some point in time*. Others have argued that we must consider not only social but individual creativity, the creativeness of the individual who makes, for himself, something that others, unknown to him, have made before, as well as the creativeness of individuals who produce something new to society or to the world.

The authors feel that the best two available definitions are Ghiselin's, on which he has worked for many years and which he elaborated in his paper at the 1957 conference, and Lacklen's, which has been used in the Space Agency and its predecessor for nearly two decades. Despite certain differences in emphasis, we consider these two definitions to be quite compatible.

It is clear that no single definition has yet been prepared that suits all workers in the field—some workers are dissatisfied, for example, with the inclusion of social judgments of value in a definition. It is not often understood that the issues in any problem of definition become clarified as research progress is made, so that these issues can be more satisfactorily resolved as total insights improve. The authors urge researchers either to choose tentatively an existing definition of creativity or to develop a definition of their own that will enable them to move ahead in their work.

It is necessary to distinguish creativity from productivity, since productivity implies quantity and creativity implies high quality of a particular kind. Research findings suggest that creativity and productivity overlap to at least a limited degree.

Our research findings and interpretations of past work imply that creativity is complex rather than unitary. A large number of different intellectual and nonintellectual test scores show some promise as predictors. Also, creativity has been measured in terms of several different criteria. It is obvious that creativity can be expressed variously in many different ways and media.

The authors assume that creativity emerges at the adult level as a complex result of many factors of both inheritance and life history. The many relevant variables within these two extremely broad categories can also interact among themselves. Current efforts could be characterized, in part, as attempts to recognize and measure the major internal and external variables that lead toward or away from creative performance.

The complexities of the total research problem might best be illustrated by describing one aspect of it, namely, the ultimate prediction problem. Here, the practical goal is to identify early in life those who have the greatest potential for creative performance, in order to set the stage so that later in life the creative process in its most extreme and rare form will be likely to occur in the individuals so identified.

The common assumption among most psychological researchers

is that all persons have some creative potential, though there are wide individual differences in degree. Lowenfeld distinguished between actual creativity and potential creativity, the former being that potential which is already developed and functioning, the latter including the total creative potential (both developed and undeveloped) within an individual (Lowenfeld, 1959).

Apparently, many lay persons have a quite different notion from that held by psychologists when they think of creativity in the arts. They believe that most people have zero potential to be creative, whereas a few persons are fortunate and have creative talent in varying degrees. An assumption held by psychologists, with which many art educators concur, is that all persons have some degree of potential to be creative in one or more ways.

It is also recognized that creativity occurs at practically all ages, in some aspects of all cultures, and to some degree in all fields of human work and endeavor, although there are general differences in the frequency, level, and type of creativity across these categories. Though some fields of endeavor are thought to require more creativity, they may not necessarily do so at all times; on the other hand, creative bursts may occur in fields not often thought of as creative. Persons who work in a more creative field *are not* necessarily *all* creative people. In other words, it is realistic to accept the notion that creativity should be expected generally in human activities and is not limited essentially to certain fields of the arts and sciences.

The distinction between the creative product and the creative process is widely recognized. Indicators of potential in both product and process are sought and used for assessment purposes. Such indicators may be of practical value as well. In the area of developing criteria for the evaluation of degree of creativity, the point of view of the present book is that assessment of the product is much more important and acceptable, for several reasons, than assessment of the process. One reason is that the product is far more tangible.

Although there are many potentially valuable indicators for identifying creative people, there is some doubt about the validity of some of them; short, highly verbal tests, for example, may not predict the highest type and level of creativity. We are also unsure about the long-range effects of education and training programs and of other environmental influences on the development and stimulation of creative potential. Good yardsticks—valid criteria of creativity —are needed if we are to have a sound basis for evaluating the effects upon creativity of such training and environmental variables. And yet the problem of the criteria of creativity—perhaps the most crucial problem in this field—has been studied less than any other aspect of our total problem. The criterion problem concerns the evaluation of the degree of creativeness of a product or a performance; it is quite separate from the prediction problem, in which the creative potential of people is estimated—for example, by means of test scores—and in which predictions about future creative performances are made, based upon the "creative potential" estimate for each person.

The authors of this book agree that the criterion problem demands the highest priority and that the most serious consideration for research support should be given to any proposals for worthwhile work on criteria. For example, a linked series of studies on criteria of creative performance at all stages of life might considerably speed up all research progress.

The reader is forewarned that the major topics discussed in the present book appear to be oriented toward applied research. Research directed toward improvement in the "state of the art" is also included; thus, research leading to improved methodology and research design and to improved criterion and predictor measures will obviously permit increasingly fruitful applied research. This general orientation reflects the emphasis in the current literature and also the fact that it is easier to write about the more tangible aspects of any field; it should not be construed, however, as questioning the need for basic research. The areas in which relevant basic research might be accomplished are necessarily broad and are not easily described or covered systematically in a report of this kind. Despite the increase in recent research, both basic and applied, it is apparent that relatively little is yet known, and that *much basic research on creativity should be supported.*

The full reports and discussions by the highly competent research participants at the Utah creativity conference series can be read in the volumes by Taylor (1955, 1957, 1959, 1963) and by Taylor & Barron (1963). The reader who is interested in other complete and explicit summaries (often uncritical, involving some topics other than creativity and, in instances, without empirical data) should see the books, monographs, and reports by Anderson (1959a), Lowenfeld (1957), Stein & Heinze (1960), and Yamamoto (1961); the *Bibliography on Creativity* prepared by the Industrial Research Institute (1955); the bibliography on creativity in research and invention in the physical sciences (Benton, 1961); *The Creativity Review* by the Dow Chemical Company; the research summaries of the Creativity Research Exchange (an Educational Testing Service program formulated and initiated by Henry Dyer at the 1955 Utah creativity conference); and the bibliographies of French and Italian contributions by Bedard (Creativity Research Exchange 9, 10). More recent books and materials include one on guiding creative talent (Torrance, 1962a), creativity and intelligence (Getzels & Jackson, 1962), readings on creative thinking (Parnes & Harding, 1962), a University of California conference proceedings on the creative person (1962), and an interestingly illustrated book on creativity in art, dealing with spontaneous versus deliberate ways of learning (Burkhart, 1962).

There has now been sufficient demonstration that useful research can be done on many different aspects of creativity, in the school room, in the universities, in research installations, and in professional activities, as indicated in later chapters. A great variety of studies have been designed and carried out in the area of prediction and also in education and training. Consequently, *it can no longer be said that fruitful research cannot be done on creativity.* There are now many leads to pursue even at this relatively early period of serious scientific research. Many examples of creativity studies are cited in later sections, illustrating what might be accomplished as well as what has already been done.

Each of the contributors to this book has selected certain problem areas as important, and these have been reviewed by the other contributors; the aim has been to identify those areas in which research seems most promising or most urgently needed. The reader should, however, be cautioned that we, as writers, are all very much aware that other researchers may find different areas more promising or more urgent. The authors hope that this book will not deter research in any area in which researchers have found important leads. Nevertheless, they feel that knowledge about creativity would be accelerated if effort could be focused in those areas identified as having high priority.

This review is based on the available literature, including the Utah conference reports, and especially upon the subgroup reports on predictors, criteria, education, and working conditions which were presented by Barron, Knapp, and Harmon at the 1955 conference; Barron, Roe, Lacklen, and Harmon at the 1957 conference; and Guilford, Sprecher, Parnes, Kuhn, and Kaplan at the 1959 conference.

A reading of the criterion and predictor (aptitude and personality) subgroup reports in the 1955, 1957, and 1959 Utah creativity conference publications and of the subgroup reports on education and environmental conditions in the 1959 report will still serve a useful purpose. To illustrate, the eleven points presented by the Barron subgroup at the 1955 conference, under the heading "New Areas in Which Research on Creativity Is Needed," were as follows:

1. The strength and the fate of originality in women.
2. The beginnings of creativity in children, with an attempt to get at things like when scientific thinking begins, how long animistic modes persist, what the overlap between them means, etc.
3. Creativity at an unlikely age. This includes both precocity and the persistence of creativity to an advanced age.
4. Periodicity of creative test performance and of creativity in general, since we think there is some sort of ebb and flow.
5. The apparently inexplicable associations of creativity.
6. Creative test performance under trance conditions, under the influence of drugs, etc.
7. Group activity and group ability as structural determinants of group creativity: (a) whether, in groups containing mixed abilities,

the diversity will result in greater group creativity; (*b*) whether democratic group structure may result in greater group creativity than authoritarian structure.

8. The educability of creativity. The question here is whether people can be taught to be more creative, i.e., whether creative thinking can be taught.

9. Identification of those high in test score but not high in actual creative performance (where the reverse pattern is at a minimum). There may be special ways in which one could approach this.

10. Variation of scoring of present tests to make them more relevant to a criterion of creativity. This is suggested by the new way of scoring the Controlled Associations test which one 1955 conference participant devised. There are probably other kinds of tests which might represent behavior of a sort which is not at present being scored and which in some cases might be more criterion-relevant for certain criteria.

11. Optimum level of creativity in an individual. "What price creativity?" is the question here. Can there be too much creative activity; can it result in some sort of diffusion of other activity and loss of effectiveness in certain important areas of personal functioning? What is too much and what is too little in creative activity? Is "perfection of the life or of the work," in Yeats' phrase, a realistic statement of the choice which a highly creative person must make?

In the same 1955 Barron subgroup report, the section on "Unresolved Issues" presents certain important technical problems still without final resolution. Knapp's 1955 subgroup report presents a long list of personality attributes felt at that time to be important, together with considerable discussion mainly from a psychoanalytic point of view. The 1959 criterion report by Sprecher and others is well worth reading, for it summarizes past work on the criterion problem and the new work at the 1959 conference. It outlines the variables and dimensions potentially involved in criteria of creativity, and it suggests in detail how future research on one important criterion, that of "breadth of applicability of a contribution," could be carried out.

It is clear that selected ideas have been given different emphases by the teams forming the successive subgroups of the conference series and that the present set of chapters differs in coverage and emphasis from those written by earlier subgroups. The present authors have built upon the previous reports, although they have not always agreed with them entirely.

In some of the work reported in the literature as well as at the conferences, it is unclear whether a creative scientist, or merely a scientist in general, is being studied and described. Readers should be cautioned that descriptions of *typical* persons involved in the more creative fields of endeavor do not necessarily apply to the *creative* persons in those fields. It is encouraging to learn that studies indicate some similarity of characteristics among people in different creative areas. Nonetheless, it is important to review such studies to determine whether *creative* performance, or *overall* performance, is the factor under investigation.

The present book is concerned with three main areas of creativity research: first, psychological characteristics (early indicators or predictors) that identify those with more potential to be creative; second, the effects of environmental factors such as education, training programs, work "climate," and other situational influences on the development or suppression of the creative potential; and third, criteria for determining the degree to which a person has produced, once or more in his life, something that could be called a creative product or a creative performance. (This last will be referred to in this book as the criterion problem.)

The authors are unanimously agreed that the research effort should continue to consider and include all three areas: predictive characteristics, criteria of creativity, and variables that can modify the relation between the predictors and the criteria, such as education and training, working conditions, and other relevant environmental factors. Almost all the creativity studies completed to date (except the rare studies solely on the criterion problem) involve at least two of these three aspects.

The functional relationships between the predictor scores, the environmental variables that can modify the predictions, and the ultimate outcome can be stated only more or less systematically at the present time. At the 1959 conference, Stein made a preliminary speculative attempt to tie together predictors, environmental variables, and criteria of creativity. The Utah studies of Air Force scientists (C. W. Taylor, Smith, Ghiselin, & Ellison, 1961; Taylor, Smith, & Ghiselin, 1963) deal with many variables from each of these three categories and some empirically determined interrelations among them.

The topics in this book have been arranged according to the sequence of events in an individual's life. This sequence has been chosen primarily for the sake of the reader, in spite of our recognition of the overriding importance of the last topic—the criterion problem. This last problem is fundamental to the other topics and is the most difficult technical problem. Interestingly enough, the importance of the criterion problem seems to be well recognized by patent lawyers—one of whom recently suggested that psychologists, well-versed in the creativity criterion problem, should join in a full exchange of ideas and findings with a highly selected group of lawyers who are well-versed in what is patentable, so that each could profit from the work and thinking of the others.

Similar teamwork among many fields seems urgently needed. For example, science and the arts can profit by working together; educators, training directors, research directors, management, and policy makers can contribute knowledge and insights to one another and can supplement and serve as catalysts for one another. As psychologists attempt research in creativity in any field, they urgently need all the help they can get from creative persons in that field.

Although man's creativity underlies all crucial movements along the frontiers of science and of other knowledge, too little is currently known about its nature. Not nearly enough empirical research has yet been accomplished. The authors hope that this book will help to increase the total effort being made both to learn more about creative talent and to develop it, in science and elsewhere. They also hope that more programs *based on the research findings* presented here will be put into effect.

# chapter 2

# PREDICTORS

# OF CREATIVE

# PERFORMANCE

*Calvin W. Taylor*

UNIVERSITY OF UTAH


*John Holland*

NATIONAL MERIT SCHOLARSHIP CORPORATION

T HE PURPOSE of this chapter is to summarize our current knowledge about the predictors of creative performance; it will include a survey of the more promising kinds of predictors and an explicit statement of our more urgent research needs. Although we cannot at this time make judgments about all predictor variables, it seems desirable to delineate the nature of those personal and situational attributes which now seem most predictive of creative performance. Future investigators may then build on such information without reworking earlier research. A certain amount of replication is needed for most findings, and it is time-consuming and expensive for each investigator to find useful variables on his own.

It is elementary, but of fundamental importance, to note that the use of predictors assumes that we have some explicit, relevant, external criterion for recognizing the creative performance that we hope to predict with our personal and situational variables. Tests of creative *ability,* often used as criteria of creativity because they appear to be valid measures of the processes tested, are at best preliminary and inadequate criteria; if we rely on them extensively, we may overlook our chief criterion: adult creative performance.

Many workers in education and elsewhere are seeking to understand the nature of creative persons and are looking for practical methods and devices that will help them immediately both in identifying creative persons and in predicting creative performance. The authors feel that this practical search is not at all opposed to that long-term search for understanding which is often called "basic" research; their position is that to distinguish between applied and basic research has little meaning. Whatever the problem, good research involves definition of terms, inventiveness and theorizing, efficient prediction, and reduction of ambiguity in the findings. Different investigators will work in different ways and in different settings, but at some point they will display an interest and competence in all these subproblems within their research. The next section gives a tentative description, based on past research and on speculation, of the creative individual.

# THE NATURE OF THE CREATIVE
# PERSON—ATTRIBUTES AND MEASURES

## *Traditional measures*

Before a tentative description of the creative person can be presented, certain widely available measures of psychological characteristics should be mentioned. It seems appropriate first to discuss the use of academic grades and intelligence tests as potential predictors of creative performance. If school grades were efficient predictors of creativity, it would be easy indeed to identify persons with high creative potential; but school grades in general have little or no validity for this purpose. Since academic performance usually involves so much that is noncreative, the nature of school work will have to change appreciably if grades are ever to become useful as predictors.

Intelligence tests suffer from the same deficiency. If traditional intelligence tests were valid measures of creative potential, again the prediction problem would be small. But the evidence suggests that intelligence tests are not very effective measures of creative potential; intelligence, as measured, accounts for only a small part of the variation in creative performance (Getzels & Jackson, 1959; Torrance, 1959; MacKinnon, 1959).

Likewise, it is helpful to speculate about the relationship between creative performance and the sheer accumulation of knowledge. It is easy to cite examples of people in the academic world who are well versed in their fields but who have demonstrated little creativity. One also can name productive and creative persons who are criticized by scholars for not being well read or for not giving due veneration to past knowledge and to the accepted orientations in their field. In other words, sheer mastery of knowledge does not seem to be a sufficient condition for creative performance. A striking illustration of this hypothesis is found in the life of Pasteur. After he had established a reputation as a researcher, Pasteur was recruited to work on a problem concerning silkworms. Shortly thereafter, a silkworms expert interviewed Pasteur and was startled by Pasteur's ignorance of silkworms—he was truly a novice. But it was Pasteur—not the experts—who reached a useful solution. Apparently, what the solution required was only a minimum of the most relevant knowledge combined with certain important intellectual and motivational attributes not usually called for in scholarly work.

### Early stage of research

Scientific knowledge about creative talent is in a very early stage, but there are many indications that some progress has already been made; we have some useful and promising beginnings. We are at the stage where it can *no longer be said* that research on creative talent cannot be done. There are now too many leads to follow rather than too few. There have been a few validation studies of selected tests (i.e., predictors of creativity) and a few criterion studies to determine the relationships among various kinds of creative contributions. Many other tests have not yet been validated, and many new ideas that have been proposed for tests have not yet been developed. Cross-validation studies have been infrequent, as have been parallel studies of creativity in different fields of science and in nonscientific fields. There have been some preliminary investigations about how different educational and training programs and different working environments may modify creative performance. As a consequence, corrections for education and for working environments may eventually be added to our prediction formulas. Constructive action to modify educational programs and environmental conditions may stimulate creative activity and reduce the problem of identifying the creative individual.

Although there have been several studies of the attributes of creative persons, very few of these have been validation studies in the conventional sense. The 1959 Predictor Subcommittee cited only three, by R. B. Cattell, Drevdahl, and Sprecher, that had been completed. It is striking, however, that in most of the studies of creative persons, a number of personal traits (e.g., independence) have emerged as being relevant to creativity with surprising consistency, although in some cases these characteristics are of minor significance. This consistency is in sharp contrast with the conflicting results usually found in the early stages of research in other psychological areas.

In the following pages, nearly all the personal characteristics found or hypothesized to date are listed. No attempt has been made to indicate the amount of empirical evidence, if any, that supports the importance of a given attribute. No attempt has been made to relate a trait to the particular techniques used to measure it or to the design of the study in which it emerged as being relevant. The reader is reminded that there may be other abilities and personal characteristics related to creativity that have not yet been identified or even recognized as psychological characteristics. As further studies are completed, some characteristics cited now will probably be found to be peripheral or of no value. It will be helpful if this long list of characteristics can be reduced and better organized and if the appropriate traits can be related to different types of creative talent. Nonetheless, it is a hopeful sign at this time that there have been discovered so many discernible characteristics that may be important in creativity.

## Intellectual characteristics

On the basis of insights derived from his own findings and those of many other researchers, Guilford has listed the following intellectual characteristics as most likely to be valid measures of creative talent: originality, redefinition, adaptive flexibility, spontaneous flexibility, associational fluency, expressional fluency, word fluency, ideational fluency, elaboration, and probably some evaluation factors. (Although their relevance as measures of creativity is still being determined, there is little doubt that the above factors measure intellectual abilities generally ignored in talent searches and in most educational programs.)

In broader terms, a few components of memory, cognition, and evaluation, more of convergent production, and even more of divergent production are involved in creative work. Divergent production, that is, the production of multiple possible solutions, is an area which has been overlooked, and it appears to be one important factor in the study of creative talent, since it includes the production of ideas in quantity and in quality, originality, flexibility, sensitivity, and ability to redefine. Pictorial fluency, another aspect of divergent production, may be an example of a characteristic needed for creative work in art but not in science.

Undoubtedly, convergent (reductive) thinking, the type of thinking which narrows down the possibilities and focuses upon producing a single solution, also has a role in creative work. Research findings on communication abilities at the University of Utah suggest that the ability to recognize a correct answer on a multiple-choice question is probably not sufficiently similar to the ability to extract a fresh generalization from a mass of data to be used as a substitute. Many useful things can be accomplished with structured questions and responses, but no one should conclude that they can measure everything. The selection among a number of alternatives of that one judged to be best and the rejection of other alternatives seem to be involved in the later stages of this divergent-convergent sequence. Compactness of thinking and expression may be related to the elegance of the final product.

Mainly as a result of a factor study on creativity by Guilford and his students (Guilford, Wilson, Christensen, & Lewis, 1951; Guilford, Wilson, & Christensen, 1952), batteries of tests, usually including many divergent-thinking tasks, are being used in some industrial and educational settings to identify creative talent. Persons selected by this type of battery tend to have intellectual characteristics different from those of comparison groups selected solely on the basis of high IQ scores: they have more fantasies; they have more ability and a greater tendency to toy with ideas; when problems arise with gadgets, they tend to suggest solutions rather than to curse the gadgets; and they are more humorous.

The ability to see patterns in data and the ability to sense problems are characteristics usually included in creativity. The capacity to be puzzled, a characteristic which has motivational features too, may be very important. A keen observer once said that part of Einstein's genius was his inability to understand the obvious. Thus the rejection of one's own and other people's superficial explanations and the ability *to know when you don't know* may be crucial to making original contributions.

The ability to sense ambiguities and to question effectively—an ability which might be described as "curiosity in action"—may be important in creative activity. Many of the components of curiosity and of motivation may be of an intellectual nature.

Revision tests, even those involving only verbal revision, are useful, since they call for a process analogous to the manipulation, restructuring, and reworking of ideas found in the earlier and later stages of creative production. They also measure the ability and tendency to strive for more comprehensive answers, another feature that has emerged in on-the-job studies of creativity. Intellectual thoroughness has also been found valid in more than one study. Unfortunately, there are probably very few occasions in our academic programs that require such revision and striving for higher quality or for more original and workable products. Likewise, most of the other creative characteristics are often ignored or are not particularly stressed in present academic programs.

A study of the products of scientists has found two quite unrelated ratings of quality: "quality without originality," and "original type of quality." Judgments of work in school may yield separate indicators of these two different types of quality, with originality the better predictor of future creative work.

Somewhat in opposition to the reworking-and-thoroughness characteristic, we find a verbal-superficiality factor. It is suspected that this is negatively related to most kinds of creative performance. Certainly in science, and perhaps in other fields, it seems unlikely that creative or profound contributions will come from superficial thinkers.

In creativity training sessions, one might design measuring devices to identify those people who show the greatest initial readiness for training and those who show the greatest gains during the training.

The creative ability so measured could, perhaps, also be validly indicated by a large gain in creativity test scores as a result of direct practice on these tests.

At least two response-set factors may measure characteristics functioning in creativity. The first, "broadly diffused attention," has often been described as preceding the insight stage of the creative process. The second, "resistance to idea reduction," may be valuable in the creation of broad new generalizations. Both the tendency to resist idea reduction and its opposite pole, willingness to reduce ideas, may be traits that contribute to creative performance.

Creative persons in many fields have stated that they work intermittently over long periods of time (though perhaps almost continually below the conscious level) on their key problems. This phenomenon of sustained interest suggested to Ghiselin that he try take-home aptitude tests to find those who continue to be involved and who jot down additional responses whenever they occur. Similarly, the ebb and flow of ideas in the creative process suggests the need for tests that assess variability in the performance of an individual over a period of time. Presumably, though the creative person may often function at low level, he occasionally functions at a very high level. Perhaps the person with the greatest variability over a period of time has more creative potential.

Other traits that should be tested include the abilities to form and test hunches (hypotheses), to foresee consequences, to infer causes, to evaluate revisions in a product, and to put forward one's ideas. The finding of a verbal-originality factor, in an interesting test designed by Ghiselin in which the subject is asked to create new compound words, leads us to hope for an analogous measure of *nonverbal originality*. Shockley has pointed out that creative thinking may require the manipulation of several ideas at a time. We lack a test for determining capacity to manipulate ideas. An interesting related question is whether this capacity can be increased by forming and training teams of workers.

The more creative scientists rate themselves high in creativity, cognition, discrimination of value, flexibility, academic achievement, and intuition. Early interest in intellectual activities and above-average breadth of interest are characteristic of the more creative physical scientists.

Thurstone suggested that a creator has good rapport with his prefocal thoughts, but this rapport is not now measurable. We also lack measures of preconscious thought, of imageless thought, of preverbal thought, and of the relationship between thinking and the expression of thinking. The ability to make good intuitive decisions on the basis of incomplete information may be relevant. Barron has suggested that we need to test the ability to express heretofore unexpressed experiences or undescribed phenomena. He feels that creative people are more open to relevant experience and more observant (seeing both what others see and what they do not see), that they place high value on accurate reporting of their observations, and that they have the ability to make such observations explicit. They sense more complexities in the world than others do, are more complex as persons, make richer syntheses, and note their own impulses more. The authors would hazard the guess that there are important unmeasured characteristics involved in the pioneering type of creativity, the ability to open the way and move ahead in unexplored areas. Perhaps our pioneers are those who show a disposition to cope with difficulties rather than to be immobilized by them. So far there is no evidence that the sheer amount of education a person has had is a good indicator of his readiness to take a new step. It is necessary, among the educated, to identify those who can absorb the lessons of the past without being held back by them, who can find new ideas and use them to improve upon the past.

To summarize our current understanding of the intellectual aspects of creativity, there seem to be many more or less distinct intellectual components. It is likely, therefore, that multiple types of creative talent exist. It is likely also that some of these intellectual components underlie some of the motivational forces in the creative person and are linked significantly to certain personality characteristics as well.

## Motivational characteristics

It is the general belief of the authors that motivation is a vital component of creativity. The great need is for better measuring instruments (for all ages), although in the Utah study of Air Force scientists (C. W. Taylor, Smith, Ghiselin, & Ellison, 1961), motivation was found to be only a small component of creative performance. It has been suggested that the creative person is curious, enterprising in his ideas, intellectually persistent, tolerant of ambiguity; he shows initiative in his area of work; he likes to think and to manipulate ideas; he has an inner need for recognition; he needs variety and autonomy; he has a preference for complex order and for challenges therein; he has an esthetic and to some extent religious orientation; he resists premature closure and crystallization of concepts, though he has a strong need for ultimate closure; he desires mastery of a problem; he finds challenging the intellectual ordering of the apparently unclassifiable; and he wants to improve upon currently accepted orders and systems. The use of passional sources of energy and kinesthetic cues may be important. High energy with vast work output through disciplined work habits is usually found.

Bloom (1963) has indicated that science students who become truly involved in research work and in the research role during graduate training tend to become the productive researchers afterwards. Conversely, those who finish their advanced-degree requirements without becoming involved in their research usually do *not* produce research afterwards; they avoid research opportunities and do not try to cultivate them. If the creative are to be found somewhere among the productive, then we can reduce our problem by looking for creative scientists among those students who become truly involved in research problems during their academic careers. Analogous situations in which the student's degree of involvement becomes clear can also be developed in nonscientific fields. We can seek out involved persons at almost any academic level if we set up the situation properly and ask for the right type of performance.

According to Kuhn, a strong commitment to and a great involvement in some particular approach have usually been important in making true progress in research, at least at certain stages of the scientific venture.

Other traits suggested as predictors are a willingness to take greater and more long-range risks for greater gain and a tendency to accumulate an overabundance of raw material for the task at hand coupled with a willingness ultimately to discard some of it in forming final products. One provocative idea presented at the 1955 conference by McClelland (on which all results have not since been positive) is that the creative person is more willing to take a calculated risk than other people are (though not an unrealistically large one) and that his estimate of the odds in research areas is actually smaller than the average estimate of other persons. The creative individual, presumably, is not interested in a sheer gamble where the outcome is left to chance, but in a risk situation where his own efforts will make a difference in the odds. The creative person does not hold man's knowledge in awe or tend to enshrine it; he is capable of revolting against some of the past knowledge and experiences of men.

Barron reports that creative people have an intense esthetic and moral commitment to their work. They may also sense, at least vaguely, a distinct sexual overtone to the act of creation.

Younger persons with creative talent, according to Getzel's findings, have a much greater variety of occupational choices; they are more interested in and aware of unconventional careers than are their fellow students. They sense that their notions of what constitutes success are not always consistent with the predominant views of society. They are willing to be nonconforming and consequently to be in the small minority.

The more creative scientists rate themselves high in drive, dedication to work, resourcefulness, desire for principles, and desire for discovery. They have high aspirations for the quality of their written work, their theoretical contributions, and the level of original work that they hope to produce.

## Group indicators

In seeking the creative person, one may find some important leads by looking slightly away from, instead of directly toward, the target. Clues for identifying creative talent may be obtained by watching the reactions of other people. The work at Minnesota gives some support to this approach. The creative person, striving for autonomy and solutions, may attempt to work his way around blocks to creativity erected by others and to overcome restrictions and organizational controls. If some members of a group appear excited or disturbed, *perhaps* there is a creative person around whose ideas and work are at least vaguely sensed as a threat to the present scheme of things. The group may attempt to eliminate or reduce this threat by developing sanctions against the person or by over-organizing and building other controls into their world. One possible way to identify the creative person is to remove one person at a time from the group, noticing in which case group tensions are most reduced. Unfortunately, one may locate disturbed persons as well as creative ones by this procedure.

Creative students may perhaps be identifiable by their problems; those who have tendencies to strive for more comprehensive answers and to be intellectually thorough may have difficulties with some of their teachers. Not only creative students but also creative teachers may encounter more than their share of complicating factors in the school setting. Frank Jex reported at the 1959 conference that high school science teachers with high creativity test scores were rated below average in overall teaching performance by their principals and immediate supervisors.

Torrance's results from using descriptions of an individual by his fellow students seem promising. Similarly, Harmon's findings in the 1957 Utah conference report show positive results for assessments made on confidential report forms. Accordingly, the possibility of using well-designed confidential reports, including ratings, check lists, and written descriptions by peers, teachers, and supervisors (as well as self-ratings), for identifying those with creative potential, should not be overlooked. One basic question here is to what degree a rater must have creative characteristics himself in order to recognize these characteristics in someone else. Another question is how to take into account any negative reactions that there may be to the more creative individual, which may influence ratings and recommendations.

In group discussions (including brainstorming sessions), individuals differ widely in their contributions to the flow of ideas. Some people merely help to set the stage; others make crucial leaps ahead, thinking "at right angles" on an unusual train of thought, rather than following the flow of the discussion. Later they may open up new and fresh avenues.

Certain persons may serve as catalysts to stimulate creative thinking in others. Other persons may be skilled in utilizing others effectively to stir their own thinking along new lines.

Unexpected but intriguing results were found in a criterion study pertaining to the working conditions of researchers in a scientific laboratory. The number of published scientific articles was found to be negatively related to ratings by supervisors on cooperation and flexibility. In other words, those researchers who go the "extra mile" and publish their completed work may pay the price of being judged inflexible and uncooperative. A second finding is more clearly concerned with creativity as distinct from productivity: those with the fastest promotion rates were credited with very few official suggestions and rated themselves low on desire for discovery. Those who had a strong desire for discovery and who made good official suggestions had a *below-average* rate of promotion.

### Personality characteristics

There is some evidence that creative persons are more autonomous than others, more self-sufficient, more independent in judgment (they go against group opinion if they feel it is incorrect), more open to the irrational in themselves, more stable, more feminine in interests and characteristics (especially in awareness of their impulses), more dominant and self-assertive, more complex, more self-accepting, more resourceful and adventurous, more radical (Bohemian), more self-controlled, and possibly more emotionally sensitive, and more introverted but bold. R. B. Cattell warns that exuberance, which decreases with maturity, should *not* be confused with creativity.

Creative scientists rate themselves high in professional self-confidence, self-sufficiency, independence, and emotional restraint, and low in aggressiveness, assertion, social desirability, sociability, and masculine vigor. They tend *not* to give a typical response on multiple-choice biographical questions.

Other personal characteristics that may be relevant to different types of creativity are: liking for ideas versus people versus things, tendencies toward socialization and interpersonal involvement, introversion versus extroversion, commitment to primary versus secondary thought processes, impulse control (suppression versus expression), and surgency versus desurgency.

Almost every time that a biographical inventory has been tried on scientists, for purposes of prediction, it has been found promising. Indirectly these inventories get at a hodgepodge of motivational and personality traits, such as work habits, attitudes, interests, values, family and academic history, etc. This complex measure of life history has proved as valid as any other device for discovering creative talent.

Creative people in different fields may have different personal characteristics. For example, it is commonly believed that the artist, struck by sudden inspiration, must get to his canvas quickly before his feeling vanishes. The special role of the spatial sense and visual imagery in art and of the temporal sense and auditory imagery in music need investigation. Many creative people have stressed the importance of mastering the techniques of expression specific to one's field. Different styles of creating within science have been studied with some success by Gough (1958), suggesting similar possibilities in other areas of creativity.

Another potentially valuable suggestion is that the creative individual tends to produce adaptive responses that are original in nature. A more extreme suggestion about adjustment is that, whereas the typical person focuses on adjusting to his environment, the creative individual tries to adjust the environment to him, to improve it in ways that he feels are urgently needed.

The Reverend Maurice McDowell has suggested that Einstein was motivated to overcome the tyranny of the unknown. Since Einstein has also been described as not seeing the obvious (or that which others saw as obvious), one may infer that he felt stimulated to reduce the tyranny of the obvious—the tyranny of other men's accepting as known what was really unknown.

As stated earlier, the "dead-wood" predictors of creative potential need to be identified and eliminated from the long list of variables reviewed here. The validity of each of the surviving characteristics and of the best weighted combination of these, for each field and kind of creativity, needs to be checked.

### Environmental influences as predictors

A recurring theme in the preceding pages has been the notion that creative attributes may possibly be modified in either positive or negative directions by environmental influences. These influences have included factors involved in educational settings, working conditions and climate, and training programs. Home environments also may be regarded as external influences enhancing or hindering the development of those attributes which have been found to be predictors of creativity. These relevant environmental factors, properly assessed, can be included in our predictor battery as indicators of future creative performance.

Alternatively, they can be viewed as modifiers of predictions; they are presented in this way in Chapters 3 and 4 of this book. It is there assumed that predictions have been made, pointing to various degrees of future creative performance; subsequently, environmental factors, such as education, training programs, and work climate, modify these predictions. These later chapters deal with the manner and the degree of this modification.

## METHODOLOGICAL PROCEDURES AND PROBLEMS

### Sources of information

Several sources may provide information useful for identifying persons with creative potential. Generally, the person himself has been the main source of information. He is asked to perform on certain tests, to do certain tasks, or to fill out forms on which he describes and rates himself in various ways. Other sources of information might include his parents and other family members, his fellow students or work associates, his teachers or supervisors, and other persons who could give relevant information in the form of ratings, check lists, descriptions, etc. These other sources have not been used as frequently in creativity studies as one might expect, in view of their usefulness in other studies. Official records and tangible products and accomplishments may also provide scores for identifying creative potential; these have shown promise the few times they have been used.

### Types of measures used

Unlike attempts to measure intelligence, which usually rely on a single measuring device such as an IQ score, the investigations of creative promise emphasize the assessment of a broad range of variables. These variables have included the following kinds of characteristics: intellectual, especially those kinds *not* measured in IQ tests; motivational; biographical; sociometric; and personality. However, to our knowledge no attempts have been made to do pattern scoring across items or profile scoring across tests in studies of creativity.

### Validation designs

As a preliminary to a main study, the approach used by Hill and by Guilford and Allen has merit. These investigators composed a list of measurable psychological characteristics and let the specialists in each field judge which of these were important for creative work in that field.

Many different designs have been used. Most of the studies have been planned to find the more creative persons within a group, rather than to differentiate groups of people in more creative work from groups in less creative work. In some studies, creative persons have described their own processes and experiences. Ghiselin (1955) discussed this method of obtaining descriptions of the creative process; more recently he developed a Creative Process Check List, in the hope that it could be scored in such a way as to distinguish more creative from less creative persons. R. B. Cattell (1959) reported a biographical study of eminent persons in the history of science, as an interesting exploratory approach to discovering characteristics of creative scientists.

In a second kind of study, groups of carefully selected creative persons are studied intensively in order to discover a set of characteristics common to the group. However, this kind of study is often highly ambiguous, since the need for appropriate comparison or control groups has been ignored. Where the tests used are standard ones, the norms for the creative group can be compared with the norms for the general population, but, usually, the use of new devices or scales makes this immediately (though not ultimately) impossible. Rarely have investigators used a control group consisting of persons who at some stage were equal in promise to the creative group but who failed to perform creatively.

A common fault of many studies is that, although great effort is put into the development and selection of psychological devices, very little effort is devoted to the criterion problem. In some studies, one or more types of achievement (such as completion of a doctorate —admittedly not always a creative accomplishment) are available as criteria, leading the researcher to look into existing files, so to speak, for predictor data to validate against the criteria. In only two or three isolated cases has intensive work been done on the criterion part of the investigation. The authors are convinced that there is no more crucial problem in creativity than the criterion problem.

Many studies have yielded concurrent validities of various predictors. One early type of study, which opened the way for much research, was the factor analysis of large, well-designed batteries of tests.

In still another kind of concurrent-validity study, a single test score or a battery score derived from a number of tests is used as a criterion, and then the correlates of this criterion are discovered. This type of study includes those investigations in which a highly "creative" group is identified by means of a "creativity" battery score and then studied for other characteristics and compared with a group selected on the basis of another type of test score. Studies of this type have certainly played an important part in arousing interest in creativity.

Another kind of concurrent-validity study includes both creativity tests and one or more external criteria of performance, usually work performance. Such studies provide individual validity coefficients. Multiple correlational and factor-analytic studies can also be done in these same projects. A modification of this plan is the comparison of two groups, formed on the basis of selected test scores, on suitable external criteria.

Some creativity studies in each of the designs reviewed here have been completed. All of these study plans have special limitations.

The results of concurrent-validity studies—in which external criteria and test data are collected almost simultaneously—need to be verified in predictive (longitudinal) validity studies using external criteria. Such predictive validity studies, in which a sample is tested and then followed up for some period before data on each person's performance are obtained, are infrequent and sorely needed.

### Sampling

Perhaps too many studies have dealt with relatively small samples. Even though some findings occur consistently in several small studies, replications on larger samples are needed for more reliable results.

The nature of the fields studied has varied, but not in any systematic way. Physical science and engineering have been more frequently studied than the biological-medical sciences, the social sciences, the arts, the humanities, or business. We need to learn to what degree findings about the physical sciences and engineering hold true in other fields and to what extent the intellectual and personal characteristics called for in one field are different from those in another. We also need to learn whether there are several types of creativity within a given field and, if so, whether any of these types recur, in other fields or in particular activities, such as administrative work. At least one study (a dissertation by Eisner at the University of Chicago) was deliberately designed to study four different hypothetical types of creativity within one field. A number of comparative studies—some completed, some in process—have focused on the differences between the physical sciences and the arts; these may yield helpful ideas.

The effects of other potentially relevant variables, such as age and amount and type of education and experience, have not always been studied or controlled. One problem that has made interpretation difficult is that of restriction of range (homogeneity of the sample). This problem is most worrisome when the variables on which the restriction occurs are related to the variables focused upon in the study. However, if the sample is homogeneous on variables unrelated to the variables investigated, restriction of range will not affect the variables under investigation. Furthermore, if zero correlations are found in many validity coefficients in a homogeneous sample, it is probable that many of these validity coefficients would remain essentially zero in a more heterogeneous sample. Consequently, investigations are needed to clarify what have been the effects, if any, of restriction of range in the completed studies.

Another problem occurs in the study of different age groups. Most studies have been done on adults, and many assessment devices must be revised before they can be administered to adolescents or young children. In some instances, entirely new measures of creative characteristics have been developed for children. In either case, we need to know whether the same characteristics are being measured in children as in adults and whether the measures are more valid in adults or in children. Guilford, in a recent unpublished study, found that the divergent-thinking portion of his "structure of intellect" was essentially the same for sixth graders and ninth graders as for adults; he found a few specific tests, however, that must be carefully watched because they change in nature in these differing age groups.

## CONCURRENT VALIDITIES OF VARIABLES RELATED TO CREATIVE PERFORMANCE

### Correlates of tests of creativity—no external criteria

Many factorial studies designed without external criteria have been instructive nonetheless. The analyses of correlations among various measures of fluencies, flexibilities, sensitivities, originality, and personality characteristics have yielded some consistent findings in studies on adults. By dividing creativity into various components (or factors), we can develop tests with known factorial content and can use a technical vocabulary for describing creative characteristics, especially the divergent type of thinking; factor-analytic studies have undoubtedly stimulated research in many ways. These studies are best summarized by Guilford (1959) and by French (1951).[1]

In another kind of study, investigators have used one or more psychological tests (including self-ratings) as criteria of creative performance. Such devices have included a battery of tests from the Guilford Creativity Battery; single tests of the same type, such as free responses to problem questions ("What would happen if?") and unusual uses of common objects; and special scorings of the TAT and Rorschach for creative responses. Barron, Getzels and Jackson, Torrance, and others have used this method to learn about

[1] J. W. French organized factor-analysis conferences at Educational Testing Service in 1951 and 1958, which yielded a standard kit of reference tests based upon factorial findings.

people who are high scorers (more creative) and low scorers (less creative) on such devices. The use of such scores as criteria has led to the development of some promising predictors. As a first step, then, this method of investigating creativity is a useful one: it usually provides a reliable and immediate criterion. The value of such a criterion lies in the degree to which it is equivalent to other more remote or more relevant criteria of creative performance. Questions of criterion bias and contamination are relevant here: unless these criteria (test scores) predict actual creative performance, they provide erroneous information about the nature of creative persons and creativity. On the positive side, test scores as criteria may be useful in isolating the nature of adult creative performance, if they are also checked in follow-up (longitudinal) studies in which they are employed as predictors.

### Concurrent validities based upon external criteria

The following subsections summarize our knowledge of the concurrent validities of several types of measuring device, based upon external criteria.

*1. High-level aptitude tests.* Special aptitude tests (such as the Guilford battery), devised to measure creative ability, have had only modest success. Evidence for the validity of such tests is still incomplete and unclear; in some instances, such tests suffer from restriction of range. Chorness and Nottelman (1957) found that an intelligence measure predicts employee "creativity" as successfully as do selected tests from the Guilford battery. However, it should be recognized that, because of the current emphasis on intelligence, people with high intelligence scores probably have an initial advantage when they take jobs or enter the academic field, which people with high scores only on more creative intellectual characteristics do not have.

Most studies suggest that the relation of intelligence tests to creative performance is generally low (.20 to .40) in unselected populations and is zero and even negative in homogeneous samples at high levels of intelligence (MacKinnon, 1959; Holland, 1961; Mullins, 1959; C. W. Taylor, Smith, Ghiselin, & Ellison, 1961; and Yamamoto, 1961).

The Remote Associates test, which calls for three-way associations, appears to be a device of special promise. Mednick has reported correlations as high as .70 between Remote Associates scores and ratings of creative writing ability for a *small* sample. At the 1955 conference, the Word Association test, scored for remote associations, appeared to be one of the most promising predictors. Since then, however, conflicting results have been obtained; in some instances, a common-associations score predicted better than did a remote-associations score. Two-way association tests have been included in factor studies and have usually been found to have a factor pattern similar to that of the Word Association test. How a three-way association test differs significantly in a psychological way from these one-way and two-way association tests remains to be determined.

*2. Motivation and interest inventories.* With a few exceptions, typical interest inventories have been poor predictors. In a battery of 69 predictors including aptitude, personality and originality scales, self and teacher ratings, etc., Holland found *simple* interest measures to be among the best predictors of creative performance. In a study of Air Force scientists, it was found that a complex motivational device had very few significant validities, whereas a brief and simple device measuring minimum aspirational level in several different aspects of scientific work had a considerably higher per cent of significant validities (C. W. Taylor, Smith, Ghiselin, & Ellison, 1961).

*3. Biographical information.* Simple check lists of background, preferred activities, expressed goals, and levels and kind of desired attainment have produced predictors of unusual validity even in cross validation (.30 to .55) (Taylor, Smith, Ghiselin, & Ellison, 1961; Holland, 1961b; Smith, Albright, Glennon, & Owens, 1961).

*4. Personality and originality scales.* The validity of personality inventories such as the CPI, 16 PF, and Saunders' experimental Personality Research Inventory is generally low, although there is considerable variation among studies by Gough,[2] Holland (1961b), and C. W. Taylor, Smith, Ghiselin, & Ellison (1961). The evidence for the validity of nonintellectual originality scales falls at about the same level, although there is again a wide range of correlations. Barron, for example, reported a correlation of .70 between his Independence of Judgment Scale and teacher ratings of creativity. More typical correlations for personality and originality scales range from .10 to .30.

*5. Self-ratings.* Simple self-ratings by adolescents and adults have moderate validity for a variety of creative performances. Terman's earlier work showed that high ratings of self-confidence, persistence, and integration toward goals were among his most efficient predictors of adult achievement. In a study of Air Force scientists, the best all-around predictor of all 17 criteria was a self-rating of creativity, which was also valid for all six creative criteria in this study. Self-ratings on several nonintellectual characteristics also had moderate validity for many of the creative criteria (C. W. Taylor, Smith, Ghiselin, & Ellison, 1961). In the 1955 Utah conference, Bloom pointed out that nonintellectual scores account for at least as much as intellectual scores in creative criteria. From the new Utah study of high school students in NSF Summer Science Institutes (C. W. Taylor, Cooley, & Nielsen, 1963), we have learned that students of this age who have had no job experience in science can make self-ratings that have some validity, though, as expected, they are not quite so reliable as those obtained from more mature and experienced scientists.

*6. Ratings by others.* Teacher ratings appear to be of little value for predicting creative performance, although they are useful for predicting other kinds of performance. Supervisory ratings, however, appear to be of some value (Buel, 1960). They have been

[2] Personal communications.

used with success as rating criteria, with psychological scores correlating significantly with such ratings in several studies, such as the study of Air Force scientists mentioned above and the current Utah biographical study of NASA scientists. Peer nominations and rankings also worked well in the study of Air Force scientists. Ratings and descriptions on well constructed forms by persons appropriately selected to give recommendations may be one of the more promising approaches to predicting creative performance.

7. *Special devices and tests.* Several investigators have begun work on unique devices and techniques. Currently, no evidence for the validity of these techniques is available. A new individual device called the "Problem Solving Apparatus," invented by John and Rimaldi (1957) and used by Stein, may have potential as a predictor. Some new tests developed by art educators may have merit. One such test consists of parallel rubber strands strung across a peg board in such a way that, by inserting pegs and interlacing strands, many new designs or a continually changing series of designs can be created. Another unusual performance test by Stipe with promising reliability is one in which examinees are given art materials and told to draw a "mess."

8. *Physical measures and effect of drugs.* Certain drugs that produce interesting reactions have been studied in connection with creativity. To what degree these drugs, or measures of physical and physiological characteristics, can contribute to identifying the creative person remains to be determined.

9. *Situational influences.* Attitudes reported by mothers [Parental Attitude Research Instrument (PARI, developed by Schaeffer and Bell, 1958)] were found to be related to the creative performance of adolescents at a very low but significant level of correlation (Holland, 1961a). Similarly, values and goals reported by fathers are related to the creative performance of their children—again at a very low level of correlation. The biographical inventory, which is usually completed by self-report but which could be partly com-

pleted by parents, also indicates that environmental factors have some validity.

The effects of institutional practices and atmospheres have been investigated by Knapp & Goodrich (1952), Holland (1957), and Thistlethwaite (1959a,b); these studies have examined the relative contribution of the student and of the college to student achievement (obtaining the Ph.D.). More recent studies (Astin, 1961; Astin & Holland, 1961) indicate that institutional influences on the number seeking a Ph.D. are negligible. The number of undergraduates seeking the Ph.D. has a multiple correlation of .92 with the percentage of students majoring in science and the average academic aptitude level of the entering class for a group of 36 colleges. The College Characteristics Index by Pace and Stern (1958) and the Environmental Assessment Technique by Astin and Holland (1961) provide devices for exploring some of the situational influences on creative persons.

## PREDICTIVE VALIDITIES OF VARIABLES RELATED TO CREATIVE PERFORMANCE

This section will be concerned only with those predictors which have been used in longitudinal studies (short-range or long-range follow-up) to predict socially relevant external criteria of creative performance. This kind of validation is valuable because it makes empirically clear whether or not a test or other psychological measure is useful as a predictor of future performance. Studies of this kind are so rare that predictors studied in this way have not been classified here in terms of the psychological attributes they represent. While validation and cross-validation studies of the concurrent-validity type are valuable, their results should be replicated in follow-up studies. Follow-up studies help to answer a number of crucial questions: Do the measuring instruments need to be revised if they are to be used at earlier ages or stages of experience? Do the tests arrange people in the same relative order at one age or stage of experience as at another? Are there significant shifts in the norms at different ages?

In a recent study, not yet published, Holland found that science achievements (winning contests, publishing papers) in high school were significantly correlated with similar achievements in college over one-, two-, three-, and four-year periods, although these correlations were of a low order (.20 to .38). This kind of predictor (past achievement) was generally superior to other kinds (aptitude, grades, originality measures). Similarly, artistic achievement in college was predicted best by a record (check list) of achievements in high school.

Other predictive investigations of creative performance are Harmon's studies of fellowship winners (one reported at the 1957 conference and a more recent unpublished one) and Bloom's brief exploratory study (reported at the 1955 conference) of the relation between the student's behavior during his graduate study and his subsequent productivity (not directly creativity). Flanagan's current talent project is a large-scale predictive study which will be used to predict later criteria of creativity.

In a recently published concurrent-validity study of biographical measures of creativity (W. J. Smith, Albright, Glennon, & Owens, 1961), there was brief mention of a predictive study. The current Utah biographical study of nearly 1,000 NASA scientists has yielded concurrent validities and cross validities—even in different laboratories in different parts of the country—with remarkably good results against on-the-job ratings of creativity. Follow-up studies on new NASA employees are planned in the near future as a more crucial check of these concurrent validities. The new Utah project on science students in NSF Summer Science Programs (C. W. Taylor, Cooley, & Nielsen, 1963), a short-range predictive study over two or three months, explores the question of the degree to which the characteristics of creative mature scientists are measurable in students and valid in predicting the students' performance in these summer programs, especially in the more creative full-time research participation programs (rather than the full-time classroom programs). In general, positive results have been obtained that are consistent with those found in the concurrent-validity studies of mature scientists. Longer-range longitudinal studies of the tested students may be possible, using the samples in the nine programs being studied.

## RESEARCH NEEDS

### *The choice of predictors*

A review of the current status of predictors of creative performance will help to make clear which predictors are the most efficient. If we look at predictors by class rather than by specific scales or inventories, we get a crude ordering. The biographical items and past achievements are our most efficient predictors. Self-ratings and direct expressions of goals and aspirations are next. Originality and personality inventories run a very poor third. Aptitude and intelligence measures rank fourth (except where restriction-of-range corrections are really applicable), followed finally by parental attitudes. Although any such ordering of promising predictors is subject to some unknown biases and errors, the consistency of these findings makes interpretation of them valuable for future research and practice. A striking exception to the above ordering occurs in MacKinnon's study of architects (1963) in which high validities were found for interest and personality inventories.

Harmon's NRC technical reports indicate that aptitude and achievement tests as well as college grades are useful predictors of scientific accomplishment. Harmon's more positive results for these kinds of predictors may be due to his use of different criteria; on the other hand, self-ratings, past achievements, and biographical scales may be even better predictors for his samples. Another puzzling question (which may be partly answerable in terms of restriction of range) is why high aptitudes have shown remarkably good results against situational test criteria (as in the Utah studies on communication abilities by C. W. Taylor, Ghiselin, Smith, Sheets, & Cochran, 1958) but have failed to show much promise against on-the-job criteria, such as ratings of scientists and of scientists' products. Such aptitude tests have recently shown promise, however, in correlating with performance in the two highly verbal fields of public relations and advertising (Elliot, 1963).

As another example, the usefulness of self-ratings suggests that greater effort might be devoted to obtaining more extensive and comprehensive self-ratings; perhaps measuring devices should cover all the characteristics ever suggested as relevant to creativity and more sophisticated scoring techniques should be developed. We do not yet know very much about how experience affects such self-ratings, nor are we yet sufficiently sure how well self-ratings will work at earlier ages. Some insights about these problems have already emerged from the above Utah study of high school students in NSF Summer Science Institutes, in which self-ratings were obtained at the beginning and at the end of these programs. However, the comparisons between the ratings before and after the program have not yet been completed or fully analyzed. Some attempt to conceptualize the development and meaning of self-conceptions might be helpful in integrating this information with the rest of our knowledge. A workable theory of self-conceptions would be a powerful tool for exploring the meaning of self-conceptions and, hopefully, for improving our predictions. As it is, the positive results for self-ratings and biographical self-reports are isolated bits of information in our psychological knowledge.

In a similar fashion, the success of biographical blanks, scales, and lists of activities suggests the need to *mine* this area and to spell out and conceptualize the meaning of this promising evidence. The designation "biographical blank" is ambiguous, since such blanks frequently contain a great variety of psychological information: self-ratings, goals and aspirations, attitudes about parents, vocations, hobbies and activities, past achievements, etc. Such information suggests hypotheses like the following: past achievement predicts future achievement; the time committed to job-related activities at home is related to work achievement; people who are original know it; activities and hobbies call for some of the same traits and personal dispositions that creative work requires. More comprehensive theoretical statements are needed to systematize this information. Presumably such statements would serve to organize this knowledge and would point to promising but neglected areas of concern.

Situational tests may prove to be very promising predictors. Such tests could be part of an educational program designed to elicit creative behavior. For instance, one might assign term papers which call not for the usual scholarly skills and treatment but for original ideas to be presented as the student wants to present them. Or students could be given credit for getting new ideas of their own while they were reading or listening during usual school activities.

Work needs to be done to determine the "best" combination of predictors of creativity. At present, there appears to be a long list of significantly valid predictors, including both intellectual and non-intellectual characteristics, but how they can be combined to supplement each other has not been studied, either theoretically or empirically. Whether a particular "best" combination of a long set of predictors would yield sizable cross-validation results or whether battery validity would shrink is still unknown, especially insofar as longitudinal studies are concerned. We now have enough available data on the concurrent validities of certain combinations to make such urgently needed studies possible.

The selection research of several national fellowship programs, including the NSF Predoctoral Program, has great promise, especially if such research includes studies of creative characteristics. The need for and value of sustained research effort by each of several organizations and universities have been clearly demonstrated. Yet single studies rather than sustained research have been the rule in the area of creativity.

Another problem of great national and scientific importance concerns the evaluation of research proposals and decisions within research laboratories and the determination of which persons and which problems will get the most budgetary support. It is quite possible that many creative proposals and individuals are turned down and that the more orthodox researchers engaged in currently acceptable, safe, and uninspired research receive financial support. (A somewhat parallel problem is the question of bias in the selection of articles for publication. It has been said that run-of-the-mill articles have a much better chance of being accepted than do really creative articles.) Moreover, research on creativity can contribute greatly to policies and practices in the areas of scholarship and fellowship administration, research support, and research publication programs.

We need to improve the devices currently used as predictors of creativity. Since many of the aptitude tests as well as the self-ratings have been relatively short in nature, they should be lengthened and expanded in whatever directions are possible and desirable. Biographical inventories have been expanded without too much difficulty; it is probable that self-reports, self-ratings, and ratings by others could be as easily lengthened. Correction scores to suppress exaggeration tendencies on biographical inventories have started to show real promise; similar correction scores might be attempted on other self-report devices. Pattern scores across sets of two or three items may add some valid measurement not yet covered. Certainly the entire area of the combination of creative scores has received only cursory attention, even though a large set of predictors that now appear to have some validity are available.

New measuring devices are also needed to test original suggestions, many of which have come from creative people outside of psychology; we need more help from persons from other fields. For example, Shockley, a Nobel prize winner for his work on transistors, has suggested that the creative person has more "idea manipulation power." Ghiselin, a poet and author of *The Creative Process,* has developed a creative process check list for which the most suitable administration and scoring systems have not yet been fully developed. Art educators have suggested several interesting new testing devices. Others have suggested the need for good tests of imagery, including auditory imagery in music.

New types of measures have been suggested by findings in other areas. For example, peer nominations have not been exploited as potential predictors of creativity, though they have often added valid variances in several areas of investigation. Tentative descriptions of creative people suggest that additional new measures are needed. For instance, creative people are often described as having a broader spread of intellectual interests; perhaps the amount and especially the spread of information that a person has gleaned can be used as a measure of his breadth of interest and of his mental set and attitude toward knowledge in a variety of fields.

## Theories of creative performance

Currently, theories of creative performance are limited to simple sets of hypotheses, which are often concerned with a few variables of a single kind: all aptitude or all personality variables. For example, Asher at San Jose State College in an unpublished paper proposes a stroboscopic model of the creative process based upon concept constancy (flexibility of closure or adaptive flexibility). More comprehensive heuristic theories may be of considerable use in organizing present knowledge and suggesting new research. Sprecher has recently written a preliminary heuristic theory of creativity, involving goals and learning activities.

Alexander, Barron, Freud, Jung, Maslow, May, Rogers, White, and others have suggested hypotheses and limited heuristic theories of creativity (see Stein & Heinze, 1960, pp. 193–261 for summaries of these theoretical contributions). The ideas contained in these writings are often provocative and serve as an important source of research ideas. At present, there is no single, comprehensive statement or report about the nature of creative behavior and related theory. The book by Stein and Heinze comes closer to this goal than any other document.

## Problems of method

It seems desirable to perform comprehensive assessments rather than to use limited sets of variables, for it is only in more complete assessments that we can learn the relative efficiency of various predictors. At this time it appears that a composite of measures is necessary to obtain efficient predictions. One of the more pressing needs is for several immediate studies of scientists on the job, using a large battery of the most promising predictors on large samples of scientists in different organizational settings; however, longer-range longitudinal studies must eventually be used to supplement and double-check such studies. As a first step we might determine the predictors that consistently identify the more creative scientists, regardless of the organizational setting. As a second step, we might determine how well the combined set of valid predictors correlates with the criteria of creativity, especially in cross-validation studies.

The Utah studies of Air Force scientists suggest that on the initial sample studied approximately half of the variance in any seventeen criteria of creative, productive, and other scientific contributions may be overlapped by a combination of 15 or more valid test predictors, although the shrinkage on cross validation is as yet unknown. Cross validation of such test batteries may yield results similar to those found for "a large battery of biographical items," in which the initial concurrent validities for empirically constructed keys were typically in the .70s and .80s and the cross validities held up in the .40s and .50s on different samples of NASA scientists at different geographical locations, even though a somewhat different criterion was used in the cross-validation study. Such approaches are similar to actuarial procedures in the insurance field and may lead to fairly efficient predictions. However, the final check of such concurrent-validity studies will be predictive-validity studies.

Studies paralleling the approaches reviewed here are also needed in other fields, such as the arts, social sciences, leadership, etc.

It is imperative that greater attention be given to separating personal attributes related to *creative* scientific performance from those related to vocational status. Many early studies of "creative" scientists were in fact merely studies of scientists.

Creativity or creative performance in different fields should be studied in order to help identify potentially creative individuals for each type of activity. Studies of the characteristics common to creative performance in all fields are urgently needed. It is likely that studies of creativity in the arts will provide invaluable leads for studies in the sciences. In addition, a knowledge of the characteristics peculiar to creative performance in a particular field would help creative people find the field or fields most compatible to them.

One of the greatest potential strengths of our nation lies in fostering creativity in *all areas* of our culture. Creative thinking is needed in many fields besides the arts and sciences: administration and leadership, political science and international diplomacy, accounting, health research and practices, old age problems, reduction of juvenile delinquency and crime, etc. In principle, creative performance can occur in any area of human endeavor.

We need to explore and develop multiple criteria of creative performance at all age levels. It is clear from the large criterion study of C. W. Taylor, Smith, & Ghiselin (1963), that no single criterion of performance is adequate or acceptable, since some criteria are relatively independent of one another.

Longitudinal studies are needed to investigate both change in predictor variables and those situations which are conducive to such change.

Finally, we need studies employing large samples, in order to secure stable results and to avoid some of the restriction in range of talent and other personal and background variables.

## The need for predictive studies

Even though research on creative processes and performance has burgeoned in recent years, there have been less than five predictive (longitudinal) studies that use relevant external criteria. But predictive studies are the only way we have to acquire valid information which will enable us to identify those adolescents who will become creative scientists. Concurrent-validity studies of tests and the use of test scores as criteria are useful intermediate steps; they help us to obtain a wide array of potential predictors. But from studies of various occupations, comparisons between concurrent and predictive validation of the same predictors suggest that a substantial number of predictors that look promising in concurrent-validity studies do not, in fact, hold up when their predictive validity is checked.

The use of scores on any particular test as a criterion of creativity is fraught with similar difficulties. Tests developed to measure creativity generally lack social relevance. Even if we can predict these test scores from other scores also designed to measure creativity, we are still faced with the problem of whether scores on these creativity tests have any real-life significance.

Consequently, we stress in our final recommendation that there is a great need in creativity research for predictive (longitudinal) studies which use a very wide variety of potential predictors, and then, after a suitable follow-up period, utilize good external criteria of creativity.

# chapter 3

# EDUCATION
# AND CREATIVITY

*E. Paul Torrance*

UNIVERSITY OF MINNESOTA

A VARIETY of forces are responsible for an unprecedented demand in education for information about creative talent. Since the 1890s there have been isolated and short-lived efforts to develop such information, many of which were promising; however, these early efforts attracted little support or attention. Recent breakthroughs in knowledge and the beginnings of sustained efforts by researchers have changed that situation. Now, because some knowledge has been accumulated and because society faces new needs, there are more demands than can be satisfied immediately.

Regardless of the forces behind these demands, education has sound, legitimate reasons for concern about all aspects of creative talent, its nature, assessment, development, nurture, and utilization. Since the development of information should be predicated upon the concerns of education, an attempt will be made to sketch some of the more important ones.

## LEGITIMATE CONCERNS OF EDUCATION ABOUT CREATIVITY

### Fully functioning persons

The development of fully functioning individuals has long been an avowed purpose of education. For many years professors of education have talked enthusiastically about the development of the unique capacities of the individual child, but most teachers have been primarily concerned with instruction in a particular subject. Furthermore, instruction often has meant teaching the child to answer specific questions in a given way, and disapproval has met those who wanted to answer the questions differently or to ask new questions.

It has been said that education in a democracy should help all individuals toward the full development of their talents. But what is meant by "talents" has never been clearly defined; consequently, there has been a tendency to develop certain "talents" such as memory, IQ, and athletic ability, and to reward these more handsomely than others less easy to identify. Currently there are pressures to limit the concern of education to the development of *intellectual* talents; those who would restrict the objectives of education in this way still urge that the schools be concerned with the *full development* of the intellect.

Despite this proposed limitation in the definition of educational goals, if the intellectual capacities of the individual are to be fully developed, the abilities involved in creative thinking cannot be ignored. Fortunately, educators have become increasingly aware that traditional measures of intelligence attempt to assess only a few of man's intellectual talents. Binet's early work (1909) showed his clear recognition of this deficiency, but it has taken the sustained work of Guilford (1959a,b) and his associates to describe how complex are man's mental operations. Certainly we cannot say that an individual is fully functioning intellectually if the abilities involved in creative thinking remain undeveloped, unused, or paralyzed.

### Mental health

Schools are legitimately concerned about the mental health of children, adolescents, and adults. Increasingly, schools have been asked to seek mental health goals. They have added social workers, psychologists, nurses, counselors, remedial teachers, and others whose concerns definitely include mental health objectives. The addition of these services reflects a growing recognition of the importance of education's role in preventing mental breakdown, delinquency, and severe maladjustment. Healthy personality growth is a positive goal.

Although we lack scientifically developed information concerning the relationships between creativity and mental health, scattered evidence from a variety of sources leaves little question but that the stifling of creative desires and abilities cuts at the very roots of satisfaction in living and ultimately creates overwhelming tension and breakdown. There is also little doubt that one's creativity is an invaluable resource in coping with life's daily stresses, thus making breakdown less likely.

In one study (Hebeisen, 1960), a battery of tests of creative thinking was administered to a number of schizophrenics who appeared to be on the road to recovery. Many of them were being considered for vocational rehabilitation by the State Department of Welfare. These individuals manifested astonishingly impoverished imagination, inflexibility, lack of originality, and inability to summon any kind of response to new problems. Their productions were the most obvious and banal of the many groups tested and gave no evidence of the rich fantasy and wild imagination popularly attributed to schizophrenics. There was only a stifled, frozen creativity.

Studies are needed to determine more definitively the intellectual characteristics of people diagnosed as having various mental illnesses, delinquents, and other types of "wasted talent." Scientifically developed information is also needed concerning the role of creative thinking or its deficiency in the genesis of various types of mental breakdown.

### Educational achievement

Almost no one disputes the legitimacy of the schools' concern with educational achievement, or learning. Their critics have constantly reminded educators that "schools are for learning." Pressures are exerted on the schools not only to help "overachievers" become "better rounded personalities," but also to influence "underachievers" to make better use of their intellectual resources: to "learn more." But, how does one tell who is an under- or overachiever? Traditionally, such judgments have been made on the basis of performance on intelligence (IQ) or scholastic aptitude tests. But recent findings concerning the role of creative thinking in educational achievement call for revision of these long-used testing procedures.

Researchers are now finding (Getzels & Jackson, 1962; Torrance, 1962a) that creative thinking can contribute importantly to the acquisition of information and educational skills. Of course, we have long known that it is natural for man to learn creatively, but in education we have generally held that it is economical to ignore this and to teach in an authoritarian manner. Recent experiments (Moore, 1961; Ornstein, 1961) have suggested that many things can be learned more economically in a creative situation than in an authoritarian one and that some people who learn little by authority can learn much creatively.

An urgent research need is to learn how to design school experiences that will foster creative acquisition of information. We need to determine which kinds of information can be learned more economically by authority and which by creative means.

Traditional tests of intelligence are heavily loaded with tasks requiring cognition, memory, and convergent thinking. Such tests have worked out quite well in predicting school achievement. When children are taught by authority, these are the abilities they require. Recent studies, however, suggest that even traditional subject matter and educational skills can be so taught that creative thinking is important in their acquisition.

Results from one of the elementary schools studied for two years in the Minnesota Studies of Creative Thinking illustrate most of these findings (Torrance, 1962a). Highly creative children (as identified by tests of creative thinking) were differentiated from the highly intelligent (as identified by an individually administered intelligence test). The highly creative group ranked in the upper 20 per cent on creative thinking but not on intelligence; the highly intelligent group ranked in the top 20 per cent on intelligence but not on creativity. Those in the upper 20 per cent on both measures were eliminated, but this overlap was small. In fact, if we were to identify children as gifted on the basis of intelligence tests, we would thereby eliminate approximately 70 per cent of the most creative. This percentage seems to hold fairly well, no matter what measure of intelligence we use and no matter what educational level we study, from kindergarten through graduate school. Although there was an average difference of over 25 IQ points between these two groups, there were no statistically significant differences in any of the achievement measures used either year (Gates Reading and Iowa Tests of Basic Skills).

These results have been duplicated in a Minneapolis public high school, in the University of Minnesota High School, and in two graduate school situations. Getzels and Jackson (1958) had earlier obtained substantially the same results in a private secondary school. They were not confirmed, however, in a parochial elementary school or in a small-town elementary school known for its emphasis on "traditional virtues in education." Even in these two schools, however, achievement was significantly related to measures of creative thinking, and the highly creative group was found "guilty" of some degree of overachievement, as assessed by usual standards.

It is of special interest that the children with high IQs were rated by their teachers as more desirable, better known or understood, more ambitious, and more hardworking or studious. In other words, the highly creative child appears to learn as much as the highly intelligent one, at least in some schools, without appearing to work as hard. The author's guess is that these highly creative children are learning and thinking when they appear to be "playing around." Their tendency is to learn more effectively by creative means than by authority. They may engage in manipulative or exploratory activities, many of which are discouraged or even forbidden. They enjoy learning and thinking, but their methods look like play rather than work.

*Vocational success*

Preparation for vocational success has always ranked high among the objectives of American education. Of course, it has long been recognized that creativity is a distinguishing characteristic of outstanding individuals in almost every field. It has been generally conceded that the possession of high intelligence, special talent, and technical skills is not enough for outstanding success. It has also been recognized that creativity is important in scientific discovery, invention, and the arts.

We are discovering now that creative thinking is important in success even in some of the most common occupations, such as selling in a department store (Wallace, 1961). In one study it was found that saleswomen ranking in the upper third in their departments in sales scored significantly higher on tests of creative thinking than those who rank in the lower third in sales. An interesting point in this study, however, is that the tests did a better job of discriminating the high- and low-selling groups in what the personnel managers considered routine sales jobs requiring no imagination than in the departments rated as requiring creative thinking. Thus, creative thinking appears to be important, even in jobs that appear to be quite routine.

## Social importance

Finally, schools are legitimately concerned that their students make useful contributions to our society and to our national goals. This recognition is quite clear in the recent statement of "Goals for Americans" by the President's Commission on National Goals (1960). Considerable importance is given to love of learning, curiosity, intellectual honesty and independence, and capacity to think clearly. It takes little imagination to recognize that the future of our civilization—our very survival—depends upon the quality of the creative imagination of our next generation.

Democracies collapse only when they fail to use intelligent, imaginative methods for solving problems. The kind of citizen here called for is a far cry from the model of the quiz-program champion of a few years ago, and he is also more than a "well-rounded individual." We ordinarily respect our well-rounded individuals, broad scholars, our men of many talents, but Dale Wolfle (1960) has made a strong case for those who develop some of their talents so highly that they cannot be well-rounded. He argues that it is advantageous to a society to seek the greatest achievable diversity of talent among all those who constitute the society, not diversity in every individual.

Henry Murray (1959) has warned that, as a nation, we have "an emotional deficiency disease, a paralysis of the imagination, an addiction to superficials." Toynbee (1962) has pointed out that, although the United States has been made a great country by a series of creative minorities, we now tend to neglect and suppress such minorities. He warns that the creative minorities and the majority must be sufficiently in tune to establish understanding, confidence, and cooperation between them. A new role for education might be the development of the skills and conditions needed for such rapport.

It should be obvious that talk about a more creative kind of education is advocacy not of "fancy frills," but of new ways of achieving education's most cherished goals.

## CURRENT EFFORTS TO DEVELOP AND COMMUNICATE NEEDED INFORMATION

Educational leaders are currently showing considerable interest in the communication of the scientifically developed information that exists. Financial support of the development of the needed information remains quite small, although the amount has increased during the past two or three years. Most of the serious retooling required to make possible the achievement of objectives involving creative growth continues to lag seriously. At the same time, there is great eagerness on the part of teachers, counselors, supervisors, and administrators for information, tests, curricular materials, manuals, and the like.

No adequate picture of the status of knowledge concerning creativity in education can be presented without at least a survey of some of these activities. Although it is not possible to take note of all of them, it should be useful at least to give examples of some of the actions taken by national educational conferences, the meetings of national associations, research activities, training programs, experimental programs, efforts to recognize creative achievement in education, publications, and development of instruments for identification.

## National and regional educational conferences

Among the national and regional conferences that have convened, perhaps the greatest impact is being felt from one held in September, 1959, at Woods Hole, to discuss how education in science might be improved. This ten-day meeting was called by the National Academy of Sciences, and brought together some 35 scientists, scholars, and educators. Considerable attention was given to the role of intuition in learning and thinking, the cognitive processes in learning, and motivation of learning.

Jerome Bruner, who summarized the conference in a significant little volume entitled *The Process of Education* (1960b), defined intuition as "the intellectual technique of arriving at plausible but tentative formulations without going through the analytic steps by which such formulations would be found valid or invalid conclusions" (p. 13). He refers to intuitive thinking as a "much-neglected and essential feature of productive thinking" and raises the question "Can school children be led to master this gift?" Many of the concepts developed in the Woods Hole conference are doubtless new to an overwhelming majority of educators. Bruner's book is being widely read by educators; evidence of its impact on educational thinking is already beginning to emerge. The thinking reflected in this book should be very useful in charting the course of educational developments that will encourage creative growth.

Another significant move in education is represented by the calling of a first conference on Productive Thinking in Education in April, 1961, by Charles E. Bish as part of the NEA Project on the Academically Talented Student. This conference brought together a group of leaders in the field of the education of the gifted. Conference participants included: Kenneth E. Anderson, Mary Jane Aschner, Guy T. Buswell, David L. Clark, Robert F. DeHaan,

Elizabeth M. Drews, Weldon T. Ellis, Susan M. Ervin, Louis Fleigler, James J. Gallagher, Miriam L. Goldberg, John C. Gowan, J. P. Guilford, Gertrude Hendrix, Esin Kaya, O. Hobart Mowrer, T. Ernest Newland, Harriet E. O'Shea, Maynard C. Reynolds, Paul C. Rosenbloom, Irving Sigel, Fred Strodtbeck, J. Richard Suchman, Abraham J. Tannenbaum, Calvin W. Taylor, E. Paul Torrance, and Virgil S. Ward. Although no document was published as a result of this conference, the assemblage of such a group as a part of an NEA Project is itself a significant step, and the resulting exchange in information has undoubtedly advanced the development and communication of knowledge in the field. A second conference on Productive Thinking in Education was sponsored by the same organization in May, 1963.

A number of regional conferences on the gifted sponsored by universities have given considerable attention to the identification and development of creative talent through education. The second Minnesota Conference on the Gifted brought together such workers as Calvin W. Taylor, Robert C. Wilson, J. W. Getzels, Viktor Lowenfeld, and several researchers from the University of Minnesota. The third conference brought together Esin Kaya, O. K. Moore, J. Richard Suchman, and Elizabeth Drews. The second Illinois Conference on Gifted Children in 1960 also gave attention to research on creative thinking.

Conferences in other special areas are also giving attention to creative thinking. For example, a conference was convened by Russell Stauffer at the University of Delaware in April, 1961, on Reading as Thinking. This conference brought together authorities in the field of reading and researchers in the area of thinking. Such conferences as this, in area after area, should be useful in developing new concepts, stimulating research, and guiding the development of curricular material of all kinds.

## Meetings and other activities of professional associations

Almost every national and regional educational conference in the past three years has included programs devoted to some aspect of creative talent or creative thinking. These include the following: the American Educational Research Association, the American Psychological Association, the National Association of Elementary School Principals, the Association for Supervision and Curriculum Development, the National Association for Educators of Gifted Children, the American Personnel and Guidance Association, the National Association for Gifted Children, the Association for Higher Education, the American Nursing Association, the National Art Education Association, the National Association of Colleges of Teacher Education, and others.

A number of the activities of the Association for Supervision and Curriculum Development manifest an enthusiastic interest in the information being developed concerning creativity in education. The October 1960 issue of its journal *Educational Leadership* was devoted to this theme and featured articles by Calvin W. Taylor (identification), E. Paul Torrance (language arts), G. G. Mallinson (science and mathematics), Margaret Woods (creative dramatics), and Manfred Keiler (art education). The Association's 1959–1960 research conference, reported in the monograph *Human Variability and Learning* (Waetjen, 1961), gave specific attention to this area, primarily through the contribution of a paper by Calvin W. Taylor. *Annotated Bibliography* no. 9 of the Cooperative Action Program for Curriculum Improvement is entitled "Creativity: A New Dimension of Intelligence" and was prepared by E. Paul Torrance and Victoria J. Punsalan (1961).

Some of the state chapters of this Association have also given specific attention to developments in creativity. For example, the Minnesota chapter in the fall of 1960 devoted about three days to the study and discussion of problems relevant to the evaluation of creative growth. In the spring of 1961, several of the school systems represented at this conference carried out experimental projects, and others have led the teachers in their systems in the study of such problems.

The National Council of Teachers of English has shown a continuing interest in creative growth and achievement. Its 1954 portfolio of materials for elementary teachers on creativity in the language arts continues to be a useful collection. Persistent and recurrent interest in creativity in education is also to be found in the National Art Education Association. Its 1959 yearbook (Hausman, 1959) reports a variety of studies of general interest on creativity in education. The American Institute of Biological Sciences has commissioned Anne Roe, with a committee of consultants (Frank Barron, Paul Brandwein, J. W. Getzels, and E. Paul Torrance), to prepare a paper on "The Creative Pupil in the Classroom."

## Research activities

As already indicated, none of the earlier contributors to research concerning creativity in education manifested sustained interest. Thus, there was little accumulation of knowledge. Since 1950, however, several research groups, primarily on university campuses, have shown signs of sustained interest. So far, fourteen or more such research groups have indicated an intent to develop programs. Occasional studies have come from a number of other sources, and work is getting under way in many other universities, school systems, and research organizations.

To date, the greatest number of relevant contributions and the most sustained enterprise have come from J. P. Guilford and his associates at the University of Southern California. Although this work has been done as part of a project on aptitudes of high-level talent and has seldom been related directly to school situations, it has had considerable impact on education. Recently, Guilford himself has given his attention to educational implications, as reflected both in his excellent theoretical article on the relationship of reading development to thinking abilities as described in his "Structure of Intellect" (1963) and also in his participation in the NEA Conference on Productive Thinking in Education and the reading conference at the University of Delaware. A number of his coworkers, such as J. R. Hills, Elnora Schmadel, and R. C. Wilson, have given their attention more directly to educational problems. Much of the work being done in other centers is based on Guilford's "Structure of Intellect," on the tests devised to measure the different thinking abilities represented in this structure of intellect, and on associated developments. Some of the work of this group is reported in the references listed under M. S. Allen, R. M. Berger, P. R. Christensen, J. P. Guilford, J. R. Hills, N. W. Kettner, P. R. Merrifield, C. E. Meyers, R. C. Wilson, and others.

Another highly productive group of workers in this field was fostered by the late Viktor Lowenfeld in the Department of Art Education at Pennsylvania State University. Long a leader in research on creativity in art education, Lowenfeld turned his attention during his last years to the interdisciplinary aspects of creativity in education (Lowenfeld, 1958; Lowenfeld & Beittel, 1959). Through factor-analytic procedures Lowenfeld and Beittel discovered in the visual arts essentially the same factors that Guilford and his team had found in the sciences. Since Lowenfeld's death, Beittel has continued to lead this group in the tradition established by Lowenfeld. Recent work by this group is reported in 1960 doctoral dissertations by P. B. Flick, V. D. Kendrick, C. E. Kincaid, A. P. Meinz, and R. C. Seelhorst. Beittel's editorial role on two of the art education journals is likely also to have considerable impact on the communication of information both within and outside the field of art education.

At Pennsylvania State, there is also interest in creativity research in the Department of Psychology. Among the contributors are Ellen V. Piers, Jacqueline M. Daniels, and J. F. Quackenbush (1960).

Although only a small proportion of the research on creativity at the University of Utah has been concerned directly with educational problems, this center is having considerable influence upon education. This influence has been felt through the five national invitational research conferences in 1955, 1957, 1959, 1961, and 1962 on the identification of creative scientific talent and the publication of the proceedings of these conferences,[1] the contributions of Calvin

[1] Since much of the basic research presented at these conferences has implications for education, a subcommittee emerged at the 1959 conference on the role of educational experience in the development of creative scientific talent, with Sidney J. Parnes as the subcommittee reporter. See also Chap. 31 in Taylor & Barron (1963).

W. Taylor to several important educational conferences, and the stimulation of research on creativity at the university and in school systems. Important contributions have come from Brewster Ghiselin, Marie Hughes, Frank Jex, William R. Smith, N. E. Wallen, G. M. Stevenson, and others in addition to Taylor.

In the field of higher education, considerable influence is being felt from the work of the Institute of Personality Assessment and Research under the leadership of Donald MacKinnon, Frank Barron, Harrison Gough, and others. This center has developed a variety of assessment devices and has made intensive personality studies of eminent creative individuals in a variety of fields, using traditional instruments such as the Strong Vocational Interest Blank, Allport-Vernon-Lindzey Study of Values, Minnesota Multiphasic Personality Interest Inventory, Rorschach, and Thematic Apperception Test. The influence of this center has been felt in education primarily through the writings of Frank Barron in such widely circulated media as the NEA Journal (1961) and Scientific American (1958) and through the contributions of Donald W. MacKinnon to the national meetings of such organizations as the Association for Educators of Gifted Children, the Association for Higher Education (1961), the College Entrance Examination Board (1960b), and the like.

Sustained research on creativity is being done at Ohio State University in a variety of fields. Among the more active contributors has been Ross Mooney; much of value has come from his theoretical work and from his stimulation and encouragement of others. For many years Laura Zirbes has made her influence felt on behalf of creativity in education, primarily through her stimulating teaching, speaking, and writing (1958, 1959). In terms of empirical research, the principal Ohio State University contributor has been Pauline N. Pepinsky (1959, 1960a,b) with her studies of productive nonconformity or independence. Manuel Barkan's book, Through Art to Creativity (1960), makes a useful contribution in the elementary education field.

A sixth center from which promising research is coming is the Creative Education Foundation at the University of Buffalo, established by Alex Osborn in 1957. Sidney J. Parnes is now providing the research leadership in this center. Much of its research has been concerned with the testing of the principles of "brainstorming" (Parnes & Meadow, 1959b, 1963; Meadow, Parnes, & Reese, 1959) and other hypotheses related to the work of Osborn (1957). Most of this work has been done with college students and adults. The influence of this center on education has been extended through the annual summer seminars and institutes of the Creative Education Foundation.

A seventh center of creativity research has been the University of Chicago, although signs of sustained effort are uncertain. In education, one of the real breakthroughs, of course, came from the work of Getzels and Jackson (1958, 1960b, 1962) with some discoveries concerning "creativity as a type of giftedness" that contributes to educational achievement. Morris I. Stein (1958, 1959, 1963) and his associates, through research with chemists (1956) and through a volume of annotated bibliographies by Stein and Heinze (1960), also developed information of interest to educators. Stein, however, has recently moved from the University of Chicago to New York University.

Sustained interest in the problems of creativity in education has been shown at Michigan State University, in the work of Harold Anderson (1959a,b, 1960, 1961) and Elizabeth M. Drews (1961). Thus far, the influence of the Michigan State group has come from the symposium organized and edited by Anderson and the effective speaking before professional groups by Drews. As yet, little reported research has come from the group, but a considerable amount may be expected in coming years.

The amount and variety of research concerning creativity now in progress at the University of Illinois give promise of a ninth center in which information may be accumulated. Under the rubric of "productive thinking," a number of projects are under way in the College of Education. James Gallagher and Mary Jane Aschner (now at Harvard) are studying the productive thinking of gifted children in the classroom, and J. Richard Suchman has been developing techniques for teaching children inquiry skills. Both of these projects involve the in-service training of teachers and make a direct attack on educational problems. Relevant contributions have been made by Raymond Cattell (1957), Fred E. Fiedler (1960), and Lawrence M. Stolurow.

The sustained, productive research of Irving Maltzman and his associates at the University of California at Los Angeles makes that university a tenth center in which there has been an accumulation of knowledge. This research, concerned with the training of originality, has involved laboratory-type experiments in which the subjects have been college students or adults. Many of the results of these studies would appear to have direct implications for all levels of education.

An eleventh center where there has been sustained interest is the University of Texas. Carson McGuire, E. Hindsman, F. J. King, and E. Jennings (1961) have reported factor-analytic studies involving various kinds of talented behavior among high school students. John Pierce-Jones and Ira Iscoe are also engaged in studies, apparently concerned with problems of the relationship between social class and creativity.

A twelfth center of research concerned with creativity in education is the National Merit Scholarship Corporation under the leadership of John L. Holland and Donald Thistlethwaite. Their concern has been largely with the selection of promising high school seniors for college scholarships and the prediction of creative achievement (Holland, 1959, 1961; Thistlethwaite, 1958, 1959, 1963).

For many years, there has been much interest in creativity in education at Teachers College, Columbia University. Some of the earlier contributions came from John Dewey (1933), Hughes Mearns (1941, 1958 reprint of 1931 work), and others. This interest is being kept alive through the teaching, writing, speaking, and research of Harry Passow, Miriam Goldberg, Alice Miel, Arthur W. Foshay, and others. A number of doctoral dissertations on various aspects of creativity in education have come from this center.

A relative newcomer among the centers, but one in which there is considerable research activity on creativity in education, is the University of Minnesota. Its work is focused directly on the problems of education, extending through all levels of education and all content areas and into specialties such as counseling and guidance, measurement, art education, home economics, industrial arts, business and distributive education, and the like. Much of this activity has been centered in the Bureau of Educational Research under the direction of Torrance. Among the contributions of this group are the following: development of instruments for assessing the creative thinking abilities at all levels of education from kindergarten through graduate school; plotting of the developmental nature of the creative thinking abilities, including cross-cultural studies; and study of conditions affecting creative growth, including both factors that can be manipulated in the classroom and laboratory and factors that originate in nature and society. Torrance's collaborators have included: Kevser Arsan, Frank B. Baker, John E. Bowers, Bert Cunnington, Kenneth DeYoung, Gordon Eastwood, Som Nath Ghei, Judson Harmon, Paul Henrickson, Richard T. Johnson, B. Luther, R. E. Myers, Necla Palamutlu, Victoria Punsalan, Herman J. Radig, Dietmar Schenetzki, and Kaoru Yamamoto. In mathematics, a number of useful contributions have come from Paul Rosenbloom and Donovan Johnson. Other contributors include: Ardyth Hebeisen, Harold R. Wallace, Gertrude Esteros, Harold Palm, and others with promising studies now under way.

A variety of long-range projects now in progress at the University of Delaware, under the direction of Wallace and Ethel Maw, Russell Stauffer, and Robert C. Ziller, should soon make this university a center of research on creativity in education. The work of the Maws deals with curiosity, Stauffer's with reading, and Ziller's with group creativity.

The stimulating work initiated by Esin Kaya at the Experimental Teaching Center of New York University and research being done by Hammer (1961), Stein, and others make New York University a potentially productive center.

Mention should also be made of work at Harvard in the Graduate School of Education, the Laboratory of Social Relations, and the recently organized Institute for Cognitive Studies. Bruner's experiments on thinking and his summary of the Woods Hole conference are especially important. The work of Anne Roe, much of which was completed before her move to Harvard, has already proved significant.

Financial support to research dealing with creativity in education continues to be at a marginal level, although there have been marked increases in the last three years. The Cooperative Research Branch of the U.S. Office of Education, the Office of Naval Research, and the United States Air Force have all provided support for this research. The Utah conferences and the work of the National Merit Scholarship Corporation have received some support from the National Science Foundation.

## Training programs

Accumulated information concerning creativity in education has begun to find its way into a variety of training programs, among them summer workshops. In the summer of 1961, Teachers College, Columbia University, held its second summer workshop on Creative Teaching under the leadership of Alice Miel and Carol Douglass. The University of Wisconsin at Milwaukee conducted a similar workshop under the direction of Louise Berman and James Mac-Donald, with E. Paul Torrance as visiting consultant. The Creative Education Foundation at the University of Buffalo conducted its eighth annual conference in the summer of 1962. Washington State University, Colorado State College, San Jose State College, and others conducted seminars in 1962, and the University of Utah initiated one in 1963.

Creativity in education is beginning to claim an important position in many conferences and courses on the education of the gifted. The theme of the second (1959) Minnesota Conference on Gifted Children was "Creativity," and all of the papers in this three-day conference pertained directly to the accumulating information on creativity in education. The theme of the third (1960) Conference was "New Ideas," and most of the papers there dealt directly with creativity. The second Illinois Institute on Gifted Children included addresses, exhibits, and discussions on creativity as related to giftedness. Many courses on the gifted are now including considerable material on creative talent. And many of the federally supported Counseling and Guidance Institutes are also including such material in their programs.

Many school systems during the 1960–1961 term used creativity in education as the theme of their in-service training programs, in some cases for the entire term. Some of these have used researchers in the field as consultants, studied research reports, tested manuals, and programmed experiences.

One of the more elaborate and carefully developed in-service programs was developed by the Milwaukee public schools and the University of Wisconsin at Milwaukee, under the leadership of Louise Berman. A feature of this program is a series of kinescopes, featuring such leaders in the field as: Harold H. Anderson, Frank Barron, Arthur W. Foshay, Marie Hughes, Alice Miel, and E. Paul Torrance. A manual of suggested projects and other supplementary materials has been developed for each of the kinescopes, and these can be rented from the sponsors of the series for use in other in-service programs.

## Experimental programs

A large number of school systems and individual teachers have instituted deliberate efforts to develop creative thinking of pupils, mostly in the elementary schools. Many of the experimental programs known to the author have been inspired by manuals, collections of suggestions, and experimental training materials prepared by the University of Minnesota Bureau of Educational Research. For example, 800 copies of a manual for elementary teachers (Torrance, 1959c) and 300 copies of *A Collection of Ideas for Developing Creative Thinking in the Language Arts* (Torrance, 1960a) have been distributed, and requests and orders continue to come in from teachers, administrators, and libraries, although both manuals have been out of print for two years. An experimental training program developed by R. E. Myers was tested in approximately 100 classrooms during 1960–1961. Experimental training material, developed for research purposes, is in demand immediately, even before its testing can be completed. Letters from individual teachers testify to the revolutionary impact and helpfulness of this material, but no formal evaluation can yet be made of its effectiveness, disseminated in this form.

## Recognition of creative achievement in education

The year 1961 saw a number of significant breakthroughs in identifying and rewarding creative talent and achievement. Such breakthroughs should reinforce and stimulate the accumulation of knowledge on creativity. One of the more significant of these was the announcement by the National Merit Scholarship Corporation that 25 of its four-year scholarships would go to students whose records suggested promise of exceptional creative performance. In addition, 20 such scholarships went to students who, though showing superior attainment and promise in one field, were not so distinguished in many fields as the typical National Merit scholar.

The students receiving these awards were not individually identified, either to the public or to themselves, as holders of the special scholarships in the experimental program. In making this announcement, John M. Stalnaker, President of the National Merit Scholarship Corporation, said, "We wished to apply the findings of research, to incorporate the lessons of experience, and to strengthen certain aspects of the Merit Program in ways not previously possible." He reported that the Corporation's research program has shown that the traditional measures of scholastic aptitude are of little or no value in predicting creativity within the very superior group.

The American Institute of Research also announced an interesting award program, an Annual Creative Talent Award for doctoral dissertations in psychology, sociology, anthropology, and education. One award of $1000 and two of $500 each will be made for the "most creative" doctoral dissertations in the fields of perception, learning, motivation, development, counseling, mental health, measurement and evaluation, and individual and group behavior.

There are also the beginnings of breakthroughs in the field of elementary education. Many have registered interest in using tests of creative thinking as one device in selecting children for special programs for gifted children. Dozens of beginnings in 1960–1961 were followed by hundreds in 1961–1962.

Measures to evaluate creative growth are now being applied in some experimental programs at various levels of education. No use of such measures has been reported for assessing creative growth in regular, nonexperimental programs. Even slower has been the development of instruments and procedures for assessing creative achievement in regard to the use of regular curricular content. This writer has been experimenting with a variety of such devices and procedures in the graduate courses he teaches. Outside the fields of art and creative writing, however, teachers have been slow to rise to the challenge of developing and using such procedures.

## Preparation of "A Literature"

The accumulation of information concerning creativity is only beginning to affect textbooks in education, children's books, professional development materials, and curricular materials.

In spite of the array of books now appearing on creativity in education, no book has yet appeared that makes effective use of the accumulation of knowledge. Even what has been known for the past 70 or 80 years has been largely ignored. Worthwhile contributions, however, have been made by Zirbes (1959), Wilt (1959), Barkan (1960), Peet (1960), and Miel (1961). Some attention to research on creativity in education is to be found in such texts as: *Education for Effective Thinking* by Burton, Kimball, and Wing (1960); *The Psychology of Thought and Judgment* by Johnson (1955); *Applied Imagination* by Osborn (1957); *Children's Thinking* by Russell (1956); *The Pupil's Thinking* by Peel (1960); and *The Psychology of Thinking* by Vinacke (1952).

In many areas, curriculum specialists, writers, and research personnel are beginning to produce special material designed to help individuals to learn creatively. Various professional groups in mathematics, physics, chemistry, and biology have included such material in experimental texts, teacher commentaries, and the like; these are producing interesting results. Popular books for children, adolescents, and adults are beginning to reflect the influence of the accumulating information and interest in creativity in education. Examples of this are Alastair Reid's *Ounce, Dice, Trice* (1958) and *Supposing* (1960); M. Munari's *The Elephant's Wish* (1959) and *Who's There? Open the Door!* (1957); and *The Poetry-Drawing Book* edited by William Cole and Julia Colmore (1960).

There have also been some beginnings toward the development of programmed experiences in creative thinking. Working with this writer, R. E. Myers (1961b,c) has been developing some workbook programs which incorporate various stages of the creative process and apply many research findings in their construction, and Bert Cunnington has been developing some audio-taped programs. O. K. Moore's (1961) work in teaching preschool children to type, read, write, and take dictation has attracted nation-wide attention. Moore is working with New Jersey's Thomas A. Edison Research Laboratory in designing automated equipment to simplify his technique, which he calls the "responsive environment." Out of this development eventually may come teaching machines with which children can learn creatively rather than just by rote.

Special professional helps are also beginning to show the influences of the accumulating information in the field. For example, the April 1961 *Professional Growth* materials published by Arthur C. Croft Publications featured three articles by this writer, one for superintendents, one for principals, and one for classroom teachers.

In conclusion, it seems obvious that education has some legitimate concerns about the guidance and development of creative talent and that there is widespread interest in the scientifically developed information that is accumulating. In the sections which follow, an effort will be made to summarize the accumulated information and to identify some of the most serious gaps in existing knowledge.

## CREATIVE THINKING IN THE EARLY CHILDHOOD YEARS

As scientifically developed information has begun to accumulate, the nature, meaning, and importance of creativity in the early childhood years are becoming clearer. Early conceptual errors concerning the nature of the mental activity of young children have been a serious block. Because many of these errors still persist, scientific information is needed to help clarify many puzzling problems. An attempt will be made to summarize the status of knowledge concerning creative thinking during the period from birth to age five by discussing the manifestations, methods of measuring, stages of development, methods of nurturing, and common inhibitors and facilitators of creative thinking.

### Early manifestations of creative thinking

Many scholars have denied the possibility that young children can think. In 1909, in *The Psychology of Thinking*, I. E. Miller discussed at length the problem of when thinking begins. He suggested that a tendency to use the terms *thinking* and *reasoning* synonymously had led to the error of underestimating the child's power to think and overestimating the importance of receptivity.

It seems clear that much of the confusion has stemmed from the ways in which each scholar has limited his observations of the manifestations of creativity. It has not been sufficiently recognized that no single test or area of observation can tap all of an individual's resources or that the same tests and types of observation are not valid or adequate at all age levels.

It is natural that many who have attempted to study creativity in early childhood have sought to do so through the medium of art. Conclusions from this research have varied, apparently according to the manifestations that have been admitted. Grippen (1933), for example, included paintings and the child's verbalizations while painting. Sources of the child's imaginative conceptions were found to be incidents in the local and immediate environment, physical aspects of the local environment, books, magazines, pictures, and travel. Since his observations were so limited, it is not surprising that Grippen concluded that "except in rare instances creative imagination does not function in children below the age of five years, but some children at the age of five exhibit a degree of it comparable to children seven years old." The total number of Grippen's subjects was only 48, another serious limitation for a conclusion of this kind.

If we observe how infants handle and shake things and twist and manipulate them in many ways, we find some of the earliest manifestations of creative thinking. We may see other beginnings of creative thinking in the infant's use of facial expression, his efforts to interpret the facial expressions of others, and the process of differentiating his own body from the environment. Since the infant does not have a vocabulary, he can learn little by authority. Thus, by necessity, much of his learning must be creative; that is, it must evolve from his own activity of sensing problems, making guesses, testing and modifying them, and communicating them in his limited way.

Excellent presentations of the literary productions of preschool children are to be found in Susan Nichols Pulsifer's *Minute Magic* (1960) and *Fun for Everybody: Songs for Children* (1949) by Bobby and Kathleen Wrenn. Both Mrs. Pulsifer and Mrs. Wrenn relate experiences that indicate a decline in creativity at about age five. Children who composed brilliant poems or songs at earlier ages were able to produce only obvious and commonplace poems or songs at ages five and six.

## Methods of measurement in early childhood

A variety of methods have been used in attempting to assess the creative products and processes of young children. McCarty (1924) used drawings. Abramson (1927) used responses to inkblots and concrete observations (enumerating objects after 20 minutes exposure).

Andrews (1930) used a variety of methods and observations, attempting to study several types of imaginative or creative activity. Three of Andrews' tests were presented tachistoscopically with the task of forming new products (transformations). The following kinds of observations were made of the imaginative play of children from two to six: imitation, experimentation, transformation of objects, transformation of animals, acts of sympathy, dramatizations, imaginary playmates, fanciful explanations, fantastic stories, new uses of stories, constructions, new games, extensions of language, appropriate quotations, leadership with plan, and esthetic appreciation.

Andrews (1930) also described some of the unpublished work of Martha Beckman Ransohoff. As stimuli, she used the Whipple standardized inkblots 1–20 and a picture test. The pictures used in the latter were taken from current magazines and were "typical of modern advertising art." Her methods of assessing responses reflect what this writer considers to be serious misunderstanding concerning the nature of creative imagination. Responses to the pictures were scored on a scale ranging from zero to two in terms of accuracy. In evaluating responses to the inkblots, she assigned the highest score to children who gave the same response to the same blot five times out of five. Since both of these measures appear to be indices of convergent thinking, it is not surprising that she concluded that the imagination of young children improves with increasing maturity. Furthermore, her conclusions are based on the study of a total of only 22 children.

Markey (1935) employed observational methods to evaluate performance in a variety of standardized situations and tasks, such as a housekeeping game, the fanciful naming of visual stimuli, leadership in imaginative games, block-building, and the like. The use of this wide range of stimuli led her to conclude that no single test taps all the imaginative resources of an individual and that the same test of imagination is not equally valid at all age levels. She points out, for example, that the decreased interest of the older children in the housekeeping game influenced the trend of the age scores, in that younger children made better scores. She contends that the housekeeping materials were better suited to the younger children because of their greater interest in games involving personification and simple make-believe uses of materials. She also maintains that the level of the child's understanding and comprehension influences the type of creative response. Thus, younger children give more fanciful names to objects, animals, constructions, and the like, whereas older children are likely to identify the stimuli in realistic terms.

From the foregoing attempts to assess the creative thinking of young children, it can be seen that there is in general a tendency for a low correlation between such measures and traditional measures of intelligence. Markey (1935) reported that the correlations between mental age and scores were slightly higher than correlations between chronological age and scores. It is interesting, however, that Markey sought in various ways to explain away the relatively low correlation between mental age and imaginative behavior (diversity of groups studied, etc.). Andrews (1930) recognized more clearly the difference between the two types of measure and concluded that the correlations between IQ and imagination and between mental age and imagination are so low as to indicate that "very little relationship exists between intelligence and the fantastic imagination of the young child." In interpreting her use of "fantastic imagination" it is important to note that her measure included transformations, analogies, and other kinds of performance now considered a part of creative thinking. Among children of two to four years of age, McDowell and Howe (1941) found that the IQ of the children was correlated positively with the degree of creative use of all the play materials (blocks, plastic clay, and paints.)

### Stages of development in early childhood

The development stages of creativity recognized in early childhood vary from investigator to investigator, seemingly according to the kinds of performance admitted as evidence.

Ribot (1906), one of the early investigators using the rubric "imagination," attempted to plot the growth and rivalry of Imagination and Reason. Reason was pictured as beginning later than Imagination and growing more slowly. Finally, they reach the same level, with Imagination giving way to Reason by the time the period of youth is over.

McMillan (1924) identified three stages in the development of the imagination. During the first stage, the young child has a sense of beauty which serves as a kind of short cut to knowledge. As she says, "the city of gold with pearly gates, with crystal fountains and unblackened skies" is real to the child at this stage. In the second stage, he comes to grips with the realities. He begins to inquire into cause and effect and to ask "why there are so many streets that are not golden, so many fountains that are turbid with filth, and so many skies that are blackened all the time." During the third stage, he begins by small degrees to harmonize the ideal of his first vision with the world of things as they are.

Andrews (1930) was considerably more systematic and thoroughgoing than other investigators in tracing the development of the imagination during the preschool years. She discovered that total imaginative scores are highest between four and four-and-a-half, with a sudden drop at about age five when the child enters kindergarten. The factor *transformation* reached a peak between three and four years of age and from then on decreased; *analogy* reached its height during the fourth year and declined during the fifth; "don't know" responses decreased steadily with chronological age up to five years and then increased somewhat. The more creative types of imagination reached a high point between ages three-and-a-half and four-and-a-half and reached their lowest ebb during the fifth year.

Markey (1935) found that the total amount of imaginative behavior increased with age throughout the preschool period. She reports, however, that performance on the housekeeping game and the fanciful naming of visual stimuli decreased among the older children, a finding which she discounts on the basis of interest and lack of information.

Ruth Griffiths (1945) identified eleven stages in the creative drawings of children and relates these to the study of imagination in early childhood. These stages are as follows:

1. A stage of undifferentiated scribble
2. Rough geometrical shapes, usually circles and squares, with names such as doors, windows, apples, and the like applied
3. Making of further objects by the combinations of lines and squares and separately of circles
4. Combination of circles and lines to make many other objects, of which one of outstanding interest is the human figure
5. Juxtaposition of many objects rapidly drawn and named
6. Concentration on one object at a time, bolder work, care taken, degree of detail present
7. Further juxtaposition, but clear subjective association, work recognizable
8. Partial synthesis, some items being shown in definite relationship to each other
9. Pure picture, one picture only
10. Multiplication of pictures, joy of representation
11. Development of a theme by means of a series of pictures

## Nurturing creativity in the early years

All the early investigators cited above recognized both the need and the difficulty of nurturing creativity during the early childhood years. McMillan (1924) commented that the hardest task of all in education is to keep alive the vision of the ideal amid the actual. Russell (1956) describes the problem of the early childhood years as one of keeping fantasy alive until the child has the intellectual development necessary in a sound type of creative thinking.

At least since the early 1900s, the recommendations of investigators for nurturing creativity during early childhood have not varied greatly. Always we seem only to be beginning, still falling far short of the goal of designing effective educational programs for nurturing creative talent. For example, in 1909 Miller wrote, "We

are already moving in the right direction in the gradual recon-
struction of the curriculum along lines which furnish concrete
material for the purpose of appealing to the child's natural impulses
of curiosity, imitation, construction, etc. Motivation is thus secured
from the start" (p. 106). Miller goes ahead to point out in some
detail the kind of opportunities that can be created in the kindergarten for this kind of development.

Andrews (1930) took the position that it is a legitimate function
of education to discover means of fostering these special abilities
(creative thinking) and to provide opportunities for their fullest
development. She suggests that vocational guidance should be begun
in the nursery, not by forcing on the child a vocation selected by
teacher or parent, but by allowing him to develop along the lines
of his prevailing interests, with encouragement for his creative acts,
whether or not they conform to adult standards.

Ruth Griffiths (1945) took a very positive attitude concerning
the functions of fantasy in solving problems of development in early
childhood. Through fantasy, the child attacks his problem indirectly,
often disguised by symbolism; he is only vaguely aware of the ends
toward which he is striving. According to Griffiths, a gradual resolution of the problem emerges from a series of imagined solutions.
She sees the result of this process as the child's acquisition of information and a change in his mental attitude. The change of attitude
is usually from a personal and subjective to a more socialized and
objective point of view.

In spite of the "very modern insights" enunciated by investigators
for many years, this writer concludes, from many strands of evidence
that have come his way, that application of these insights has lagged
seriously. Letters from parents, interviews with parents, and observations of preschool programs all suggest that Miller's optimism in
1909 has not been fulfilled—except perhaps in a very small percentage of schools. There is still a wide gap between "insight" and
application.

This lag in bringing about a more creative kind of education for
young children is characteristic also of other cultures, such as Western Samoa. Following her studies in Samoa in the 1920s, Margaret

Mead described how almost all creativity was suppressed from birth. Younger children were disciplined by the older ones, who were punished if they permitted the infants to cry, make noises, or explore their environment. According to data collected in one of Torrance's recent cross-cultural studies, this practice remains relatively unmodified. Thus, it is little wonder that the originality of the Western Samoan child is lower at the time he enters the first grade than in any of the six cultures studied (Metropolitan, USA; Negro, USA; Australia; India; Germany; and Western Samoa).

## Inhibitors and facilitators in early childhood

From reported investigations, the two most powerful inhibitors to creativity during early childhood seem to be premature attempts to eliminate fantasy and "holding-back operations" that prevent children from learning more than they are "ready" to learn. Emphasis on sex roles, which appears as a powerful inhibitor after age five, seems to have little measurable influence before five. McCarty (1924), for example, found no statistically significant differences in creative drawings between boys and girls before the fifth year. McDowell and Howe (1941) found no differences in creativeness displayed with blocks and plastic clay, but found girls superior to boys in the creative use of paint.

All the investigators cited recognized that children must learn to distinguish between fact and fancy, but maintained that it is possible for education to devise methods by which this learning may proceed without sacrificing creative growth. Andrews (1930) points out that such methods would require the "finding of legitimate channels in which imagination might move forward unfettered, such perhaps as art, music, literature, and even the sciences." She insists that hypotheses are nothing more than an active imagination resting on a foundation of knowledge and experience. She suggests that the teacher or parent who can "become as a little child" and with him enter into the world of his imagination may, by doing so, nurture a creative genius, or at least make possible a kind of development that will later become an endless source of enjoyment. This kind of empathy may become at the same time a means whereby the child learns how to differentiate the "world of fact" from the "world of make believe."

Especially among educators of the gifted, signs of willingness to revise some of our concepts regarding readiness are emerging. From Mayer's book, *The Schools* (1961), one would conclude that such progress has been most slight. Mayer quotes an assistant superintendent in charge of elementary education in New York City as saying, "Research shows that children's eye muscles are not capable of the fine adjustments necessary for reading until they are six and a half years old" (p. 66). Mayer points out that, at the same time that this was being said, Omar Moore at Yale was teaching three-year-olds to read by the ingenious use of an electric typewriter and that, nearly sixty years earlier, Maria Montessori had written that "almost all of the normal children treated with our method begin to write at four years, and at five know how to read and write, at least as well as children who have finished the first elementary."

The concepts presented in Bruner's *The Process of Education* (1960) may have a great influence in helping educators successfully work through conflicts concerning the readiness issue. Bruner develops the concept of *structure of knowledge* and some interesting ideas about intuition and motivation which support his revised concept of readiness. About readiness, Bruner says, "Experience over the past decade points to the fact that our schools may be wasting precious years by postponing the teaching of many subjects on the grounds that they are too difficult. The essential point often overlooked in the planning of curricula . . . [is that] the basic ideas that lie at the heart of all science and mathematics and the basic schemes that give form to life and literature are powerful." For this purpose, Bruner suggests "the spiral curriculum," one that turns back on itself at higher and higher levels of complexity.

Research concerning facilitators of creativity among young children is rather sparse. The Union College Studies in Character Education (1954) found a significant relationship between increase in the number of the possessions of two- and three-year-olds and increase in dramatic and pretend play (with props). Markey (1935), on the basis of her observation of children in nursery school, concluded that more adult-directed imaginative activities and more closely supervised creative activities at earlier levels might better foster the development of creativity than undirected freedom of expression. These are areas badly in need of further investigation.

## Suggested research priorities

In terms of both urgency and promise of potential "pay off," a problem of high priority is to determine the factors responsible for the drop in creativity that occurs at about age five. Such information could provide guidance toward making learning and thinking in school more exciting to children and also toward prevention of mental illness, delinquency, and many kinds of learning and personality problems. An important but perhaps more difficult area to investigate, in which "pay off" might be slower, is the study of preverbal and nonverbal manifestations of creative thinking, especially in the first three years of life. This area is recommended as important, not only for its potential to yield means of identifying creative talent, but also for possible contributions to our basic understanding of creative thinking and the influences in infancy that might affect it.

## CREATIVITY IN THE ELEMENTARY SCHOOL YEARS

There is rather general consensus that the elementary school years are critical in the development of creative talent. Sensitive observers have long noted and deplored the rise and decline of the child's creative powers during this period. Most of them have done so in a spirit of helpless resignation or have made arbitrary pronouncements concerning the solution to the problem. Sustained, imaginative research concerning these problems is lacking. Many important *beginnings* have been made, however, and an attempt will be made to summarize the status of the knowledge that has accumulated as a result.

## Manifestations of creativity in the elementary school years

Of the many manifestations of creativity among children during the elementary school period, greatest attention has been given to creative writing and art. More and more, adults are finding delight in the writing and art of children. More and more, teachers are coming to value the creative writings and art of children over the reproductions of adult models. Aside from the walls of school rooms, however, there are few places where such manifestations of children's creativity can be enjoyed. A bibliography of children as authors by Kupferberg and Topp (1959) lists 450 titles. Most of these, however, are poorly presented, difficult to obtain, and published in few copies. Here and there exhibitions of children's art have achieved unexpected success, and exchange exhibits with other countries have attracted considerable attention.

Throughout history, in spite of the "holding-back operations" which seem always to be with us, there have been some dramatic examples of outstanding creative achievement at a tender age (Cole, 1956, p. 27). Newton spent his childhood making water clocks and windmill models. James Hillier constructed his first microscope as a boy. Louis Braille at approximately age ten became obsessed with the idea of developing a better system of writing for the blind to replace the enormous and heavy embossed books then in use. By age 15, young Braille had almost perfected the system that now bears his name.

Nearly all of the studies of creativity during the elementary years, like those studies of preschool years, have limited the scope of their observations of the manifestations of creativity, and so seriously curtailed the accumulation of knowledge.

*Methods of measurement during the elementary school period*

As might be expected, more varied materials and tasks have been used in assessing the creative capacities of children during the elementary period than during the preschool years. With the child's increased ability to communicate ideas through speech and writing this becomes possible.

Typical of many of the early efforts was Kirkpatrick's (1900) work with four inkblots. Colvin (1902) used compositions, giving attention to such factors as invention, sense of humor, imaginative power, and perceptive power. Simpson (1922) used 50 sets of four small round dots, representing the four corners of squares, as stimuli for constructions; fluency, originality, and flexibility were assessed. The methods of McCarty, Abramson, and Grippen have already been mentioned. Harms (1939) employed a test requiring the representation of words (mostly names of various actions) by single lines in grades one to twelve. Stephenson (1949) reports the use of a poetry-writing test and an Art Form Test.

During the past three years, Torrance (1962a) and his associates at the University of Minnesota have been engaged in a continuing program of development and research related to the identification, development, and utilization of creative talent. Concentration has been on the elementary school period. A variety of tasks have been devised, and though the work is far from complete, an attempt is being made to develop a comprehensive approach to the measurement and development of these abilities.

At first, Torrance and his associates sought to adapt for use with children some of the tasks developed by Guilford and his associates (Guilford, Wilson, Christensen, & Lewis, 1951). Their first work was with forms consisting of the following six Guilford-type tasks: Unusual Uses, Impossibilities, Consequences, Problem Situations, Improvements, and Common Problems. Adaptation was accomplished by substituting objects or situations more familiar to children. Thus, subjects were instructed to think of unusual uses of "tin cans" or "cardboard boxes" instead of "bricks" and to imagine all the things that might happen "if animals and birds could speak the language of men" instead of "what would happen, if all national and local laws were suddenly abolished?"

Almost simultaneously, experimentation was begun with several other kinds of task. These tasks were constructed on the basis of analysis of the experiences reported by eminent scientific discoverers, inventors, creative writers, and the like. An attempt was made to construct tasks that would be models of the creative process, each requiring several types of thinking. This approach differs in two major ways from Guilford's, yet makes direct use of Guilford's work. First, instead of seeking measures to represent single factors, the strategy in the Minnesota studies has been to develop complex tasks presumed to involve the whole creative process and then to evaluate the products in terms of the kind of thinking or factors manifested. Second, the Minnesota group has tried to build into the tasks and instructions certain features that make use of what we know about the nature of creative thinking. A calculated attempt has been made to develop tasks which will grip the interest of subjects and which permit "regression in the service of the ego."

The Minnesota researchers have become increasingly aware of the need for enlarging the scope of test tasks by including a greater variety of stimuli, by involving a larger number of the senses, and by expanding the limits of the kinds of observations made of behavior. From the very outset, they used materials that could be examined and manipulated—as in the Product Improvement Test, in which the subject is handed a toy, and in the Ask-and-Guess Test, in which the subject is given a picture about which he is to ask questions that cannot be answered by examination of the picture and to formulate hypotheses about possible causes and consequences of the pictured behavior. They have now adapted the concept of Guilford's Consequences Test (originally verbal) by presenting its improbable situations both in words and with drawings, and have called it the "Just Suppose Test." The new Sound Effects Test makes use of tape-recorded sound effects, a progressive series of warm-ups, and other features.

The nature of a test task can be changed by modifying the instructions, the timing, or some other feature. In a three-task, nonverbal battery, the first task, Picture Construction, is calculated to stimulate originality and elaboration. The ten-minute time limit is more than most children will use. Children outstanding as elaborators, however, do not have enough time, and some of the highly fluent and highly original individuals keep thinking of new ideas, either adding to or completely changing their first ideas. The two succeeding tasks bring out increasing variation in fluency, flexibility, originality, and elaboration. There is not enough time to complete all the possible units and make all of them elaborate. The Sound Effects Test has been presented with and without cues or examples as a part of the warm-up and with and without invitations to regress. Versions have also been produced to appeal to imagination as related to all of the senses.

The performance of many children will vary greatly depending upon whether the administration of the test is individual and oral or group and written, especially with tasks requiring multiple verbal responses. At the fourth-grade level, scores on group-administered tests of creative thinking correlate more highly with scores on tests of intelligence and achievement than do scores on individually administered tests. It is doubtful, however, that the group test in this case is really a test of creative thinking. The thinking processes of some children are seriously hampered by difficulties in committing their ideas to writing.

Even at the ninth-grade level, there is little or no relationship between scores on tests of intelligence and group measures of creative thinking within the range of the upper 25 per cent in intelligence, but there is a relatively high relationship between these two variables within the lower 25 per cent in intelligence. Such results probably occur because the group test of creative thinking does not give a valid measure of the creative thinking abilities of ninth graders falling in the lower ranges of intelligence. On the Ask-and-Guess Test, test-retest reliabilities range from .46 to .61 in grades four to six when one test is written and the other oral, whereas the reliabilities range from .75 to .85 when both are written, with different stimulus pictures.

Whether one gives clues or examples also appears to make a difference. Present indications are that the giving of examples reduces originality and increases fluency. A similar issue pertains to emphasis in the instructions upon quantity without attention to quality, as opposed to stress on some quality, such as "unusual, original, or exciting." Children in the primary grades actually give more responses when instructed to think of "unusual, original, exciting" responses than when instructed to think of as many ideas as possible without regard for quality. This tendency is reversed in the intermediate grades, in some cases, but emphasis on originality usually increases originality of response without significantly influencing fluency.

Much experimentation is needed with different time limits. It is important that we determine the effects of different time limits on scores for such qualities as fluency, flexibility, originality, and elaboration; we also need to know how the varying of time limits can affect the task's validity. Determining the most desirable length of a battery of tasks to be administered at one sitting poses a similar problem. On productive and creative thinking batteries of about 60 or 70 minutes' duration, many individuals reduce both the quantity and quality of their production near the end, while others maintain about the same pace throughout. We do not now know whether performance on the first tasks yields a better index of potentiality than performance on the last tasks, nor whether performance on a lengthy battery administered at one sitting yields a better index of potentiality than the same battery administered at two or three different sittings. Perhaps a better question would be: What *kinds* of potentiality does each condition enable us to identify?

Experimentation with different scoring schemes must be continued. At first, there was an inclination in the Minnesota studies to score responses to a single task in as many ways as possible. Such elaborate scoring would be prohibitive in a practical situation, but it was felt that this elaborate scoring was necessary in order to develop an effective and efficient procedure. More recent efforts have been in the direction of simplification and systematization.

There are dangers in oversimplification, but there are also reasons for pessimism about constructing tests of creative thinking that can be used with IBM answer sheets.

Test-retest reliabilities and inter-scorer reliabilities have in general been quite satisfactory. With the use of scoring guides, scorers quite readily reach a point at which inter-scorer reliabilities exceed .90. On test-retest reliability, battery totals range around .85 in the intermediate grades, with alternative forms of the stimulus materials. In the primary grades, reliability coefficients generally range from around .45 to .70. Test-retest reliabilities for single tasks or scores drop somewhat over a period of one year. Perhaps we should be more concerned about conditions that cause low reliability than about the reliability of the tests themselves.

In designing test tasks and in developing instructions and scoring systems, an effort has been made to incorporate characteristics that make use of what is known about creativity. This knowledge has been gleaned from the history of invention, discovery, and other creative achievements, as well as the results of experiments. Most attempts to establish the validity for measures used have involved one or the other of the following two approaches (Torrance, 1962a):

1. Identifying high and low groups on some test measure and then determining whether or not they can be differentiated in terms of behavior that can be regarded as creative

2. Identifying criterion groups on some behavior regarded as creative and then determining whether or not they can be differentiated by appropriate test scores

Researchers using the Minnesota measures found that elementary school children who achieved high scores on the tests of creative thinking also initiated a larger number of ideas in small-group situations that involved creative problem solving than did their less creative peers. When matched for intelligence, sex, race, and teacher, the most creative children (one boy and one girl in each of 23 classrooms), far more frequently than their controls, were found to have reputations for having wild or fantastic ideas, produced drawings and other products judged to be unusual or original, and did work characterized by humor, playfulness, and lack of rigidity. Through psychiatric interviews, Weisberg and Springer (1961) found that highly creative fourth-grade children (identified by the same tests) were rated significantly higher than their less creative peers on: strength of self-image, ease of early recall, humor, availability of Oedipal anxiety, and uneven ego development. On the Rorschach Ink Blot Test, they showed a tendency toward unconventional responses, unreal percepts, and fanciful and imaginative treatment of the blots. Their Rorschach responses characterized them as being both more sensitive and more independent than their less creative peers.

Through numerous partial replications of the Getzels and Jackson (1962) studies at the elementary school level, it has become clear that the Minnesota Tests of Creative Thinking (Torrance, 1962a) identify a type of individual different from those identified by traditional intelligence tests. These individuals differ from "intelligent" individuals in ways which may indeed be regarded as "creative." In most schools (five out of seven), the achievement of the "creative" individuals equals that of their more intelligent peers. In addition, in a large number of teacher and peer nominations, the "creative" persons are characterized as having many original or unusual ideas, including many ideas for being naughty, and as showing playfulness and a sense of humor.

Children nominated by their teachers on various criteria of creative thinking, curiosity, and the like, achieve higher scores on the appropriate measures of creative thinking than do their peers not so nominated. In one pilot study, high and low groups of children were differentiated on a nonverbal task (Circles), and their language behavior was studied as manifested in their imaginative stories. The more creative children wrote longer stories, used a greater variety of words, and more frequently used first-person pronouns, verbs like "said" and "was," and conjunctions indicating cause or consequence.

The Minnesota researchers have increasingly recognized the need for exploring "nonpsychometric" methods of identifying creative individuals. Some highly creative children have difficulty in writing down their ideas. Factors such as the immediate testing conditions, motivating circumstances, personality disturbances, and unfavorable reactions to time pressures prevent some highly creative individuals from revealing their creative potential. Holland (1961) has reported the use of indicators of creative achievement at the high school level, and some exploratory work has been done with various kinds of check lists of creative activities, life-experience inventories, reading questionnaires, etc. With the help of about 90 experienced teachers, this writer has recently compiled a list of observable kinds of behavior that appear to aid in identifying creative children.

Developers and users of tests of imagination and creative thinking with elementary school children have consistently found little or no relationship between such measures and tests of intelligence. Simpson, in 1922, declared, "By joining a creative test, such as we have outlined, with a 'reproductive' test such as any general intelligence test, we shall get a more accurate statement of the worth of an individual." In studies using the Minnesota Tests of Creative Thinking, coefficients of correlation between creative thinking scores and scores on intelligence tests tend to be higher for boys than for girls, higher for unselected groups than for highly talented groups, higher for group-administered tests than for individual, orally administered tests, and higher within the lower ranges of intelligence than for the higher ranges. In unselected groups of elementary school children, coefficients of correlation are about .16 with performance on the Stanford-Binet, about .25 with scores on the California Mental Maturity Test and the Kuhlmann-Anderson, and about .32 with the Otis Quick-Scoring.

There seems to be little doubt that the abilities measured by both traditional tests of intelligence and scholastic aptitude are important. Here John Anderson's (1960) concept of "ability gradient" seems to be useful. According to this concept, ability level can be thought of in terms of thresholds. Once we learn what amount or degree of an ability is needed to carry out a task, we can then consider the factors that determine function beyond this threshold. There are cut-off points, that is, levels above which the demonstration of ability is determined by the presence of other factors. For example, we might determine where the cut-off point is in terms of Intelligence Quotients by discovering how high the IQ must be before a point is reached when a higher IQ makes little difference and the creative thinking abilities become determiners of success. From his own work and that of others, this writer's guess is that the critical point as far as academic success is concerned is at an IQ of approximately 120 or perhaps 115. Anne Roe and Donald W. MacKinnon, in their studies of eminent individuals, have also suggested 120. Very early in the Minnesota research, it was noted that many of the most creative children had IQs about 120 and that their measured achievement was generally quite high. In most schools studied the Getzels-Jackson phenomena were found: children scoring high on creative thinking tests but below the high IQ cut-off score achieved as much academically as the high IQ group. But even in schools where these phenomena were not present, highly creative pupils with IQs between 120 and 130 performed as well on achievement tests as those with IQs in excess of 130.

Much careful work needs to be done in determining the kinds of stimuli and tasks necessary to yield an adequate inventory of a child's creative thinking capacities. Caution needs to be exercised in trying to lump into one score an assessment of the productions resulting from the varied tasks used. Although there are some apparently all-round creative children, a few appear to be primarily fluent; a few others, especially good elaborators; others, original. Some apparently respond better to word pictures; some, to visual stimuli; others, to nonverbal auditory stimuli. Almost untouched is the area of achievement tests that involve creative thinking definitely and directly. It is this writer's contention that measures of creative achievement in almost all content areas can be constructed along much the same lines as those along which tests of creative ability are being developed.

### Stages of development during the elementary years

Research concerning the stages of creative development during the elementary years has been remarkably consistent, considering the variety of measures, samples, and periods in history involved. In the culture of the United States, one peak in development seems to be reached approximately at age four-and-a-half. A drop, at age five when the child enters kindergarten, is followed by increases in the first, second, and third grades. At age nine, near the end of the third grade or at the beginning of the fourth, there is a rather severe decrement in almost all of the creative thinking abilities. Then comes a period of recovery, especially for girls in the fifth grade. This recovery, however, is primarily in fluency and not in originality. The recovery in originality comes largely in the sixth grade. After this, there is another decrease between the sixth and seventh grades.

The shape of the developmental curve differs from culture to culture. Present indications are that, where there is a high degree of cultural continuity, development of these abilities is continuous. Drops in the curve appear to occur where cultural discontinuities coincide with severe discontinuities in development. Thus, the evidence indicates that drops in the developmental curve are strongly influenced by cultural forces as well as by purely developmental forces. Longitudinal studies now entering their fifth year are expected to clarify some of the issues concerning the course of creative development.

### Nurturing creativity during the elementary years

The accumulated evidence in American education leaves little doubt but that nurturing creativity during the elementary school years is a difficult problem. Or at least the evidence suggests that teachers, administrators, psychologists, and other school personnel generally have not been very successful in solving the problems involved.

Mayer (1961) in his recent book about the schools refers quite interestingly to Rice's famous articles about American classrooms in *The Forum* in 1892. Rice tells of seeing a Chicago teacher shout at her class, "Don't stop to think! Tell me what you know!" Rice asked a New York principal whether children were permitted to move their heads in class and was told, "Why should they look behind when the teacher is in front of them?" Much concern has persisted about "punishment for original sin," and many still follow the advice of John Wesley to "break your child's will in order that its soul may live." Mayer found numerous incidents reminiscent of those reported by Rice, but he also reports many bright incidents of teachers who have mastered the art of helping children to learn creatively. Bruner (1959) paints a rather gloomy picture concerning the extent to which elementary school teachers encourage or permit children to think.

### Discipline problems of teachers

The difficulty of permitting spontaneity, initiative, and creativity in the classroom while maintaining control has been described by Jules Henry (1959) on the basis of research data involving direct observations of teacher-pupil interaction and interviews with teachers on their ideas about classroom discipline. Henrickson and Torrance (1961a) have also examined a number of research findings for their implications concerning school discipline. Although the accumulated research findings suggest a number of possible solutions, there appears to be no body of information that deals directly with the problem of discipline and creativity.

Many observers have noted that young children come to school with an insatiable curiosity and an enthusiasm for learning, both of which diminish as they proceed through school. Sanders (1961) has questioned whether the validity of such observations has been established. He points out that, even if we are certain that desire-to-know diminishes, we still do not know whether it is a natural phenomenon in child development or whether the school actually dulls enthusiasm for learning. Sanders (1961) and many before him (Boraas, 1922; Brandwein, 1955) have viewed the intellectual curiosity of the teacher as the possible determining factor. In an experiment conducted by Torrance, it was found that the pupils of teachers scoring in the upper half of the sample on a measure of creative motivation or intellectual curiosity showed significant growth in creative writing during a three-month period. Pupils of the teachers scoring in the lower half failed to show any gain in creative writing during this period.

## Other problems of teachers

In addition to the problem of maintaining discipline, a variety of other problems faced by teachers in nurturing creativity have been identified. These include the following:

1. When allowed to do so, children propose unexpected solutions which may disconcert teachers who anticipate more prosaic responses (Sanders, 1961).

2. There is a strong temptation to tell the child what is "best" in order to "save time" (Sanders, 1961).

3. When the creative approach is used, children see relationships and significances that the teachers and even professionals in the subject matter field might miss (Hohn, 1961).

4. Children ask questions that the teacher cannot answer (Hohn, 1961).

5. Teachers may feel guilty about permitting children to guess (Bruner, 1960; Hohn, 1961).

6. Time pressures and scheduling problems at times make it difficult to permit and consider the many questions that children want to ask (Sanders, 1961).

7. Quite realistically, teachers have to help children to conform in many ways "just to get along."

## Suggestions to teachers for nurturing creativity

On the basis of some exploratory research, including a review of the relevant literature, Torrance (1962b) compiled the following 20 suggestions to teachers for nurturing creativity in the elementary school:

1. Value creative thinking.
2. Help children become more sensitive to environmental stimuli.

3. Encourage manipulation of objects and ideas.
4. Teach how to test each idea systematically.
5. Develop tolerance of new ideas.
6. Beware of forcing a set pattern.
7. Develop a creative classroom atmosphere.
8. Teach the child to value his creative thinking.
9. Teach children skills of avoiding or coping with peer sanctions without sacrificing their creativity.
10. Give information about the creative process.
11. Dispel the sense of awe of masterpieces.
12. Encourage and evaluate self-initiated learning.
13. Create "thorns in the flesh," making children aware of problems and deficiencies.
14. Create necessities for creative thinking.
15. Provide for active and quiet periods.
16. Make available resources for working out ideas.
17. Encourage the habit of working out the full implications of ideas.
18. Develop skills of constructive criticism.
19. Encourage acquisition of knowledge in a variety of fields.
20. Be adventurous-spirited yourself.

Although almost all these suggestions would pass most tests of "common sense" and some research evidence can be cited to support each of them, there is still a need for scientifically developed information concerning each one. To implement these suggestions would in some cases require considerable retooling and reorganization in education. In many cases, we have mere hypotheses about *how* they can be implemented. These hypotheses need to be tested, modified, and elaborated.

From the examination of imaginative stories by children which involved divergency and from studies of the needs of creative children, Torrance (1961h) formulated a set of frontiers of relatively unexplored areas of educational practice.

*Self-initiated learning.* Torrance (1961h) places provisions for giving credit for self-initiated learning at the head of his list of promising areas of development. Earlier writers have recognized the promise of this approach, but the literature concerning educational practice and research gives little or no evidence that anyone has ventured to do very much about it. Boraas (1922) discussed the problem of developing initiative and proposed two fundamental principles, stated essentially as follows:

1. Initiative can be developed only through practice on the part of pupils. Teachers must begin by letting them think for themselves and by allowing them to initiate projects.

2. Pupils must begin by practicing those forms of initiative which they naturally incline to and like—for example, curiosity, wonder, and questioning.

Boraas in 1922 recognized that these were trite and commonplace principles. Nevertheless, it is probably fair to say that we do not yet know how to apply them and do not really know what would happen if they were applied. Many individual teachers who have sought to test them, however, have described their own techniques and the results they have achieved. Natalie Robinson Cole (1940) says she has found that when children are engaged in what they love to do, the barriers are down and their creative abilities develop. Some of the teachers observed and interviewed by Mayer report similar experiences. For example, one of them described some of the exciting things that happen when children are permitted to think about the infinite (Mayer, 1961, p. 81).

For the greatest "pay-off," self-initiated learning must be supplemented by the development of skills in research, or how to learn. This means that the child should begin to develop research skills quite early in his school life and should acquire them both in depth and breadth. The development of these skills should be accepted consciously as an instructional goal. Although there is little accumulated information about what research skills can be taught elementary age children and how they can be taught and practiced, there has been enough experience to indicate that many such skills can be taught children during this period, and that they can become powerful tools for the acquisition of knowledge. This writer has for the past three years taught to a group of elementary children many of the concepts and techniques of educational research. They even conducted with great care and enthusiasm an experiment in the lower grades, developed and tested scores of hypotheses, and prepared without delay well written reports.

Examples of the kinds of studies that are needed if we are to teach research skills to children are: the study of inquiry training by Suchman (1960a, 1961), the studies of the discovery method in mathematics by Hendrix (1961), experimental studies by Bruner (1959) at Harvard, and studies of the relationship between teacher questions and the productive thinking of pupils (Aschner, 1960).[2]

*Learning on one's own.* A closely related new approach is to be found in provisions to permit children to do things on their own and to learn on their own. The University of Minnesota Bureau of Educational Research (Hiller, 1961) conducted an exciting study in which it was found that children will do a great deal of writing on their own, if encouraged to do so. Many observations suggest the potential value of such provisions, but as yet there is little or no firm, scientifically developed information concerning their actual value.

*Responsive environment.* Another promising new approach may be identified by the phrase "responsive environment." In responsive environments, children are propelled by their own curiosity, the adult or the environment only responding promptly to the child's efforts to learn. This concept of the responsive environment is illustrated in the experimental work of O. K. Moore at Yale. Appealing

[2] On the basis of an educational theory worked out by C. W. Taylor, Ghiselin, Wolfer, Loy, & Bourne (1963), William L. Hutchinson has just completed a dissertation at the University of Utah on creative and productive thinking in the classroom which resembles Aschner's work in some respects. His dissertation was designed to determine whether at least as much subject matter was absorbed by a class when a wider than usual range of thinking and learning abilities (as indicated by verbal exchanges) was used by the students. All his findings were significant and positive, except one which was at the borderline of significance.

to the children's natural curiosity about electric typewriters, Moore (1961) has demonstrated that preschool children can learn to read, write, type, and take dictation. Here we find skills being learned creatively which everyone had assumed could be taught more economically by rote. An attempt is now being made to create responsive environments that are completely automated. The author believes that our failure to provide a responsive environment may often have led to the very early destruction of much of the excitement of learning.

*Revision of readiness concepts.* A fourth area for exploration would be a thorough revision of many of our concepts of readiness—already an area of much controversy in education. A recent report of the Educational Policies Commission of the National Educational Association and the American Association of School Administrators is favorable to open-minded exploration in this area. Bruner's *The Process of Education* (1960b) presents some concepts that should be useful in attacking this problem and in testing possible solutions. The usual defense of "holding back" operations is the fear that the child will become frustrated by failure. The ability to cope with frustration and failure, however, is a characteristic shared by almost all outstanding individuals. Certainly, almost all highly creative scientists, inventors, artists, and writers attempt tasks that are too difficult for them. If they did not attempt these overly difficult tasks, their great ideas might never be born. The research findings on acceleration (the advancing of students ahead of the accepted readiness stage) are rather clear and consistent, but do not satisfy the need for information concerning the extreme creative reaching out involved here.

*Self-concepts.* A fifth new approach is that of helping children to develop their self-concepts. Usually, we have ignored the child's natural concern about his own potentialities; at best we have tried to "correct" his self-concept by authority. Some children may despise an outstanding "gift," if their giftedness makes them different from others. This makes far too many highly creative children willing, consciously or unconsciously, to hide or destroy their talents. Considerable study has been made of the self-concepts of adults and adolescents, but not of children. Longitudinal and experimental studies of the process by which children develop their self-concepts are badly needed, especially in relation to their creative potential.

*Recognition of uniqueness.* A sixth frontier for exploration is the recognition of the uniqueness of the individual and its consequences for the nurture of creativity. Educators have long been interested in individual differences, but this concern has definitely been overshadowed by an emphasis on adjustment to a norm and the development of the well-rounded personality. Some schools now are exploring the possibilities of strengths-and-weaknesses programs in elementary schools. In one curriculum for academically gifted children, the afternoons every other week are devoted entirely to such a program. Opportunity is given for developing further the special enthusiasms, talents, or hobbies of the children. Guidance is also given in strengthening neglected educational skills that might cause these children to bog down even in pursuit of their enthusiasms, both vocational and avocational. These programs need to be studied and evaluated.

## Roles of specialists

This section on nurturing creativity during the elementary school period has so far been devoted largely to the role of teachers and administrators. Attention needs to be given also to the roles of such specialists as the school counselor, social worker, psychologists, and nurse. Although the roles of these persons differ somewhat, at least six special roles in nurturing creativity, especially in the highly creative child, may be performed by teams of specialists. These are (Torrance, 1962a):

1. Providing for highly creative children a refuge, a safe relationship
2. Serving as "sponsors" or "patrons" for certain highly creative children

3. Helping highly creative children understand and accept their divergence

4. Listening to the ideas of highly creative children

5. Recognizing creative talent and seeing that it is given a chance to develop

6. Helping parents and fellow workers understand the problems of highly creative children

All of these roles require the development of theory and research to accumulate information necessary for greater understanding and for effective implementation.

## INHIBITORS AND FACILITATORS

First, an effort will be made to identify from research and observation some of the forces in society that inhibit creative growth. Then, a number of suggested ways for dealing with these forces will be identified.

### Inhibiting forces

*Success-orientation.* It is frequently alleged that we have in the United States one of the most success-oriented cultures in the world. We are reminded that our military and civilian education prepares individuals only for success, not for coping with frustration and failure. Every frustration must be prevented, and almost any failure is dreadfully serious. Evidence of the inhibiting effects of this tendency is seen again and again in the individual testing of children on tasks of creative thinking. The resolution of this problem would seem to be to give pupils more difficult problems—problems they have a chance of solving, but difficult enough to challenge them and to make them think. Much information is needed concerning the construction of problems of varying difficulty, the determination of the effects of problems that are too difficult, and the identification of the characteristics of difficult problems.

The problem of success orientation has long engaged the attention of educational reformers and experimenters; yet little firm information exists to guide us. Most of the relevant studies have been concerned with norms and "safe limits" rather than with "testing the limits." Herbart (quoted by Grozinger, 1955), for example, stated, "One must take risks with boys." He argued that one must let children get into natural crises, blind alleys, and other threatening situations. When the child realizes that he has involved himself in such a situation, he will usually find his way out; if not, teachers and counselors can find suitable ways of helping him. Educational researchers should experiment with the question of what risks need to be taken, instead of devoting all their energies to such problems as determining the ages at which most children can cope with a given task.

*Peer-orientation.* Anthropologists tell us that we have in the United States the most peer-oriented culture in the world. Evidence of the inhibiting effects that peer pressures toward conformity exert on creative thinking is too obvious to need enumerations; it appears when we observe children, when we conduct experiments, when we do sociometric studies, and when we study the creative writings of children. It is likely that pressures for conformity are responsible in large part for the sharp drop found in the developmental curves in the fourth grade and again in the seventh. At about the time a child reaches the fourth grade, his need for consensual validation is intensified. He becomes almost afraid to think until he learns what his peers are thinking. Unusual or original ideas are common targets of peer pressures to conformity. Investigations into this problem have as yet barely scratched the surface.

*Sanctions against questioning and exploration.* Although educators generally recognize that children need to ask questions and in other ways to inquire about the wonders and mysteries around them, tendencies to do so are often brutally squelched. Teachers have many devices for putting the curious child in his place. Even in laboratory experiments (Torrance, 1962a) significant relationships were found between the amount of manipulation of objects and the quality and quantity of ideas produced about them. Examples of useful ideas and research projects in this area are: the work of the Maws (1959, 1960) on curiosity, H. H. Anderson's (1961) concept of the open system, Suchman's (1961) inquiry training, and Mork's (1959) ask-and-guess method of teaching. Lines of investigation such as these need to be continued long enough to accumulate a useful body of information.

*Overemphasis or misplaced emphasis on sex roles.*   Both boys and girls suffer in their creative development from our society's overemphasis or misplaced emphasis on sex roles. Both simply shut out certain areas of awareness and refuse to think about them. Creativity, by its very nature, requires both sensitivity and independence of thinking. In our culture, sensitivity is definitely a feminine virtue, and independence is a masculine one. Thus, highly creative boys are likely to appear more effeminate than their peers and highly creative girls, more masculine than theirs.

During the elementary school years, the inhibiting effects of this cultural block emerge in many places. In the Minnesota Studies, it was first observed in the Product Improvement Task. In the first grade, boys excelled girls on the fire truck, but girls excelled boys on the nurse's kit. Some boys refused to think of anything to make the nurse's kit more fun, protesting, "I'm a boy! I don't play with things like that!" Some of the more creative boys, however, first transformed it into a doctor's kit which they felt quite free to deal with. By the third grade, however, boys excelled girls even on the nurse's kit.

These inhibiting effects of sex-role conditioning also showed up in experiments involving small groups working with science toys. Girls were quite reluctant to work with these science toys, frequently protesting, "I'm a girl; I'm not supposed to know anything about things like that." In the 1959 studies, boys demonstrated and explained over twice as many ideas as girls. In 1960, however, it was found that some changes had taken place. Girls were less reluctant to work with these materials, showed enjoyment in doing so, and equaled the performance of boys. The contributions of boys continued to be more highly valued by peers than those of girls, however.

*Divergency equated with "abnormality."* Once even leading thinkers believed "genius" and "madness" to be associated with each other. Many inventors, composers, creative scientists, and other creative individuals were regarded as insane. Although all these beliefs were discredited long ago, somehow the belief has persisted that any divergence from behavioral norms is an indication of something abnormal, unhealthy, or immoral which must be corrected at all costs. Evidence from the Minnesota Studies indicates that children are taught very early the harsh consequences of divergent behavior, even outstanding performance in many areas of life. They feel that the pressures of society to rid children of divergent characteristics are relentless.

It might prove fruitful for investigators first to toy with and then to test the idea that many individuals might contribute far more to society and be far happier if they capitalized upon unique strengths, instead of spending fruitless energy in trying to compensate for some so-called weakness. At the same time, attention should be given to the problem of helping such individuals master the basic skills necessary to prevent their becoming bogged down later on in their chosen areas of specialization.

*Work-play dichotomy.* Another characteristic of our culture which seems to block creative development is a work-play dichotomy. One is supposed to enjoy play; he is considered queer if he doesn't. Also, one is supposed to dislike work, and something is felt to be wrong if he doesn't. There is supposed to be no playing around in work. This appears to be one important reason why more teachers do not give children more opportunities to learn creatively. Children enjoy creative experiences, and their pleasure makes teachers uneasy. School is supposed to be work, and work is no fun. It has been this writer's observation that in schools with an austere, no-fun atmosphere there is the least evidence that the creative thinking abilities are used in learning.

An important clue concerning this problem comes from Torrance's (1962a) study differentiating the highly intelligent from the highly creative child. In one school there was a difference of 25 IQ points between these two groups (the upper 20 per cent on IQ but not creativity, and vice versa), but no difference in their measured achievement. Ordinarily we would have to say either that the highly creative group was "overachieving" and working too hard or that the high-IQ group was "underachieving" and ought to work harder. Teachers, however, rated the highly creative as less ambitious and less hardworking. Yet, with IQ's averaging 25 points lower, they still learned as much (measured by standardized tests) as their more "intelligent" classmates. Apparently they had been learning through activities that appeared to their teachers to be "playing around."

A rich field for research could be opened by exploring, through laboratory and field experiments and studies in natural situations, the effects of the work-play dichotomy on creativity and ways of modifying it. A number of interesting concepts have been suggested in the literature. Schafer (1958) has given as interesting discussion of the nature and role of "regression in the service of the ego." Maslow (1956) and McPherson (1960) have discussed the nature and role of "primary creativeness" (which involves the ability to play, fantasy, and laugh) in relation to productivity. Snyder (1959) has used the concept "area of playfulness" which he sees as essential to the "authentic life" and creativity. LaPiere (1959) delves into some of these problems in *The Freudian Ethic*.

*Facilitating forces*

In this section, a number of facilitating forces, which might counteract some of the inhibiting forces just discussed, will merely be enumerated, since they have been discussed in detail elsewhere

(Torrance, 1962). The results of a series of experiments designed to facilitate creative development in children will be summarized briefly.

Some of the most important facilitating procedures that this writer has been able to identify are as follows:

1. Rewarding varied kinds of talents and creative achievements
2. Helping children recognize the value of their creative talents
3. Teaching children to use creative problem-solving processes
4. Developing creative acceptance of realistic limitations in a problem situation
5. Avoiding the equation of divergency with mental illness and delinquency
6. Modifying the misplaced emphasis on sex roles
7. Helping highly creative children become less objectionable
8. Developing school pride in creative achievement
9. Reducing the isolation of highly creative children
10. Providing sponsors or patrons for certain highly creative children
11. Developing values and purposes
12. Helping highly creative children learn to cope with anxieties and fears
13. Helping highly creative children to develop courage and to tolerate the anxieties of being in the small minority, of exploring the uncertain, etc.
14. Reducing the discontinuities that seem to be associated with entrance into kindergarten, the fourth grade, and the seventh grade

Most of the Minnesota studies involving experimental manipulations have concerned the role of evaluation in the development of creativity. These experiments have been organized around three problems:

1. How can teachers and others create an environment that places a high value on creative thinking and achievement?

2. What is the most effective kind of evaluative behavior teachers and others can use to promote creative growth?

3. How can children be helped to develop values conducive to creative thinking?

Following are some of the conclusions that now seem to be justified, on the basis of approximately 20 experiments involving elementary school children:

1. After an orientation course such as that contained in the manual, *Rewarding Creative Thinking*, classroom teachers seem to want to reward creative thinking in their pupils, but many of them are unable to do so effectively because of such factors as their own personality characteristics and their perceptions of social expectations.

2. In projecting plans for discussions with children about their creative writing, teachers seem to be preoccupied with the critical and the remedial.

3. Teachers participating in in-service training programs for developing creative thinking do not tend to initiate any more creative activities than their colleagues under control conditions.

4. Even though elementary school teachers volunteer to carry out creative thinking programs, they tend to be inhibited in doing so, unless the principal is involved in the experiment and gives his direct approval.

5. Boys and girls are rewarded differentially for their creative thinking, and this appears to interfere with the full creative development of both boys and girls in certain areas.

6. The type of evaluative practice (criticism and correction, suggestions of other possibilities, or a combination of criticism and constructive suggestions) does not affect performance on subsequent tasks requiring creative problem solving. Too frequent use of evaluation during practice sessions, regardless of type, seems to interfere with subsequent performance on similar tasks.

7. Unevaluated ("off-the-record") practice tends to produce

greater originality, elaboration, and sensitivity than evaluated practice in most instances, except at the sixth-grade level.

8. When peer-evaluated practice is used, creative evaluation (constructive possibilities) rather than critical evaluation (defects) tends to be more effective in producing originality, elaboration, sensitivity, and the like, except in the kindergarten through the third grade.

9. Competition in grades one to six increases fluency, flexibility, and originality in creative thinking tasks. Practice and "warm-up" do not completely eliminate the advantage achieved by competition. (This does not, of course, include an assessment of various side-effects of competition.)

10. Individuals tend to achieve along those lines in which they are rewarded. When rewarded for originality, sixth-grade children produced about twice as many original ideas as when they were rewarded for quantity regardless of quality. When rewarded for the originality and interest of their stories, other groups of sixth-grade children wrote more interesting and original stories but made more errors in usage, spelling, and mechanics than children rewarded for correctness.

11. If one member of a group is definitely superior to the others in creative thinking abilities, he almost always experiences pressures to reduce his productivity and/or originality and is frequently not given credit for the positive contribution he makes to the group's success. The repertoire of group strategies for controlling creative members and of the counteractive techniques of creative individuals can be identified and used in characterizing the evaluative conditions of a group.

12. Homogeneous grouping for tasks requiring creative problem solving reduces the social stress, enables less creative members to become more productive, and increases the enjoyment of members.

13. Imaginative stories by children about both animals and persons with divergent characteristics provide a promising technique for studying cultural pressures against divergency and consequently against creative thinking. Among the cultures sampled, urban cul-

tures appear to be more intolerant of divergency than rural cultures. Children in special classes for the gifted seem to feel freer of these pressures than children in regular classes. Minority groups seem to feel rather strong pressures for conformity to the larger society.

14. Children in grades three to six can be stimulated to do a great deal of writing on their own, if they are given reasons for doing so. A vehicle such as a school magazine seems to increase the value children place on their own ideas and those of their peers.

## Instructional materials beyond textbooks

When this writer discovered that in-service training efforts were unsuccessful, he turned some of his attention to the development of instructional materials that might assist teachers in developing the creative thinking abilities of their pupils. This first took the form of workbooks. Myers devised large numbers of exercises, tested them on his own fourth-grade pupils, and obtained the cooperation of other teachers in trying them out. Some of these were then put together into what might have been termed an experimental "training program" and were made available to about 100 teachers for testing. The reports were encouraging, and, where pre- and post-tests were made, the data showed that the use of the materials resulted in significant growth in creative writing and in attitudes relevant to creativity. The materials were then revised and made available for further experimental use (Myers & Torrance, 1961b,c). A second workbook and manual at the junior high school level, *Invitations to Speaking and Writing Creatively,* has been produced and is now being tested.

Attention was turned next to taped materials. It was thought that such materials might aid teachers in overcoming their own difficulties in becoming "warmed up" and in helping pupils to become "warmed up." The first set of these experimental materials was tested during the 1962–1963 term in three school systems. Central to each recording is a dramatized story around which some programmed experience in creative thinking revolves. One-fourth deals with great moments of scientific discovery and invention, one-fourth with historical achievements, one-fourth with the relationship of man to his environment (geography), and one-fourth with fantasy material. In all four areas, the materials are designed to facilitate the "warm-up" process and to help children become more fully alive. Each category also has some unique secondary objective. The material on great moments of scientific discovery and invention is designed to acquaint children with the nature and value of the creative process, with emphasis on the present-day value of these achievements. The material on historical achievement is designed to familiarize children with the historical importance of creative achievements; the material on man and his environment, with the importance of creative problem solving in survival; and the fantasy material, with the enjoyment and value of imaginative activities.

Materials have also been devised for teaching gifted elementary children many of the basic concepts and skills of creative research and for teaching some of the principles of creative thinking.

In all this developmental work, there are implied no delusions that creative teaching can be "canned." It cannot. This writer believes, however, that research findings in this area are not likely to exercise much influence unless they are translated into tested materials and procedures. He also hopes that, as teachers use these materials, their own creative energies will be galvanized into action, so that they will develop new ideas of their own and will value more highly than before the ideas of their pupils.

## RESEARCH PRIORITIES IN THE ELEMENTARY YEARS

At the moment, the most urgent research need in relation to the elementary school years is for the standardization of one or more batteries of tests for assessing creativity. The need is for a battery that will give an adequate inventory of the creative thinking abilities, yet will be simple to administer, score, and interpret. At the same time, there is need to experiment with alternative administrative and scoring procedures and to develop tasks that will continue to explore the boundaries of the creative thinking abilities of children. Such tasks should use a variety of kinds of stimuli and should seek to exhaust the response repertoire of elementary school children, so that an adequate taxonomy can be created. Along with this work, there should be parallel developments in the construction of achievement tests that could be used to assess creative growth and assess the outcomes of experimental educational programs.

Perhaps one of the most promising areas of research concerns the factors responsible for the slump that seems to occur in most elementary schools at about fourth grade. Information on this problem should be important in salvaging creative talent, in preventing mental illness and delinquency, and in avoiding many learning difficulties. Experimental, longitudinal, and cross-cultural studies are needed.

## CREATIVITY IN THE HIGH SCHOOL YEARS

Of the different educational levels, the high school years have perhaps been the most neglected in creativity research. Information has accumulated concerning the preschool and elementary school years because of interest in "creative imagination." Apparently, educators have not had much interest in the "creative imagination" of high school students. Information has accumulated concerning creativity during the college years, because many outstanding creative scientists, writers, and performers of many kinds begin their productivity during these years and because it has been deemed appropriate for colleges to produce professionally trained people who will make creative contributions. No such expectations exist for high schools.

Creative growth has rarely been recognized as an objective of secondary education. Although many promising changes in objectives seem to be occurring, especially in high school mathematics, physics, biology, and chemistry, the results of a 1959–1960 sample survey of Minnesota social science teachers probably reflect with accuracy the current status of high school objectives. Each social science teacher in the survey was asked to select a course or unit and list its three most important objectives. The objectives listed were then classified according to Guilford's five mental operations with the following results:

*Cognitive* (recognize, realize, become aware of, become acquainted or familiar with, be conscious of, etc.) ........ 70.7%

*Memory* (remember, acquire distinct or thorough knowledge of, learn thoroughly) ............................. 5.3%

*Divergent* (independent thinking, constructive, creative, liberal, inquiring, etc.) ............................. 1.7%

*Convergent* (behavioral norms, right attitude, right solution, etc.) ................................................. 18.7%

*Evaluative* (critical thinking, assessing, selecting, comparing, judging, deciding, etc.) ........................... 3.6%

## Manifestations of creativity during high school years

Although a few creative scientists, writers, and inventors won eminence while still of high school age, the number has been too small for much study, and in most cases they did not achieve their eminence in the high school setting. High schools have long had provisions for recognizing creative writing and speaking talent. In recent years, there have been many provisions for recognizing scientific and inventive talent. In studies by the National Merit Scholarship Corporation, a five-item Creative Science Scale and an eleven-item Creative Arts Scale based on high school experiences have proved quite valuable in predicting later creative performance (Holland, 1961). The following achievements are recognized in its Creative Science Scale:

1. Giving an original paper at a scientific meeting sponsored by a professional society
2. Winning a prize or award in a scientific talent search
3. Constructing scientific apparatus on one's own initiative

4. Inventing a patentable device
5. Having a scientific paper published in a science journal

The following achievements are included in the Creative Arts Scale:

1. Winning one or more speech contests
2. Having poems, stories, or articles published in a *public* newspaper or magazine (*not* a school paper) or in a state or national high school anthology
3. Winning a prize or award in an art competition (sculpture, ceramics, painting, etc.)
4. Receiving the highest rating in a state music contest
5. Receiving one of the highest ratings in a national music contest
6. Composing music that is given at least one public performance
7. Arranging music for a public performance
8. Having minor roles in plays (not high-school- or church-sponsored)
9. Having leads in high school or church-sponsored plays
10. Winning a literary award or a prize for creative writing
11. Having cartoon published in a public newspaper or magazine

These are but a few of the manifestations of creativity among high school students, but they are sufficient to indicate the feasibility of criterion research at the high school level.

### Measurement of creative thinking at the high school level

Devices for assessing the creative thinking abilities of high school pupils have tended to be in the direction of group-administered tests with verbal stimuli requiring verbal responses. Although some of the devices originally developed for use with children have been extended into or through the high school years, most of the instruments used with high school students were initially developed for use with college students or adults. Some of the major efforts will be summarized briefly.

Colvin (1902) made more use of his measures, which were based on compositions, with high school students than with younger groups. Abramson (1927) used inkblots and concrete observations (enumerating objects after 20 minutes of exposure) with high school students, as well as with grades three to six. Harms (1939) applied his test in which subjects draw lines to represent words (mostly action words) throughout grades one to twelve. M. D. Vernon (1948) used his Imaginative Construction Test (stories based on four-colored pictures) with high school subjects, as did Stephenson (1949) with his Poetry Writing and Art Form Tests.

Most of the recent work with high school students has involved adaptation of Guilford's tests with a few innovations here and there. Getzels and Jackson (1958) used four adapted tasks (Word Associations, Uses for Things, Hidden Shapes, and Fables) and constructed one of their own (Make-Up Problems). In the latter task, subjects are presented with four complex paragraphs, each containing a variety of data. Subjects are then required to make up as many mathematical problems as they can which can be solved with the information given. Scores depend upon the number, appropriateness, and originality of the problems.

With seventh-grade subjects, McGuire, Hindsman, King, and Jennings (1961) used the following Guilford tests: Rhymes, Unusual Uses, Consequences, Common Situations, Seeing Problems, Mutilated Words, and Gestalt Completion. Piers, Daniels, and Quackenbush (1960) administered the following Guilford measures to seventh and eighth graders: Consequences, Plot Titles, and Unusual Uses. Guilford, Merrifield, and Cox (1961) recently reported work in which they administered a battery to ninth graders and found essentially the same factors as had been found with adults.

Some of the Minnesota batteries have been used with high school populations. In addition to adaptations of Guilford's Unusual Uses and Consequences tasks and Getzels and Jackson's Make-Up Problems Test, these have included: the Ask-and-Guess Test, the Product Improvement Test, the Circles Test, and others.

### Developmental phenomena during high school years

Although developmental phenomena during the high school years have received little attention, most of the existing evidence is fairly consistent. Most investigators have reported a decline in imaginative functioning between the sixth and seventh grades and in some studies on into the eighth. There follows a period of fairly steady growth until about the end of the high school period, at which time there is a leveling off or a slight decline.

Colvin and Meyer (1906) reported a general decline in creative writing during the entire high school period. Simpson (1922) found a peak which extended through the second half of the sixth grade, after which there was a decline in the seventh and a still further one in the eighth. Mearns (1931), on the basis of experiences in stimulating creative writing but without any measurements, maintained that a decline which set in during the sixth grade continued throughout the high school period, unless counteracted by special encouragement.

In the Minnesota Studies (Torrance, 1962a) the abilities measured show a decline between the sixth and seventh grades, after which there is a fairly steady rise until near the end of the high school period. Most of the growth curves then show either a leveling off or a slight decline.

There are some clues indicating that the decline at the beginning of the high school period is the result of new pressures to conformity inherent in the tradition. There is a need for studies in schools having seven- and eight-grade elementary schools and for longitudinal (follow-up) studies to obtain clarification of the major causal factors. In a thorough search of the literature, no longitudinal studies of any type have been found.

### Nurturing creativity during high school years

A search of the literature reveals an almost total lack of laboratory or field experiments at the high school level designed to nurture creativity. Almost all of the reported studies at this level have used measures of creative thinking as predictors of later performances rather than as criteria of present creative performance. In two current studies at Minnesota, measures of creative thinking and creative achievement are being used as criteria. In one, pre- and post-tests of creative thinking are being used as one of several devices to assess the effectiveness of a team-teaching project. In another, a similar pre- and post-test design, involving both measures of creative thinking and measures of creative application of the subject matter, is being used to assess the effects of highly creative versus less creative teachers (as measured by a battery of creative-thinking tests).

Although there has been an absence of the kinds of experimental studies that we find in the elementary school and in industry, there are descriptions of a number of special programs designed to promote creative growth. Perhaps most adequately described is a program in science reported by Brandwein (1955) in *The Gifted Student as Future Scientist*. This description is rich in hypotheses concerning those conditions which nurture creativity during this period.

Extracurricular or cocurricular activities have always made claims of nurturing creativity in high school. Some of the new programs in mathematics, physics, and chemistry represent built-in attempts to stimulate creative growth through these disciplines. Many summer camps for high school youths are planned with a view to stimulating creative growth. Special seminars and workshops also have such aims. Seldom, however, have these been evaluated. Torrance has evaluated two eight-month seminars on perception for high school students conducted by the Walker Art Institute. Although the participants for whom there were pre- and post-measures showed significant growth far beyond that found under ordinary conditions, the attrition in these groups has been so great during the eight-month period that the evaluations are of limited value.

Some educators maintain that there must be fundamental changes in the way schools are organized if they are to foster creativity, independent responsibility for learning, inquiring minds, and ability to solve problems, in contrast with mere familiarity with facts. Some, like J. Lloyd Trump (1959), associate secretary of the National Association of Secondary School Principals, have suggested organizations involving team teaching, varied class size, provisions for individual study, resource centers, and programs emphasizing creativity and independence in learning. Evaluations of programs such as those proposed by Trump and others should include assessments of creative growth and achievement.

## Facilitators and inhibitors during high school

It is to be expected that most of the forces seen as facilitators and inhibitors during the elementary school period persist as facilitators and inhibitors during the high school period.

Many of the inhibiting and facilitating influences are reflected in the Getzels and Jackson studies, already mentioned. These studies have done much to dramatize the fact that there are other types of giftedness among high school students than that represented by the high IQ. As already indicated, they studied two groups: one exceptionally high in intelligence (IQ) but not concomitantly high in creativity, and one exceptionally high in creativity but not concomitantly high in intelligence (IQ). Although the two groups differed by an average of 23 IQ points, they did not differ in achievement as measured by appropriate standardized achievement tests. The high IQ student was rated as above average in desirability as a student; the high creative was not (Getzels & Jackson, 1958). In their fantasy productions the creative students made significantly greater use of stimulus-free themes, unexpected endings, humor, and playfulness. The values of the highly intelligent subjects correlated highly with those of teachers; those of the creative subjects were negatively correlated with those they attributed to their teachers. The career choices of the creative students were far more unconventional than those of the high-IQ group. In summarizing the data comparing the family influences of the two groups, Getzels and Jackson write, "The over-all impression of the high IQ family is one in which individual divergence is limited and risks minimized, the over-all impression of the high Creative family is one in which individual divergence is permitted and risks are accepted" (1961, p. 359).

Many clues concerning inhibitors and facilitators in American high schools are to be found in Coleman's (1961) studies of social climates in high schools. In the ten high schools studied by Coleman, he found in the social climates evidence of forces that inhibit and facilitate various kinds of achievement among pupils. Coleman suggests that changes be made in the reward structures of high schools to shift from interpersonal competition to intergroup competition in which group rewards reinforce achievement. In other words, he advocates procedures whereby schools will take pride in the creative and intellectual achievements of its student body, just as they now take pride in members of athletic teams, bands, and the like.

The work of Elizabeth Drews (1961) has also revealed a number of interesting clues concerning the forces that impede and facilitate creative growth. For one thing, her studies indicated that homogeneous grouping can be a far more facilitating factor than is popularly thought. In homogeneously grouped ninth-grade English classes, slow students read more, recited more, were more confident, liked school better, and were better accepted socially and intellectually than slow students in heterogeneous classes. Superior students wrote many more compositions, did more research, discussed at a more mature level, used more difficult words, expressed more complex and abstract thoughts, and were more interested in learning. (They were also more modest in their ratings of self in relationship to others.)

Among gifted high school students, Drews (1961) identified three types: social leaders, studious achievers, and creative intellectuals. Of these, the studious achievers attained the highest grades and the creative intellectuals, the lowest. The creative intellectuals, however, excelled the other two groups on standardized achievement tests, sampling a wide range of content and educational skills. During the times when preparations were being made for examinations, the social leaders were studying those things on which they would be graded, though they read relatively little in general. The studious achievers were also studying those things which would earn good grades from teachers. The creative intellectual, however, might be reading a book on philosophy or a college textbook, neither of which would earn him much credit in the teacher's grade book.

Pressures toward conformity have been named by a number of observers and groups as a major inhibitor of creativity. In one of the 1961 publications of the NEA Project on the Academically Talented Student (Ziegfield, 1961) it is pointed out that "strong trends toward conformity and uniformity are increasing in our culture." He enumerated as powerful pressures such forces as: developments in communication which bring to millions the same printed material, musical presentations, etc.; complexity of structure, both social and mechanical; and pressures against deviation or irregularity.

Similarly, C. W. Taylor (1962b) has pointed out some of the possible negative and positive effects of new instructional media on creativity. He indicated that it is quite unlikely that areas heretofore neglected in education will automatically receive attention with the emergence of new instructional devices. He emphasized the need for deliberate techniques to develop creativity and to determine which instructional media might be most effective in developing various characteristics, including creativity. The Philosophy of Education Association has also called attention to the need for determining whether or not some of the new instructional media can be used in such a way as to stimulate creative thinking. Unless attention is given to these problems through research, many of the new teaching media can become inhibitors rather than facilitators of creativity.

At least as recently as 1952 and 1957 (Mead & Métraux, 1952; Heath, Maier, Remmers, & Rodgers, 1957; Remmers, 1957) the image that high school students had of the scientist could be counted a serious inhibitor of creativity. In a study by Mead and Métraux, using projective material, and in a national survey by Remmers and his associates, it was found that high school students had a very unfavorable image of the scientist. This image is so unfavorable that it is likely to create a negative reaction to almost any career requiring a high degree of creativity. There is now need for replication of the Mead-Métraux and Remmers studies to determine the extent to which this image has been modified by the events of the intervening years. There is a further need to determine what image is held by high school students of other careers requiring creative performance.

## CREATIVITY IN HIGHER EDUCATION

Much has been written concerning the need for developing creativity in higher education, and college students have served as subjects in experiments concerning creativity phenomena. Yet there is almost no evidence of experimentation in admissions practices, college teaching, or evaluation of achievement. As in the preceding sections, an effort will be made to summarize the accumulated knowledge and to indicate some of the gaps in knowledge.

### *Manifestations of creativity in higher education*

Undergraduate college students have been known to produce almost all types of creative products—inventions, medical discoveries, books, monographs, musical compositions, dramas, operas, and the like. Usually, however, such manifestations occur outside of college requirements and activities. The term paper is usually a digest of known facts or opinions of experts and is graded primarily for correctness of form and content. The research of others is almost always evaluated in terms of correctness of methodology and is done in a critical rather than a constructive manner. Dissertations and theses, usually regarded as original contributions, tend to be evaluated in terms of the correctness of the methodology rather than in terms of originality, power, and worth of the ideas developed and tested.

There are, and perhaps always have been, dramatic exceptions to these generalizations which appear to represent the consensus of many observers of the higher education scene. The field of medicine, for example, has one of the richest traditions of discoveries by undergraduate students. This was called to our attention by W. C. Gibson (1958) in an exciting little book entitled *Young Endeavour*. Gibson presents rather compressed biographical sketches of approximately

150 medical students who made significant scientific contributions. Their discoveries were made while they were still undergraduates, or they conceived ideas during the undergraduate period and worked them out later. Gibson (1955) has maintained that "the inquiring, restless mind of the uninhibited undergraduate is still our greatest asset in medicine and the greatest deterrent to smugness in research." Gibson also used history to show how teachers and administrators brush aside some of these young discoverers as "nonconformists." He presents Jenner as an example of a medical student who became very unpopular with his instructors "because he kept bringing up his fantastic theory, as from a back pasture." Even after he had worked out his ideas and turned to the Royal Society for an audience, he was rebuffed and advised that he "should be cautious and prudent . . . and ought not to risk his reputation by presenting to the learned body anything which appeared so much at variance with established knowledge, and withal so incredible." The same advice, interestingly enough, was given Benjamin Franklin when he reported on his derivation of electricity from the clouds. Such advice was also offered Frank Whittle, a jet propulsion pioneer, on the grounds that he was still only a Cambridge undergraduate and his theory was "incredible."

## Measures of creative thinking in higher education

Although no reports have been located of colleges or universities in the United States that use measures of creative thinking as a functional part of their programs, a great variety of such measures have been developed for use with college students and have been in existence for many years.

In 1916, Laura Chassell reported rather detailed data concerning a battery of twelve tests of originality. This battery included: Word Building, Picture Writing, Analogues, Original Analogues, Chain Puzzle, Triangle Puzzle, Royce's Ring, Completion Test, Economic Prophecies, Code Test, Invention for Sheet Music, and Novel Situations (Consequences).

In his book, *Teaching to Think,* published in 1922, Boraas described and discussed the following eight types of tests of "imaginative thinking":

1. The interpretation of inkblots
2. Word-building test
3. Sentence-building test
4. Making of similes or metaphors by combining any two of a given series of words
5. Completion of mutilated sentences
6. Painted cube test
7. Imaginary journey test
8. Production of rhymes

Examples, scoring directions, and norms are given in most cases. Boraas also reported what is now an extremely interesting analysis of examinations for teacher certification and state high school examinations. According to his analysis, teachers' state examinations given in Minnesota during the years 1907 to 1914 contained 75 per cent memory questions and 5 per cent thought questions. The State High School Board Examinations given in Minnesota during the years 1899–1912 included 76 per cent memory questions and one per cent thought questions. Recent analyses of a somewhat similar nature indicate that shifts in examination construction have been only in the direction of more recognition questions instead of memory questions (Getzels, 1960).

Hargreaves (1927) described and presented data concerning twelve tasks which he scored for fluency and originality: Word Building and Composition, Ebbinghaus Test, Invention of Stories, Indeterminate Picture Completion, Unfinished Pictures, Ink Blots, Indeterminate Language Completion, Unfinished Stories, Writing Words, Probable Situations, and Imaginary Situations.

Maier and his associates (McCloy, 1939; McCloy & Maier, 1939) experimented with a variety of measures closely related to their interest in art education. Their tasks included: interpretative titles to pictures, critical appraisal and interpretation of completed works of art, compositions, and opinions and interpretations of paintings.

Welch (1946) has made several interesting contributions on the assessment of creativity involved in seeing new combinations. His tasks include: Block Constructions (make as many pieces of furniture or home furnishings as possible from ten blocks), Sentence Construction (from ten words), Letter Construction (from three straight lines), and Short Story Construction.

Owens and his associates (1957) have developed a series of tasks to assess creativity in machine design. These include: Power Source Apparatus test, Design-a-Machine test, Three-Dimensional Space Relations test, and Figure Matrices test. This battery is supplemented by a Personal Inventory and a Personal History form. Harris (1960) has developed two forms of a 20-item test of creativity in engineering which has been standardized on engineering students. The content is oriented to engineering, and the tasks require subjects to list possible uses of various objects and to guess "What is it?" Scores are obtained for fluency, flexibility, and originality. Buhl (1961) and others have used the AC (Sparkplug) Test of Creative Ability to study creative thinking among engineering students.

Barron (1958, 1963) and his associates at the University of California have developed a battery of tasks for assessing originality among college students and adults. Among the tasks described in the literature are: Mosaic Constructions, Anagram Test, Drawing Completion (Franck), Figure Preference test (Welsh), and Inkblot test (uncommon responses).

Other instruments that have been used with college subjects include the following: Flanagan's (1958) Ingenious Solutions to Problems, one of the few attempts to assess creative thinking through multiple-choice items; Frederiksen's (1959) Formulating Hypotheses test, an attempt to elicit creative-type responses and transfer them to machine-scorable answer sheets by having subjects code their own responses; and Burkhart's (1961, 1962) Divergent Questions test, which requires subjects to ask questions about a given object such as an apple or a paper clip.

The elaborate battery of tasks developed by Guilford and his associates has been used with college subjects not only by Guilford's laboratory but also by other groups. Because of the length of this battery, most groups have used only a portion of the Guilford tasks, a number of which were originally developed by Thurstone, the United States Air Force, and Educational Testing Service. Since his presidential address before the American Psychological Association in 1950, Guilford has continued to modify his conceptualization of the creative thinking abilities and the tasks used to assess them. In a recent monograph by Guilford and Merrifield (1960), these modifications are summarized. This work has been done within the framework of Guilford's "structure of intellect." Earlier, Guilford had hypothesized that the thinking abilities involved in creativity are those he had defined as divergent productions and transformations. He now includes also the redefinition abilities, which are in the convergent-production category, and sensitivity to problems, which falls in the evaluation category.

The revised conceptualization of creative thinking includes the following factors, and there are several tasks to assess each: sensitivity to problems, flexibility (figural spontaneous, figural adaptive, and semantic spontaneous), fluency (word, expressional, and ideational), originality, elaboration, and redefinition (figural, symbolic, and semantic).

The Minnesota tests already described have also been used with a wide variety of college groups.

As with the lower age groups, work with college subjects has shown very low correlations between measures of creativity and measures of intelligence or scholastic aptitude. In general, the findings reported by Hargreaves in 1927 have continued to be supported. When he scored his tests of imagination for fluency of ideas, with emphasis on quantity rather than quality, he obtained fairly high correlation with intelligence tests. In addition to the appreciable amount of what he felt was Spearman's general factor $g$ (the so-called general intelligence factor), he found a considerable group factor in common with other measures of imagination. The "speed" factor was also found to be important in fluency. When these same tests of imagination were scored for originality, denoting novelty and uncommonness, Hargreaves found very little relationship. Barron (1957) reports a coefficient of correlation of .33 between his measure of originality and the Concept Mastery test. Torrance and his associates (1962a) found correlations of .10 and .11 with the Miller Analogies and −.02 with the Ohio State Psychological Examination among graduate students in education.

Replicating, in part, the Getzels-Jackson design, Palm and Bentley (Torrance, 1962a) found that highly creative graduate students achieve about as well as those high on the traditional measures of scholastic aptitude. Although graduate students ranking high on the Miller Analogies tend to perform better on multiple-choice tests than do those ranking high on the tests of creative thinking but not high on the Miller Analogies, the reverse is true on creative applications of knowledge, decision-making problems, original projects, and self-initiated activities.

In spite of the evidence on hand and the forceful arguments of Getzels (1960), Mednick (1961), and others for the development of admission criteria for colleges and universities that will not eliminate such applicants as the "bright nonconformist," there seems to be no move to use measures of the type described in this section in admission programs. Perhaps the single most significant move has been that of the National Merit Scholarship Corporation already described.

A report by Nishibori and Shibuya of the National Institute of Educational Research in Tokyo (1961) describes a battery used in Japan between 1953 and 1955, which apparently included creative-thinking problems. One section consisted of problems requiring definition of possibilities arising from data, comprehension of the change in the whole structure arising from the change in one of the conditions, comprehension of the relationships of the facts expressed by words or graphs, and the like. Although these tests were discontinued as a means of selection for higher education in 1955, research has shown that these tests (known as Shin-Teki type tests) are more valid than the achievement tests now used in Japanese universities.

*Nurturing creativity during the college years*

Insofar as deliberate attempts to nurture creativity during the college years are concerned, various types of honors programs seem to be the most widely used and studied. Many of these programs have been described and evaluated in the various issues of *The Superior Student,* the newsletter of the Inter-University Committee on the Superior Student. The evaluation of these honors programs, however, has been difficult and elusive. A number of studies fail to show significant differences in the achievement of students in independent study programs and those in regular classes. McKeachie (1960), summarizing studies in this area, concluded, "Independent study is not a panacea, and we still know little about the type of students, teachers, previous training, or objectives necessary for its success."

Most of the evaluative investigations of independent study have limited themselves to traditional kinds of final examinations which measure retention of factual textbook material. One of the most encouraging projects is that of Weitman and Gruber (1960) and Gruber and Weitman (1962) at the University of Colorado. Students in freshman English, physical optics, educational psychology, and a number of other fields who spent part of the class time meeting in groups independent of the instructor emerged superior to students in conventional classes in such strengths as making difficult applications, learning new materials, and curiosity.

It is difficult to assess the long-range effects of such experiences. Some accumulated data suggest that honors programs increase the number of students deciding to do graduate work. It is also interesting to note that in Anne Roe's (1952) study of eminent scientists, many in this outstanding group indicated that what determined their career was a college project in which they were given free rein to find out things for themselves.

There have been reported a few studies of natural situations at the college level designed to determine the relationship between some of the creative thinking abilities and achievement and to determine the effects of various curricula upon "general creativity." An example of the former is a study by Hills (1955) of the relationship between originality and success in college mathematics. This study seems to indicate that, in a situation where faculty members feel that originality is important, where the subject matter permits originality on the part of students, a positive relationship will be found between originality and success in course work. An example of the latter is Meinz's (1960) study of the differential effects of industrial arts and art education on the general creativity of elementary education majors. Students in the art sequence designed to promote creativity made significant gains in general creativity, as measured by a battery of tests, whereas students enrolled in an industrial arts sequence designed to teach the use of tools and processes showed actual losses in fluency and flexibility.

In some colleges, courses in creative problem solving have been established and evaluated. Perhaps the best known of these is the one at the University of Buffalo under the auspices of the Creative Education Foundation. Studies reported by Meadow and Parnes (1959), Meadow, Parnes and Reese (1959), and Parnes and Meadow (1959) have shown that such a course has a significantly positive effect on the performance of students on creative problem-solving tests. A study by Parnes and Meadow (1960) has shown that the effects produced by such a course persist, at least from eight months to four years after the completion of the course. A number of special, short courses or training programs have produced significant, positive changes in creative performance (True, 1956; Nicholson, 1959; Maltzman, 1960).

Taking a somewhat different approach, Torrance and his associates have conducted a number of experiments in regular classes in educational psychology. In one, students who read research articles creatively excelled those who read research articles critically, in the quality of their original projects and in their ability to make creative applications of the subject matter of the course. In another, students who worked in groups, compared with those who worked alone on original projects, made greater gains on multiple-choice tests and on creative applications of subject matter. In another (Torrance & Harmon, 1961), memory, evaluative and creative reading sets had differential effects on performance on tests assessing various kinds of achievement (recognition or multiple-choice), memory or completion, creative applications, and decision making or evaluation. Hyman (1961) has also conducted experiments which have shown that a "constructive attitude" toward prior information compared with a "critical attitude" produced solutions, on both related and unrelated problems, which were rated significantly more creative.

In summarizing a variety of evidence, Torrance (1962a) listed the following as changes that must be made before colleges can effectively nurture creativity in students:

1. Development and use of instruments and procedures to supplement present devices for selecting and guiding students
2. Changing the objectives of courses to include the development of skills in creative thinking about course content
3. Curricular changes that will permit students to learn creatively many of the things now taught by authority and give experience in creative application of scientific information
4. Development of methods and materials that will stimulate students to learn creatively and will foster creative growth
5. Development of instruments for assessing achievement in courses that involve creative thinking
6. Development of concepts of teacher-pupil relationships and principles for rewarding creative thinking (other than through grades)

Stein (1958), Dougherty (1960), McNeil (1960), and others have outlined some of the changes needed in order to nurture creativity in higher education.

## Inhibitors and facilitators in higher education

Since the forces that inhibit and facilitate the development and expression of creativity appear to be cumulative, all of the forces mentioned in the earlier sections probably operate in one way or another in higher education. The evidence seems to indicate, however, that creativity may be revived, at least to some degree, at any age (Mearns, 1941; Osborn, 1957). In fact, most of the studies cited in the preceding section demonstrate that even brief periods of training and the establishment of certain optimal conditions in higher education can improve the quantity and quality of creative thinking.

Knapp and Goodrich (1952), Thistlethwaite (1959a,d) and others have studied college environments as facilitating or inhibiting to the development of creative talent and find tremendous differences among colleges in this regard. Thistlethwaite (1959c) has studied the effects of social recognition upon college students. Holland and Kent (1960) have called attention to the possible effects of the concentration of scholarship funds upon a restricted type of giftedness.

H. H. Anderson (1959b, 1961) has used the concepts of "open" and "closed systems" in discussing the facilitators and inhibitors of creative development in higher education. The open system permits originality, experimentation, initiative, and invention. In higher education, some of its features are the seminar, the class discussion, the term paper, the original experiment, and student progress. The closed system is concerned mainly with the acquisition of knowledge, memorization of facts, and finding already known answers to problems. Its features include the required curriculum, fixed-answer problem solving, intelligence testing, and normative individual differences.

The problem of facilitators and inhibitors can also be approached from the viewpoint of individual personality—the forces within oneself. Excellent theoretical treatments from this viewpoint have been offered by Rogers (1954), Tumin (1954), Maslow (1956), Snyder (1959), and others. Interesting clues are provided by a variety of personality studies comparing the characteristics of highly creative and noncreative students. Among these are the studies of Drevdahl (1956), MacKinnon (1960, 1962), Pepinsky (1959), Torrance (1962a), and others.

Pepinsky (1959, 1960) has contributed some especially good leads through her studies of the strategies used by what she calls "productive non-conformists." She has concluded that "the occurrence of constructively independent behavior will be maximized where nonconformity is: (1) logically instrumental to task accomplishment,

(2) phenomenally compatible with the maintenance of the individual's own system of motive and defense, and (3) where independence is compatible as well with the conditions under which the group, in the process of social assessment, is willing to give favorable consideration to the exceptional case" (p. 85).

A few experimental studies are beginning to appear which will help to detail the conditions necessary for creativity among college students. Fiedler, Meuwese, and Oonk (1960) found that homogeneous grouping, based on religious and collegiate affiliation, resulted in less social stress and superior group creativity among college students. Ziller, Behringer, and Goodchilds (1960) found that open groups are more creative than closed groups.

Many exciting leads for research with student teachers have been provided by the work of Robert C. Burkhart (1962) in his studies of spontaneous and deliberate ways of learning. In his interesting book based upon work in art and art education, he contrasts rather fully in color illustrations the art products of spontaneous learners and of deliberate learners. He presents evidence that in his field the spontaneous learners tend to produce the more creative products. In his chapter on the interacting theory of creative education he raises many challenging points about the role of teachers in bringing about more creative ways of learning and producing in students. He also deals with positive and negative experiences during the creative process and is engaged in searching (with some reported success) for teaching techniques that will prove to have positive rather than negative effects when used as probes during the creative process in art work.

### Research priorities in higher education

At the level of higher education, perhaps the most urgent research need is for experimentation with admissions practices and selection devices that will not eliminate promising creative talent. The arguments of Getzels (1960) and Mednick (1961) are provocative, and the recent action of the National Merit Scholarship Corporation in granting scholarships for promising creative talent that would not otherwise have been rewarded may pave the way for other experiments. One promising type of experimentation would be to screen for creative promise applicants who would otherwise be rejected, admit them, and follow their success through college and into careers. Such experiments are needed both at the undergraduate, professional school, and graduate school levels.

Perhaps the most promising area, if we are interested in what can be done to encourage the unfolding of creative talent, is that of experimentation with teaching procedures that will stimulate students to think independently, to test their ideas, and to communicate them to others. This would entail a program of research involving both laboratory-type experiments and classroom experiments conducted by regular instructors with power, prestige, and status. Especially needed is creativity research related to the education of teachers, the supervision of student teachers, and the in-service training and development of teachers.

# chapter 4

# ENVIRONMENT
# AND TRAINING
# FOR CREATIVITY

*J. H. McPherson*

**DOW CHEMICAL COMPANY**

THERE ARE many problems involved in studying the various aspects of behavior that are related to creativity. It has been necessary for those working in this area to recognize that a scientist's creativity is the result of a fortunate combination of intellectual characteristics, emotional dispositions, and a particular climate that is favorable "for him." The authors recommend that scientists doing research on one aspect of this total field maintain an awareness of the other variables that are operating.

At the third (1959) University of Utah Conference on the Identification of Creative Scientific Talent, J. P. Guilford reported on the results of research that have led him to revise his concept of the structure of the intellect. As he views it, intellect involves five major kinds of mental activity, which can operate on four different kinds of content to produce six different kinds of product. In addition to the intellectual characteristics, it is possible to posit several personality or emotional traits that are frequent among creative scientists. These are the traits that seem to emerge consistently from studies reported at the Utah conferences. The issue of climate or environment arises with some frequency, but studies of the "climate" variables are less numerous than studies of the intellectual and emotional variables.

The total of creativity can be simplified by means of the outline (p. 131) as a guide to thinking about research needed in the future.

By using this frame of reference, one can see that a given individual's performance may be influenced by any one of the many possible combinations of these factors. For example, a scientist who is able to use the major mental factors effectively and who is problem-centered, spontaneous, and independent may thrive in a supportive and stimulating environment but flounder in a hostile climate.

The framework described above will be used to integrate the balance of this chapter, which is divided into two main parts. First, an overview will be presented of the kinds of training courses now in use to stimulate adult creativity, partly in order to see the direction of future research. Second, some of the major factors involved in assessing the industrial research climate will be reviewed, again

| Mental activity factors | Emotional factors | Climate |
|---|---|---|
| 1. Cognitive thinking | 1. Self-concern versus problem concern | 1. Stimulating |
| 2. Memory | 2. Spontaneity versus inhibition | 2. Supportive |
| 3. Divergent thinking | 3. Independence versus dependence | 3. Neutral |
| 4. Convergent thinking | 4. Acceptance of mysticism versus denial of mysticism | 4. Hostile |
| 5. Evaluative thinking | 5. Democratic character structure versus authoritarian structure | 5. Destructive |

in order to see what must be learned and what must be done to improve that climate.

## TRAINING METHODS NOW IN USE

Perhaps in the 1970s or 1980s many of the young adults in our society will have had (1) secure early lives that provided them with the freedom required for creative activity, (2) rewarding experiences in educational climates that supported creative efforts, and (3) sufficient experience with social groups that knew how to create conditions conducive to the nurture of creative people. Such conditions would alter considerably the nature of the adult training courses of the future. At this time, unfortunately, it seems that most adults reach maturity with much of their creative potential buried as a result of their educational and social experiences. Therefore, we must now provide training that will develop the creativity of people whose potential has hardly been tapped. In other words, creativity-training programs for adults are now remedial in nature;

they are attempts to overcome previous deficiencies in education and training.

Current training programs may be classified as follows: (1) those designed to develop sensitivity to problems, (2) those providing experience with a variety of problem-solving approaches, (3) those providing individuals with a knowledge of the various rationalizations used to hinder or block the creative process and the methods for reducing the effect of these rationalizations, and (4) those preparing individuals to influence others to accept and support their ideas.

## Development of sensitivity to problems

At the college level various methods are being used to give students experience in locating problems. In a report, "Individual Creativity and the Corporation," produced by Manufacturing Group 25 (1958) of the Harvard Graduate School of Business Administration, some of these efforts are reported. According to this report, Professor Leo B. Moore of M.I.T.'s School of Industrial Management provides his students with opportunities to visit industrial firms to locate problems. At the Harvard Business School, in a program entitled "Creative Marketing Strategy," it is common practice for students to meet with business executives to discuss a general problem, which they must probe in order to discover specific problems. At the U.S. Steel plant in Gary, Indiana, groups of eight salaried employees with varied backgrounds are given the task of studying various production facilities to locate problems that need solution. Scientific personnel of many laboratories keep "idea books," which they use as a method of recording the ideas or problems that serve as a source. One group of chemists and chemical engineers at the Dow Chemical Company (called the Innovation Group) takes this approach. They consider those problems on which they are currently working to be "first-order problems." These problems are examined for their problem-stimulation value until "second-order problems" are developed.

The second-order problems are examined as a source for third-order problems.

## *Various problem-solving approaches*

The problem-solving methods now being taught could well be classified as "traditional" and "new." Traditional methods are more rational, and logical; the "new" methods attempt to train the individual through freeing him from his emotional inhibitions. Some of these methods concentrate specifically on some *portion* of the creative process—on the problem-statement part, for example.

The concept of the creative process used in General Electric's program, reported by E. K. von Fange, seems to be a traditional one involving the following nine steps:

1. Define the problem
   a. Establish the problem
   b. Investigate approaches
2. Search for methods
3. Evaluate all methods
4. Generalize the results
5. Select method
6. Make the preliminary design
7. Perform test and evaluation
8. Generalize the results
9. Find the best solution

This approach does not attempt to release the force of the unconscious or the preconscious for use in the creative process.

Two methods which seem to differ from the usual problem-solving approaches but which apparently do not attempt to alter emotional dispositions are "attribute listing" and "morphological analysis."

"Attribute listing" is defined by Robert Platt Crawford (1954) of the University of Nebraska. An example of "attribute listing" can be seen in the search for a better method of cutting cheese. Here, the initial problem was how to develop a better knife; this problem led to another, how to arrange to use more knives on each piece of cheese. Then the attributes of a better wedge were listed; next, the undesirable attributes—to be eliminated—were listed. Finally, the familiar five-and-dime cheese cutting wire was produced. The attribute-listing method involves looking at all aspects of a situation: by progressive examination of the desirable and undesirable attributes of the various aspects of the problem, the solution is reached.

A somewhat similar method is "morphological analysis" (proposed by Fred Zwicky of the Aerojet Corporation in California, 1957). This method involves combining the major attributes of the major variables of a problem into a grid so that all possible combinations can be considered. For example, when the problem of how to fabricate a new type of building material is at issue, the essential attributes of the material, the methods of bonding material, and methods of fabricating are plotted on an extensive grid which provides over 1,000 combinations to consider. This technique facilitates the imagination by enabling the individual to focus on one aspect of the situation at a time.

There are two approaches: "brainstorming" (Osborn, 1957) and "synectics" (Gordon, 1961) which contain within their methodology the objective of freeing a person from the usual inhibitions that operate to block his creative process. The primary aim of the "brainstorming" approach is to free the individual, whether working alone or as a member of a group, from the effect of using critical judgment prematurely. Either an individual or a working group is asked to express ideas readily, spontaneously, and uncritically until a quantity of ideas is available to be judged. The research of Sidney Parnes (1959) of the Creative Problem Solving Institute indicates the positive effects of "brainstorming"; this research also provides evidence that individuals working alone often accumulate more and better ideas than they do when working in a group. Osborn and his colleagues have developed a variety of methods for stimulating the imagination. One of these, called "Check List for New Ideas," provides the individual with a series of questions to ask himself about the product he is examining, such as: How could it be put to other uses? How could it be modified? etc. Within the "brainstorming" context we find methods similar to the "attribute listing" methods given above.

In a recent book, *Synectics: The Development of Creative Capacity,* W. J. J. Gordon (1961) outlines a training program for helping people become more creative. The word "synectics" means the joining together of different and apparently irrelevant elements. The word is used in the context "synectics theory" to describe a view of man's creative process; it is also used to describe a training program developed from the theory.

Synectics theory is based on three assumptions: (1) that the creative process in human beings can be concretely described and that this description can be used to develop teaching methods that will increase the creative output of both individuals and groups, (2) that invention in the arts and in the sciences are much alike and are achieved by the same fundamental intellectual processes, and (3) that the individual creative process is much like the creative process in a group.

The advocates of synectics theory believe that people who understand what psychological processes are required can markedly increase their own creative efficiency. In the creative process the emotional aspects of the task are seen as more important than the rational aspects. Understanding these emotional aspects of the task is considered most necessary if success in problem solving is to be increased.

From research that began in 1944 and has continued since that time with various groups, Gordon and his colleagues have analyzed the thought processes of a person's activity during invention, and have selected four psychological states that characterize the creative process. The first of these states is called "detachment-involvement"; in this state a person tries to remove a problem from its usual context, in order to see it differently, and then to become sufficiently involved with it to develop new insights. In one instance, involvement requires one to imagine how he would feel if he were a spring. The second mental state is "deferment," which is resistance to the first solution that comes to mind in favor of waiting to see if a better one comes along. The third mental state is "speculation" or permitting the mind to run free. The fourth mental state is called "autonomy of the object," which is what happens when ideas about the solution of a problem seem to crystallize and develop a life of their own.

The members of synectics group are very wise in their recognition of the futility of merely recommending to people that they become involved, or speculate, or detach themselves. Accordingly, they have developed what are called "operational mechanisms" to help produce each of these mental states. Making the familiar strange and the strange familiar are synectic goals. Four mechanisms are used to help make the familiar strange. *Personal analogy* is used, as in imagining how one would react if one were a molecule. *Direct analogy* is used, as in studying the way a clam opens and shuts in the process of designing a self-closing dispenser. *Symbolic analogy* is used, as in making a comparison with the Indian rope trick in the process of designing a hydraulic jack. And finally, *fantasy* is encouraged— the free and capricious use of the imagination. In synectic training, efforts are made to go beyond the traditional or "expert" way of viewing the world to a "fresh" view of things, or to see things as they were before they became coated with layers of opinions about how they ought to be. Hasty attempts to say "That is irrelevant to this problem" are discouraged in synectics training. Play with apparent irrelevancies is used extensively to generate energy for problem solving and to get new views of the problem. Members of synectics training groups are taught to be on the lookout for the pleasurable feelings that signal the arrival of insights.

The approach of the training outlined above goes considerably beyond "brainstorming" methods and provides specific techniques for using the vast storehouse of man's vivid associations. This approach is quite foreign to the usual concept of the scientific method, but it seems most logical when compared to the processes remembered by inventors. It is based upon analysis of these processes, and particularly on A. H. Maslow's (1957, 1959a) concepts of "primary creativeness" and "secondary creativeness." "Primary creativeness" is seen as coming from those who can play, fantasy, and be spontaneous. "Secondary creativeness" is seen as coming from those who over-control their emotions, those who can't play very well.

Perhaps the newest training methods for unlocking the unconscious forces for use in the creative process will come from experimentation with drugs such as psilocybin, which has been isolated as an active principle of the mushroom used by Mexican Indians in religious ceremonies for many centuries (Hollister, 1961). Evidence indicates that dreamy, ruminative, and introspective periods are some of the somatic effects of this drug. Timothy Leary has been an active researcher in this area.

## *Programs to provide personal insight and to reduce hindrances*

Since creativity is primarily individual, it is wise to assume that some training focused on the individual rather than on the group will be effective in facilitating creativity. Some programs are, therefore, designed to help individuals gain insight into their own personality attributes, interests, and abilities, as they relate to the creative process. Each individual needs his own program, constructed on the basis of knowledge of the inner conditions that hinder or even inhibit creativity.

Lack of self-confidence, fear of being dominant, and tendencies to be too dependent are some of the emotional factors that block. Professor John Arnold (1962) of Stanford University lists a number of difficulties which he calls "perceptual barriers." Among these are: isolating a problem from its natural context, narrowing a problem too much, and failure to use all the senses in getting data.

Many people have a self-concept that poses a dilemma: on the one hand, they hold exceptionally high standards for their work; on the other hand, they expect to engage themselves in a wide variety of projects. Some persons caught in this dilemma have learned effective methods for handling the conflict. For example, one can learn to "package" one's projects into manageable parts; by completing one part at a time, one can handle a number of tasks without lowering of standards.

Others have a self-concept involving exceptionally high standards not of work but of social conduct; they may be partially blocked, for example, by firmly held values, which do not allow them to be aggressive toward others. Some of such people have learned to distinguish aggression that stems from a particular idea from generalized aggressive behavior and so have been able to alter their approach.

Some scientists permit their work to be blocked by boredom, which they often attribute to external circumstances. Others profess a desire for research freedom, yet do not know how to use it. Some are so eager for success that their own eagerness blocks them from reflective thought. Others are so busy fighting off administrative opposition that they have little energy left for creative activity.

Individual training programs will require that each individual be provided with information about himself to use in his self-appraisal. As indicated in Chapter 2 of this book, many psychological tests and questionnaires for self-appraisal are available. And private sessions will be needed with psychiatrists, psychologists, or others qualified to assist individuals in self-examination.

Groups of scientists can either facilitate or hinder the creative process of the individuals included in their group. Supervisory and management personnel can also either facilitate or block. Training programs designed to increase individuals' sensitivity to how they affect and are affected by others in a group program, such as those conducted every summer at Bethel, Maine, by the National Training Laboratories of the National Education Association, have as their primary aim the "freeing" of the individual in the group situation.

It is quite possible that programs in the entire area of individual development will be most rewarding.

### Preparing to influence others to be receptive

It is quite possible that some of the best ideas in the nation are held by individuals who are not able to gain an audience. Programs have therefore been organized to help scientists learn to influence others to accept and support their ideas. In some instances young scientists are given opportunities to try out various methods of expressing their ideas in efforts to get resources to do research. Other programs are designed to help the scientist describe his findings so they can be understood and used.

## The direction of future research

This brief survey of methods suggests that the *top priority* task in this area is to discover other methods *now in use* in various disciplines and to assess the utility of these methods. The growing awareness of the need for increased creativity leads one to expect that many unpublicized methods exist at this time. These methods should be shared and evaluated against suitable criteria in well-designed research studies.

Another major task is to match the content of such training methods with the intellectual and emotional qualities thought to be needed. A survey of methods suggests that more training is needed in the development of divergent thinking skills. There seems to be even more evidence that our people need training in the development of the qualities of independence, spontaneity, and reduction of self-concern, all of which seem necessary for creative problem solving. Appropriate techniques in the emotional areas might represent the greatest innovation in training methodology.

A third major task is to increase cooperation between psychology and other disciplines. Each discipline may require training in a variety of problem-solving approaches. These disciplines may also require different constellations of emotional dispositions and environmental conditions. It may be wise for the National Science Foundation and other agencies to encourage separate studies of creativity training for physicists, for example, rather than to assume that the same training methods will be applicable to all fields.

A fourth major task to be undertaken is to study the duration of training results. How long-lasting, for example, are the results achieved from training designed to increase problem-solving flexibility?

A fifth major task is to relate the training needs of youth with the training needs of adults. This is the task of discovering how to relate training programs geared to developing the intellectual and emotional dispositions necessary for creativity to the developmental processes of adults and children.

Five major tasks have just been stated. Using the "thinking factors–emotional factors–climate factors" analysis posed at the beginning of this chapter, one can develop a host of specific questions that might be asked and hypotheses that might be tested. For example, what is the relationship between the ability to do divergent thinking and democratic character structure? Does an authoritarian classroom climate have a stimulating, neutral, hostile, or other effect on the ability to assimilate cognitive material versus the ability to do divergent thinking?

A series of questions offered below might be used in preliminary assessment of the quality and quantity of creativity stimulated in a college course.

1. How often does the student have the experience of receiving data that are incompatible with conclusions he had previously reached on the basis of earlier data, in order to test his ability to integrate the new evidence? (Such exercises should provide him with experience that is considerably like the reality he will ultimately face; the "Now what do you think?" type of question.)

2. How often is the student required to consider what would happen if the recommendations he suggests were carried out? (Rather than have him merely make recommendations based on the application of his scientific knowledge, he should be required to consider the effects of his recommendations; the "What would happen if?" type of question.)

3. How often has the student been asked to combine two old ideas and come up with something new? When his performance is measured, is this kind of creative activity rewarded?

4. How often has the student had the experience of taking a theory, a finding, a product, etc., and asking himself such questions as, "In what other ways could this be useful? What else would this explain?"

5. Has the student been taught the wisdom of interspersing work on one problem with work in some other area, to permit the incubation period that seems so necessary for the production of creative solutions? (When the individual engineer, his peers, and company pressure all combine to force a solution, this useful practice is often lost in the momentary urgency. Acceptance of the value of interspersed work should permit the reduction of guilt when a man is working on a project which has no perceived social urgency. "Am I pushing too hard on this particular problem?" and "Is now the time to let it stew awhile?" are pertinent questions.)

6. Since considerable evidence indicates that some of the most ingenious problem solutions come at "off beat" moments and are often classified as intuitive insights, have scientists been taught to respect their intuitions as a genuine thought process? Can we hope that the next generation of scientists will have as much respect for their emotions and intuitions as they have for their reason? Does the scientist respect his own ideas well enough to take the trouble to write them down?

7. Has the student been taught that it is appropriate for him to strive to be creative; or has he determined, from the models he sees before him, that when creativity is mentioned, it is assumed to be the province of other fields? (Some men seem to believe either that creativity is something to which only the brilliant should aspire or that it is monopolized by the arts. Some read the growing volume of literature as an academic exercise rather than for hints about improving their own creativity. Some admire being productive and remaining an Indian among chiefs; they then argue in favor of allocating creative activities to others. "I'll aspire to be creative too," should be a more common resolve.)

8. Has the student been taught that creating is a hazardous social activity, and has he prepared himself for the negativism he will encounter? (Experience indicates that for every innovator there is

a host of critics. Many highly trained men have suppressed their ideas because they hate to appear a fool. Training courses should provide experience in standing up to or working around criticism, so that the student will not enter cold reality without some effective tactics. It may be easier to prepare a young scientist to meet his critics than to hope to dampen the critics—there are just too many of them.)

9. Has the student been taught the likelihood that the conditions he finds most conducive to the emergence of creative ideas may be unique to him? (We hope that, once he discovers such conditions, he will feel free to accommodate himself even if his behavior seems odd. We can also hope that his colleagues will respect his idiosyncracies.)

10. Has the teaching environment provided sufficient materials, models, etc., so that the student can manipulate the materials as well as think about them? (There is some evidence to suggest that some persons get their best ideas when they are actually handling materials.)

11. How much is the student taught to ask questions, and to what extent is asking questions that the professor can't answer rewarded as an intellectual activity?

12. How often does the student finish a course with several problems in mind that the course couldn't answer? (Perhaps it would be an innovation in teaching methodology if one of the questions on a final examination were, "Outline three problems in this field that are on the horizon, and indicate how you might try to solve one of them.")

13. Since "reflective thought" is a necessary ingredient for the emergence of creative ideas, is the individual provided with the time and other necessary conditions to indulge in this activity?

14. Since the problems in the reality he will face when he embarks on his professional career are likely to have a long history and to defy quick solution, what simulated long-range problem has he faced in his training? (Perhaps it would also be a fruitful innovation if each sophomore were expected to select a problem on which to work during the rest of his undergraduate days, with one of the

criteria for determining the adequacy of his preparation being the nature of his success on this long-term problem.)

It is also possible to visualize that each major curriculum could be examined to determine the range of problem-solving techniques employed and the relative effectiveness of each of them. Calvin Taylor's paper, "Effects of Instructional Media on Creativity: A Look at Possible Positive and Negative Effects" (1962b, prepared for the St. Louis seminar on a theory of instructional materials, in connection with the ASCD, NEA project supported by the U.S. Office of Education) contains valuable information that could be used to develop methods for measuring the "creativity stimulating" aspect of various instructional media.*

## ASPECTS OF THE INDUSTRIAL RESEARCH CLIMATE THAT AFFECT CREATIVITY

The first two paragraphs of the subcommittee report by Kuhn and Kaplan (1959) on environmental conditions affecting creativity in the report of the third Utah Conference report provide the orientation of this section:

* *Editor's Note:* One of the many points raised in this paper is the potential value of live discussion materials in texts and other scholarly reports. To our knowledge, no one has made a study to determine whether the more formal parts or the live discussion parts of a report have more creative material in them per unit of publication space. We feel that discussion material serves both to provoke more thoughts in the minds of readers and to show them how crude or how well-grounded is the subject matter being presented. During the small conference which preceded the final preparation of this book, McPherson suggested that the material finally used might prove to be less creative and refreshing than those comments which somehow did not become a part of the written volume.

This criticism, however, could not be strongly leveled at the 1955, 1957, and 1959 Utah creativity reports, since nearly all the discussion was transcribed and published. We strongly suspect that the liveliness and unexpectedness of the discussion in the Utah reports is one of the main reasons that these reports have been almost self-propelling. In fact, students in creativity seminars

Unlike the problems of criteria, predictors, and education in the sciences, the problems of environmental conditions have hardly been studied. There are several useful discussions of the socio-economic conditions that promoted the Scientific Revolution of the seventeenth century, as well as a few recent studies of working conditions, morale, and productivity in individual industrial and government laboratories. But almost no other guide posts exist. The man who wishes to understand, for example, why some cultures, like our own, have been particularly productive of technological innovation but conspicuously backward in contributions to basic science can scarcely find basis for even an educated guess. The same is true for the man who wishes to discriminate between the sorts of scientific work effectively undertaken by a group and those that respond best to concentrated individual work. Yet the ability to answer questions like these will inevitably affect the nation's ability to utilize its creative scientific potential.

Under these circumstances our committee's first and most important recommendation is a plea. Research on the general environmental conditions—cultural, professional, and institutional—conducive to first rate scientific research needs major encouragement. We are aware of no area in the social sciences where research is simultaneously so vitally needed and so much neglected. Clearly most of the participants in this conference can not and should not undertake that research themselves. Some will contribute significantly to it, but the joint efforts of sociologists and social psychologists, of economic historians, and historians of science will also be required. Nevertheless, this group can help to see that such research is undertaken by recording its conviction that both the fruitful direction and the application of its own research will benefit from a greatly increased understanding of the role of the environment in the effective utilization of potential scientific talent.

The immediate climate for the scientist may be looked at from the point of view of the effects of the following: (1) corporate

---

have repeatedly stated that they felt as though they could step right into the discussion about creativity as they read these three transcribed conference reports. We doubt that a teacher could teach solely by authoritarian means if his students had texts with such discussion materials.

policies, (2) immediate laboratory policies, (3) laboratory supervision, and (4) laboratory group. To these can be added the effects of the community (how much involvement with science the community will sanction) and the effect of the wife and family. It is also possible to examine all aspects of a scientist's climate and make an overall research-determined evaluation of it (stimulating, supportive, neutral, hostile, or destructive) as indicated at the beginning of this chapter.

William Reed Smith (1959) reported at the third Utah Conference on some possible favorable and unfavorable conditions that affect scientific creativity. This report of conditions came from an analysis of attitudes expressed in interviews obtained from over 200 physical research scientists in two basic research centers. The following favorable and unfavorable conditions were reported by Smith:

The Stein Research Environment Survey, developed by Morris I. Stein and currently being published and administered by Science Research Associates, Inc. in Chicago, is perhaps the most comprehensive device for use in systematically appraising the research environment. This 189-item anonymous survey asks the scientists for judgments about the following aspects of his environment: (1) the effect on the scientist of the company for which he works, the research organization in the company, the particular sub-organization he belongs to, and his individual influence, (2) the scope of the problems undertaken by the various levels of research organizations, (3) the kinds of abilities and activities that make for success in the organization coupled with a judgment of how well he individually meets these requirements, (4) the quality of certain conditions and auxiliary services (e.g., patent-tracing facilities and service), (5) methods of problem selection, (6) amount of pressure experienced, (7) the distribution of time in various activities, (8) the nature of the relationships between people in the laboratory, (9) competence of colleagues and superiors, (10) quality of communications, and (11) factors that facilitate or impede creativity. A Survey of Administrators also accompanies this survey. When the results of this survey are reported, along with studies of relationships between these results and such factors as the disposition of the individual scientist

| Unfavorable conditions | Favorable conditions |
|---|---|
| 1. Instability of the budget | 1. Certain individual freedoms |
| 2. Conflict between the demands of management activities and research activities | 2. Intellectual challenges of the work |
| | 3. Location and certain facilities |
| 3. Inadequacies in supportive groups and procedures | 4. Relative stability of civil service employment |
| 4. Inadequacies in compensation and other attractions | 5. Encouragement of continual training |
| 5. Lack of professional internship for young scientists | |
| 6. Poor communications with scientists | |
| 7. Inadequacy of physical facilities | |
| 8. Dearth of suitable recognition | |
| 9. Exclusion of scientists from high-level decision making regarding scientific problems | |
| 10. Insufficient long-range planning in the total scientific program | |
| 11. Interference between contract monitoring and regular research activities | |
| 12. Inefficiency in selection and placement programs | |
| 13. Lack of personnel counseling for scientists | |

and the success of the organization taking the survey, the "climate area" of the creativity domain should be considerably illuminated.

It is wise to assume that the psychological needs of scientists are much like those of other human beings. At times, apparently, scientists have been treated as a breed apart, who would produce if they were left alone and not bothered. It has become increasingly apparent that capable supervision, adequate rewards and recognition, sensible communication, and an organization that does not frustrate their efforts are needs vital to the success of most scientists. It is perhaps not so much in his basic needs but more in the detailed means by which his needs are met, that the scientist differs from persons in other occupational endeavors. If one accepts this idea, then the current findings of social psychology can be easily translated into the creation of a climate conducive to scientific creativity and to creativity in nonscientific endeavors.

By using an accumulation of evidence from current articles (some of which result from fairly well-controlled studies and some which might best be classified as of the "arm-chair" type), one can develop a list of questions that may be useful in appraising the climate for scientific creativity at different levels. Analogous questions could be raised about the climate for creativeness in nonscientific fields.

## Climate at the national level

1. How is the public informed about needed inventions?
2. How well is the public informed about how to seek either federal or foundation funds to support their ideas?
3. What funds are available for the support of private inventors?
4. How easily can inventors become aware of how to seek a patent?
5. What funds are available for the protection of the inventor's ideas? (No doubt there are many other questions that could be asked at the national level, and perhaps the answers to the questions listed here are available but are not adequately communicated to the people.)

## Climate at the corporate level

1. Do top-management officials appear to operate on the belief that creativity is to be expected from everyone? (There is some evidence to indicate that having creative ideas is considered the province of the organization's scientists. So many nodules of creativity are required to bring an idea from its initial stages to its final

productive stages that it is much healthier if all members of the organization are treated as creative or potentially so.)

2. Do top-management officials realize the relative effects of various kinds of business organizations on creativity? (The usual rigid pyramidal structures seem to inhibit, whereas the structure of many small businesses overlapping within the large corporation seems to give freedom.)

3. Do corporate officials recognize the possible effect of urgency on the creative process? (It would be wise if pleas for action were based upon such recognition. There is perhaps a range of problems that respond differently to the effect of pressure.)

4. What system of rewards does the corporation use to motivate its scientists?

Some organizations recognize the scientists' need for evidence of progress. Various solutions are used. In one corporation the following three channels for advancement of scientific personnel are available: (1) scientific advancement, (2) supervisory advancement, and (3) administrative advancement. Within the scientific-advancement category there are these levels: chemist, associate chemist, research associate, senior research associate, research scientists, and senior research scientist. We could wish that the concept of the "ideal scientist" would exclude the kind of status-seeking such a system implies, but scientists too live within our society. There is evidence also that those researchers who fight for ideas are often rewarded no more than the passive researchers who do what they are told.

### Climate at the supervisory level

1. Does the supervisor possess the skills required to help a subordinate define a problem? (Often laboratory supervisors, asked to assist in defining a problem or to appraise a scientist's progress on a problem, are not sufficiently aware of the nature of the problem area to fulfill either request.)

2. Does the supervisor understand the emotional requirements of creative activity sufficiently well to interpret the normality of these reactions to his subordinates? (The wisdom of not pushing too hard for a solution, the depression that occurs after problem solution, and the need for what appears to be "irrelevant activity" must be understood.)

3. Does the supervisor understand that when his ideas of how the project should be done differ from his subordinates' ideas, there need not be a conflict? Does he understand that there are times when the joining of his ideas with those of his subordinates gives rise to a more imaginative solution than that possessed by either of them at the beginning?

4. Does the supervisor teach the value of high-level personal involvement in a task, or does he seem to ignore the need for involvement by assuming that it is easy for a researcher to shift his research emphasis?

5. Does the supervisor see the virtue in providing some scientists with partners who can help "promote" ideas with influential persons, or see the virtue in helping with promotion himself? Or is he apt to leave all promoting up to the scientist, who is often unable to perform this activity effectively?

6. Does he recognize that, although lack of enthusiasm for the work may be an individual problem, he can, by bringing in new personnel with different ideas or consultants with a different point of view, increase the enthusiasm of his group?

7. Does the supervisor understand the nature of individual differences in the needs of his personnel?

There is some evidence that industry has spent much more time in the selection and training of foremen and production managers than in the selection and training of research supervisory personnel. The laboratory supervisor needs to realize that certain of his personnel will thrive under a hands-off policy while others will flounder. He needs to maintain a sensitivity to the effects of policies on individuals. Scientists, like all industrial personnel, desire an adequate mutual appraisal of their work. Supervisors need to develop a repertoire of skills to meet the idiosyncratic evaluation needs of their personnel.

8. How well is the supervisor prepared to teach the young scientist about the nature of the industrial research reality? It seems inevitable that management personnel will evince more enthusiasm about ideas that hold the promise of immediate profit. Young researchers need to learn how to "endure" under such circumstances. At best, the odds are that "only one out of every eight [industrial researchers] is successful," and therefore the young researcher must be prepared to engage in a difficult endeavor.

The work of Rensis Likert and his colleagues at the Institute for Social Research at the University of Michigan is the primary source for the following questions, which can be used to evaluate the supervisory personnel in research laboratories (Likert, 1961). The other questions are derived from other sources as well as the author's own experience.

9. Is the supervisor able to define his efforts to build an effective work group?

10. Does he help maintain high-performance goals for his group?

11. Does he show an active interest in the work of the members of the group, yet still maintain a "hands-off" policy?

12. Does he exert too much pressure on his group?

13. Can his supervision be characterized as being "too much close supervision"?

14. Are the objectives for his group clear and understood?

15. How is he seen by his subordinates? Cooperative? Democratic?

16. Does he participate in training his subordinates for better positions?

17. Does he take the time to discuss personal problems with his subordinates when they solicit help?

18. Does his group believe he wishes to get their ideas, and does he take appropriate action on their ideas?

19. Does he give information freely to his employees or does he tend to keep things "close to the chest"?

20. Is he successful in getting a hearing for his group's ideas with the higher levels of management? Does he have influence?

## Climate at the level of group functioning

The following list of questions has also been derived from the work of Likert and his colleagues. Research needs to be done to explore the relationship between these group aspects and the nature and amount of the creative products produced by the group members.

1. When you look at the group, can you see that it contains members who can perform a variety of needed roles? (It has initiators, information givers and seekers, opinion givers and seekers, coordinators, orientors, evaluators, energizers, encouragers, harmonizers, compromisers, etc.)

2. Is there a relaxed working relationship among the members?

3. Is the group loyal to its membership and loyal to the leader?

4. Do the members and leaders have a high degree of confidence and trust in each other?

5. Have they managed to make their values and goals mesh with those of neighboring groups?

6. Will each member extend himself to meet the objectives of the group?

7. Does a supportive climate exist in the group?

8. When there are the inevitable and useful differences of opinion, is the focus on arriving at sound solutions or on interpersonal conflict?

9. Are the efforts for personal achievement channeled constructively?

10. Is the group eager to help each member develop to his full potential?

11. Does each member accept willingly and without resentment

the goals and expectations that he and his group establish for themselves?

12. Does the group set high performance standards for itself? Are these goals high enough to elicit top performance and not so high as to produce too much anxiety?

13. Does the group carry with it the feeling that "we can accomplish the impossible"?

14. Do the members of the group give each other help in meeting the work goals?

15. Does the group attach high value to new creative approaches and solutions to its problems and to the problems of the organization?

16. Does the group also value "constructive conformity"?

17. Is there a strong motivation on the part of each member to communicate fully and frankly to the group all the information that is relevant and of value to the group's activity?

18. Is there a high motivation to receive information?

19. Is there a high level of communication to the leader directly (or indirectly by expressions to the group) about what needs to be done?

20. Is there a desire on the part of group members to influence and be influenced?

21. Is the group too easily swayed? Or does it examine carefully the ideas that it welcomes?

### Future research on "climate"

The *major* task in this area is to work toward programs designed to change people's attitudes toward those who are creative and to increase the creative expectations of persons in all disciplines.

A second major task is to emphasize the idea that neither manipulation of facilities nor arguing of pros and cons of decentralization versus centralization is nearly so important as improvement in the quality of interaction between the potentially creative person and the "significant others" in his environment—namely, his boss and his work group.

A third major task is to learn more about the other significant aspects of the research climate that seem central for the promotion of creativity.

A fourth major task should be research into the ways and means of reducing time spent in sending and receiving communications and in other administrative activities. Coupled with this effort is the need to prepare our young scientists to use the freedom they are given.

A fifth task is for some organization to attempt to incorporate into its climate all the factors felt to be generally positive according to the best educated estimates, to see whether large or only minor or negligible changes in creativity occur through "proper" manipulation of the total external environment.

In a sense the conclusion of this chapter returns to its point of departure. Progress in improving the creativity of our people will be obtained most effectively if we remember that we must simultaneousy progress in the preparation of the individual, from both an intellectual and an emotional point of view, and in the provision of a stimulating climate.

*chapter* **5**

# CRITERIA

# OF CREATIVITY

*Hubert E. Brogden*

**U.S. ARMY PERSONNEL RESEARCH OFFICE**

*Thomas B. Sprecher*

**WESTERN ELECTRIC COMPANY**

THE AUTHORS believe that, of the general research problems discussed in this book, the most pressing is the determination of criteria of creativity. The quality of research on predictor tests and other measuring devices, on education, on training, and on environmental conditions depends, in the last analysis, on the adequacy of the criteria used. Since the criterion is the yardstick by which other measures tentatively advanced as predictors or manipulators are evaluated, establishment of criteria of creativity is fundamental to all research in this area. In spite of this importance, research studies specifically directed toward criteria of creativity are rarely found in the literature; furthermore, most investigators devote little time or attention to the development of the criteria that they use. The need for research on criteria of creativity is therefore great.[1]

The contrast between the investigator who looks for a single criterion and the investigator who looks for *criteria* may be only of degree, but it is important. For to assume that *creativity*—or *success, salesmanship, or leadership*—is unitary may be to overestimate the possibilities for coordination of thinking at our present state of knowledge. "Creativity," a controversial and nebulous word, has different meanings to different people, and the existence of multiple criteria should be recognized.

This chapter is concerned more with scientific creativity than with the creativity of teachers, administrators, artists, authors, and others;[2] this limits the problem, but, even so, a variety of possible criteria emerge. Almost all workers agree that one important characteristic of the creative scientist is the *originality* of his product; most would add that the *value* of his product, variously conceived, is also important. But is the creative person the same as the productive person? Minimal productivity is probably necessary before a person's creativity can be identified and recognized by society. There may

[1] This chapter covers the major ideas and comments reported in the 1959 University of Utah Criterion Committee Report. Those participating in that committee report were Allen Gamble, Lindsey R. Harmon, Cecil Mullins, Plinio Prioreschi, Thomas B. Sprecher (main reporter), and Calvin W. Taylor.

[2] The authors believe that most of the discussion in this chapter is applicable to other disciplines and activities as well as to science.

also prove to be at least a moderately high correlation between productivity and creativity. Nevertheless, many researchers choose to emphasize the exceptional cases: the very productive worker whose contributions are not individually creative, the creative worker whose quantity of production is small.

Discussions of who is creative or what products are creative are frequently heated and emotional. There are at least two causes for this. One cause is the importance of these questions. The second, however, is the absence of empirical knowledge; for, in the subjective opinion and absence of knowledge, personal anecdotes hold sway.

Basic studies devoting broad-scale attention to criterion problems have been few, although at least one criterion is usually involved in any empirical research study published in psychology. Studies that are specifically devoted to criteria or to a thorough study of a single criterion, and studies that invest a substantial part of their resources on aspects of the criterion problem are identified with only fourteen investigators[3] in the area of scientific creativity.

The earliest investigator was Terman in 1925; the next was Flanagan in 1949; the next was Taaffe in 1953; and the remaining ten all reported in the period from 1957 to 1961. Buel, Flanagan, Harmon, Herman, Sprecher, Stoltz, Calvin Taylor, and Donald Taylor have all applied major portions of their study resources and/or consistent effort to the study of criterion problems as such. But the contributions of at least four of these fourteen investigators have centered around doctoral dissertations—which hardly implies concerted institutional effort.

As an example of the complexity of the criterion problem, con-

[3] The complete list is as follows: Buel, 1960, 1961; Flanagan, 1949; Guilford, 1963; Harmon, 1958; Herman, 1959; Holland & Astin, 1961b; Shockley, 1957; Sprecher, 1959a, 1959b; Stoltz, 1958, 1959a, 1959b; Taaffe, 1953; C. W. Taylor, Smith, Ghiselin, Sheets, & Cochran, 1958; C. W. Taylor, Smith, & Ghiselin, 1963; Donald Taylor, 1958; Terman, 1925b, 1957b; Torrance, 1963.

Although Flanagan's work was concerned primarily with productivity in research, the importance and thoroughness of his study and the high degree of overlap with creativity make it extremely relevant.

sider the study by Calvin Taylor, Smith, and Ghiselin (1963) of 56 variables characteristic of 166 research scientists. Included in this extensive list of criterion variables were many aspects of research products, a variety of ratings from different sources which included self-evaluations, and a number of variables related to organizational status. Taylor's results show that a set of criteria as inclusive as this requires many dimensions by which to show its interrelations, and is not readily simplified to any single criterion. Agreement between ratings of individuals and ratings of products was not necessarily high. In the light of Taylor's findings, it appears that many criterion variables often used alone for purposes of evaluation are in reality incomplete, failing to cover factors that should be included.

A guide to the variety of criterion variables that can and should be considered is presented in the accompanying outline. This outline of variables will be the basis for discussion of the varied aspects of criteria in this chapter.

It is no accident that, in the outline under Area I, What Is Measured, the *products* category is placed before the *persons* category. Although the goal of this chapter is to indicate a variety of approaches to criteria, there is little question that the approach through the product will most closely approximate the ultimate criterion. We know that certain individuals are creative because they have produced one outstandingly creative product or have consistently produced many such products. Despite the fact that products lie at the heart of criterion problems, little work has been done with them. This neglect should be corrected. To our knowledge, no experimentation either with product rating or with deliberate changes in products to determine the effect of such manipulation has been carried out in connection with scientific creativity, productivity, or research work in general. In art, some promising work was presented in Burkhart's second chapter (1962). But the heart of the criterion problem has almost always been neglected. Later in this chapter, in connection with product rating, specific suggestions will be presented for such research.

Problems in Methodology, referred to in Area II of the outline, are vital. Standard and perennial problems in psychology are reliability of measurement and the avoidance of bias in measurement.

Area III in the outline, Control Variables, is useful primarily for completeness. At the present state of knowledge, despite work by Mosing (1958) which showed that different educational backgrounds neither cause individuals to perform differently on a creativity test nor substantially change that test's validity for any of the disciplines studied, our safest assumption is that the criteria suitable for a physicist are different from those for a biologist, those for a professor in a university different from those for a supervisor in an industrial organization, etc.

As various areas of research activity are discussed in this chapter, emphasis on some of these will be apparent. The emphasis here is on what is now important, but this is not to deny the value of work in other areas—no best guess at any one time is likely to be a best guess for all time. And, any day, someone's creativity in dealing with the criterion problems of creativity may provide important new concepts of which the authors of this report are unaware. Such creativity and experimentation must be encouraged. The repeated neglect, however, of the core of the criterion problem does suggest that real opportunities for major advance lie there.

## OUTLINE OF VARIABLES INVOLVED IN CRITERIA OF CREATIVITY[4]

I. What is measured
  A. Products
    1. Direct products
        a. Absolute value regardless of input cost
        b. Relative value, taking input costs into account
    2. Supplementary products (serendipity)
    3. Aspects of products
          Novelty (personal or social); number of products; comprehensiveness; generalizability; new implications;

---

[4] This outline was adapted from that presented by the criterion committee at the third (1959) University of Utah conference on the Identification of Creative Scientific Talent (C. W. Taylor, 1959).

surprise; value (immediate or long range, and social, economic, or scientific); informational value
  B. Persons
    1. As representative of products
    2. As representative of processes
II. Methodology
  A. Source of the value judgment
    Supervisors; peers; monitors; organizational records; self; historical records; honors and awards
  B. Qualifications of the source
    Scientific knowledge if a person; general scientific-society acceptability if a particular formal kind of recognition; opportunity for observation; objectivity; skill in making judgments; "takes one to know one"; importance of various qualities rated to the judge himself
  C. Reliability and bias
  D. Overlap of criteria
  E. Scaling and weighting methods
III. Control variables
  A. Conventional biographical variables
    Age, length of service, sex, organizational level, position
  B. Time dimensions
    1. Stage of developmental process of individual or organization studied
       Successive or simultaneous samples at age level; cultural changes over time; concurrent versus predictive validation
    2. Successive refinement of criteria after initial approximation
    3. Time for adequate basis for judgment
       Need to get acquainted; sheer availability of observations of performance; time to settle into job to enable productivity
  C. Employer
    1. University or college

      2. Industrial organization
      3. Independent research laboratory
      4. Government
      5. Other
  D. Dimensions of field
      1. Mathematics
      2. Physics
      3. Chemistry
      4. Electronics
      5. Aerodynamics
      6. Biology
      7. Psychology
      8. Social Science
      9. Other
  E. Dimensions of research functions
      1. Theory
      2. Experimental
      3. Basic
      4. Applied
      5. Invention
      6. Design
  F. Opportunity variables
      1. Material resources
         Equipment; library; money available; etc.
      2. Psychological and social environment
         Change of cultural conditions; teamwork versus solitary
         work; compatibility with particular boss or work as-
         sociates; organizational policy and security regulations;
         etc.
      3. Difficulty or potential of problem area studied
         Amount of previous research in this area; availability
         of basic concepts in this area; complexity of field and
         variables studied; clarity of definition of the problem;
         ease of identifying and controlling stimulus or environ-
         mental characteristics of the problem; etc.

## DETAILED CONSIDERATION OF WHAT IS MEASURED

### Products

What do we mean by a product? A product may be a physical object—an article or patent—or it may be a theoretical system of the design of a mechanical linkage which is independent of its representation in a particular physical diagram. The product may be an equation or a new technique for controlling heat flow, but, in any case, it has an existence separate from the person who produced it. It can be transmitted and is not uniquely bound up with the life of an individual.

The distinction between the absolute value of a product and its relative value may be important, given a specific operational setting. In large part its importance is in reference to the input costs that must be taken into account in judging the product.

Sometimes input costs may be neglected. For many types of product it is difficult, impossible, or irrelevant to calculate the amount of input cost; for instance, the input cost in personal effort, time, and emotional stress that results in a work of art may, for society's purposes, be irrelevant. But where deliberate resources are allocated to achieve a given end, as on a production line or in the refinement of a particular invention, the likely or actual cost of the product is important. Excessive use of manpower, time, or money decreases the value of a solution to a problem, especially when these resources could be more profitably invested elsewhere.

One distinction, not made explicitly in the above outline, should nevertheless be mentioned, namely, that between products that occur naturally in the course of normal organizational effort and those which are specifically produced on request. Samples of a scientist's work can be deliberately obtained under a wide variety of circumstances with various controls and with various experimental manipulations, and can be used to measure the various aspects of creativity and productivity. A large number of criterion variables can be collected, using this approach. With work-sample measures, it is possible to ensure uniformity, equality of opportunity, and introduction of controls, which might otherwise be difficult or impossible to attain in testing.

Work samples may lack realism. Since they are obtained in a test-like situation where motivation is usually high, they may fail to show differences in productivity resulting from differences in motivation, work habits, and the like. It has been suggested that realism can be achieved without sacrificing the major advantages of the work sample: standard work assignments can be introduced into the on-the-job situation, with appropriate handling to ensure that the subject is unaware that he is being tested. This might be an excellent way of combining the best features of conventional work-sample measurement and assessment of the actual regular productivity of an individual.

Several specific proposed steps in research concerning scientific products will be listed here.[5] These are important for a full investigation of how well the various characteristics of products do indeed measure creative scientific accomplishment.

1. The question: What is the relation between amount of creative productivity and level of creativity? should be investigated.

2. The question: What is the relation between the diversity of an individual's products and the level of his creativity? should be investigated.

3. Scales for the evaluation of level of creativity of products, such as those suggested by Ghiselin and Lacklen,[6] should be developed.

4. Abbreviated procedures for product evaluation should be worked out, as a by-product of step 3 above.

[5] These proposals, adapted from the section of the 1959 Criterion Committee Report written by Lindsey R. Harmon, were worked out originally by the 1957 Criterion Committee for the University of Utah creativity reports.

[6] As noted in the 1959 Utah report (and in the introductory chapter of the present book), "Ghiselin's dictum was that the measure of creativity of an idea is the 'extent to which it restructures our universe of understanding.' Somewhat related is Lacklen's definition that the creativity of a contribution may be measured in terms of the extent of the area of science which it underlies; the more basic the contribution, the wider its effects."

5. Scales (as developed in step 3 above) should be "validated" against ratings of individuals who vary in their judged creativity.

6. The adequacy of official records for product evaluation should be investigated, to determine the amount and nature of errors of commission and omission.

## Supplementary products

Evaluation of the "supplementary products" of an individual's work involves the concept of "serendipity"—the art or knack of finding useful results when one is not looking for them. The distinction between direct products and supplementary products may or may not be important in a given setting. It is of potential importance, however, in distinguishing between creativity in research, where products are not immediately to be put to use and supplemental or indirect products are welcome, and creativity in applied science, where such results are often felt to be out of place. Supplemental results may, in long-range terms, be more important than direct results, but often, in an industrial setting where a specific operational problem or need is urgent, no supplementary products can be accepted as substitutes for direct products. The immediate goal must be met first, and a product or result that pays off in the distant future or for another division of the plant may be judged to be of very little value.

## Aspects of products

A variety of views may be taken toward a given product. A product may be valued for its novelty, for its size or quantity, for its breadth of application, or for its sheer value in terms of a more independent standard, such as number of dollars saved, or errors or accidents prevented.

One useful aspect of products, which Gamble brought out in the 1959 Criterion Committee Report, was "breadth of applicability." Gamble suggested that a "truly creative product or contribution has a characteristic of being itself creative in the sense that it generates additional creative activity. Other creative contributions follow in its wake. For example, an important new scientific theory provides new solutions to problems hitherto unsolved, new perceptions of problems hitherto unperceived, and new discoveries." As Gamble notes, this could provide a basis for measurement of levels or degrees of creativity: the lowest creative product simply solves the immediate problem to which it was directed; the highest creative product opens up a wide range of related problems and affects broad areas of thought.

## Persons as criteria: as representative of products

The next broad type of criterion, that of particular *persons,* is widely used by psychologists. The distinction between persons as seen through their products and persons as seen through their processes of work may be a somewhat arbitrary one, but it is useful. Attainments such as eminence in a field, training and educational status, and organizational responsibility are also thought of as "products" in this context, for they usually are rewards for achievements. These achievements are the central point, and the honors and awards, the higher stature, the widespread reputation, are secondary; they measure indirectly the "production" of these individuals. Studies such as those by Roe (1951a,b, 1953), Barron (1956, 1958), and K. E. Clark (1957), in which eminent individuals were nominated by peers in their field of endeavor, exemplify this approach.

Difficulties are sometimes encountered in working with ratings of individuals as such, because of complications arising from the halo factor. The importance and the obtainability of these kinds of data challenge experimenters to develop procedures that will maximize their usefulness. The hypothesis that creativity ratings provided by persons who are themselves creative will be superior (in the sense of being more consistent or more predictable) can be checked, in part, by empirical research.

Self-report techniques, whether the self-report is of traits or of more specific achievements and activities, should be a promising approach. Holland states that reports of a great number of specific achievements and activities in school can be obtained from college students, and that these are both consistent and capable of being predicted. Work by Van Zelst and Kerr (1954), Stein (1959a, 1963) and by Calvin W. Taylor, Smith, Ghiselin & Ellison (1961) suggests that self-ratings on characteristics may be at least as predictable as more conventional ratings.

Self-report of critical incidents, collected over an extensive time period, would be an interesting supplement to and contrast with other forms and sources of criteria.

Another approach possible in studying persons *as persons* involves the use of film clips. The same or equivalent research reports could be read by persons who vary in manner of reading, in poise, and in other personal characteristics. The object would be to determine the degree to which these factors influence the ratings of the person (or the ratings of the product presented, namely the report).

The critical-incident technique, as developed and used by Flanagan (1949) and his students, offers another procedure for determining the amount and kind of characteristics present in creative versus noncreative individuals. Its primary use so far has been to form generalized descriptions of occupational groups. Supervisors (peers could be used also) are interviewed frequently over a period of weeks; they are asked to report outstanding characteristics of their men not in the form of traits assessed but in the form of actual incidents (good or bad) noted. These are then tabulated under some acceptable set of categories. The tabulation could, however, be by individual rather than by group, and weighting of the various incidents reported for an *individual* might identify both types and levels of creativity among the group. For such purposes, the collection of incidents would need to be quite extensive. Telephone contact with the supervisor(s) might be an alternative to face-to-face interviews; this would leave more follow-up control with the investigator than he would have if he depended on the supervisor's own clerical record of incidents.

Observation of men at work by trained observers can be another approach to assessment of creative work. If a tentative agreed-upon definition of creativity is used (or later applied to a full record of the work activity observed and inferred), the estimating of the extent to which various individuals approximate to that definition could approach objectivity. Certainly estimates so standardized would supplement in a useful way the more conventional global and residual impressions of individuals that constitute "ratings" of scientists in most studies.

## *Persons as criteria: as representative of processes*

Process measures are one step further removed from the ultimate criterion of creativity, which is, presumably, bound up primarily with products. Brogden, in particular, believes that, at least in applied science, research should be concerned almost entirely with those things of practical importance whose production it seeks to facilitate. The aim of applied science is to produce end effects, and when the end effect in question has been defined and a measure of it found, this is the criterion. A criterion so developed is by definition made up of products or aspects of products, not of processes. Note, however, that the product need not be a physical object.

The term *process* is often used in contradistinction to *product;* it refers to aspects of on-the-job behavior that are necessary in order to achieve products. This, at least, is the way Brogden and Erwin Taylor (1952) have used the term in considering classification of criterion bias. Process variables in a job primarily concerned with motor skills might include deftness in the use of the hands or the grace, poise, and coordination with which the individual handles himself.

From this point of view (Brogden's), process variables are not, on their face at least, criterion variables. They do not, in other words, in themselves have social value, and they do not contribute directly to the stated objective.[7] It is, of course, possible that one could

[7] But Sprecher adds his view that they may. For example, an agreeable secretary has more social value than one who is equally "productive" but disagreeable.

demonstrate through empirical analysis that a process variable, or a set of them, was equivalent to a product variable but more reliable. From Brogden's point of view, however, process variables have no more standing as criterion variables than do predictors—or any set of variables taken at random.

It is Sprecher's belief, on the other hand, that process measures may well be involved in ultimate criteria. Process measures may help to identify people whom one would want to call more "truly" creative. If someone produces novel and valuable ideas with ease, he seems to be more creative than the individual who produces comparable ideas by dint of perseverance and hard work. *How* a product or end is achieved is of tremendous social (as well as moral) importance. Because of this, process information may frequently be central in studies of creativity in applied science. The practical man may want to know not only what has been achieved, but how: at what organizational, economic, or psychological cost. Too great a cost in process variables can negate product value.

Also, an experimenter may want to know how to identify people who are truly "independent" or "fluent," so that he can further refine the groups he uses to study the extremes of these aspects of creativity. And, if one's goal in studying creativity is training in more effective methods of work, it is reasonable to presume both that one wants to identify creative individuals who produce through more effective techniques than other people and that these techniques are one factor to look for in identifying creative individuals. Crude and unimaginative techniques of work are undesirable.

## METHODOLOGY IN THE CRITERION PROBLEM

### Source of the value judgment and qualifications of the source

The first two sections of this chapter have specified certain variables that might be considered control variables in some sense; but they are more than controls. Since they are basic sources of variation in criteria, they will be included in this section.

It cannot be assumed that a professor judges a student the same way his students judge him, nor that a supervisor judges his employees the same way his employees judge each other. These differences are likely to be sources of differences in perception, each of which will have to be taken into account, because each is of considerable importance in its own right as a criterion variable. The source of the value judgment and the qualification of the source may be major contributors to criterion variability and heterogeneity.

## Reliability and bias

Miminum reliability is of course necessary for psychological studies that involve criteria, since they are no exceptions to the need for verification of basic consistency of technique (see criterion reliabilities reported by Donald W. Taylor in the 1957 Utah creativity report, p. 24). Generally speaking, reliability studies may serve to eliminate certain variables or certain ways of measuring criterion variables. After a certain minimum standard has been met, however, reliability is of less importance than validity. The establishment of satisfactory reliability is not in itself sufficient to prove that the variables in question are useful as criteria.[8]

Experimental manipulation of products as well as of film clips of persons might be useful in identifying possible biasing elements in criteria. Such experimental manipulation is one of the few areas in which experimental, as distinct from correlational, research is possible. In order to study the sources of values attributed to research reports, a series of rewrites of such reports could be utilized in which

[8] As a side product, reliabilities over time could test the hypothesis that several measures covering, say, four different time periods would yield intercorrelations showing a simplex-like pattern. A simplex-like pattern involves high entries adjacent to the main diagonals of the correlation matrix with gradually lower values as the corners are approached. The implication of this is that measurements closer in time would be more highly related than those farther apart in time.

specific writing qualities are injected. An analysis of variance design could be used involving a number of variables relating to facility of presentation, such as clarity, grammar, organization, and impressiveness. Experimental manipulation of writing quality in this fashion would permit a more thorough study of a variety of writing or communicating dimensions. Such studies would be designed to yield mean differences in judged quality for the various dimensions manipulated. However, although findings would indicate whether such manipulations do affect judgments of products, they would not give conclusive evidence of the importance of this as a biasing factor, since such factors might be present to a lesser degree in the natural state of such reports. Common sources of bias, frequent in psychological research, such as the error of central tendency, the halo tendency, the leniency error, etc., should also be taken into account in working with such judgments.

## Overlap of criteria

The methodological problem of how much overlap or interrelationship there is among criteria could be investigated in two ways. The first way is through a factor analysis, which attempts to show the underlying dimensions that simplify a matrix of intercorrelations to a smaller number of more basic variables. The factor-analytic method adds what seems an intuitively valuable understanding to the structure of criteria.

It is further suggested that factor-analytic studies themselves could be carried out in two ways: first, in the conventional manner, which uses all the available variables and attempts to resolve them to a simpler number of more basic variables, and, secondly, by using only the predictor variables (and any construct variables) without the use of the criterion variables themselves. Adding the criterion variables later into the results of the predictor factor analysis could check on the equivalence of certain criterion variables, since if they are equivalent they should be collinear in the factor space.

Another possible approach to determining the overlap or consistency of criteria is to use the criterion-equivalence approach of R. H. Gaylord (1953). A direct correlation between two criteria, of course, reveals their agreement. In a case where the same predictors are available for both criteria, equivalence of these criteria can be determined by writing separate multiple-regression equations, using these predictors first for criterion *A* and then for criterion *B*. If these regression equations are similar, then the criteria are similar to that extent. In any event, information about the nature of the particular variables and their different weights for criterion *A* and criterion *B* would be instructive.

Such multiple-regression equations could be written for the major variables involved in a study of, for instance, gross scales on an interest test; they also might be determined through an item-analysis procedure which develops item keys against these criteria separately. Keys would be developed against criterion *A* and criterion *B* in an analysis sample, and the validity of both keys would then be determined against both criteria in a cross-validation sample. If the regression equations or the keys generalize without loss of validity from criterion *A* to criterion *B* and vice versa, the two criteria may be said to be equivalent, in that they have yielded essentially equivalent end products.

In basing the criterion-equivalence approach on equality of regression equations for a battery of predictors, one should recognize that the findings of equivalence cannot be generalized with certainty to new sets of predictors. Two criteria can also be equivalent in these terms even though one of them is less predictable than the other. The *pattern* of correlation in the cross sample will reveal this.

## Scaling and weighting methods

Scaling and weighting methods are particularly important because conventional methods of rating give no explicit recognition to the value or importance assigned to the dimensions being rated. Without explicit recognition of this problem and an explicit technique for handling it, the effective weights assigned to rated dimensions of, for example, a report on a research study may vary widely from those intended. In combining rated quality of a report with quantity (number of reports), known characteristics of ratings might well lead to overemphasis on quantity. While this might be the legitimate object of the rating system, it could occur by accident because the leniency tendency of most raters would lead them to give some credit for mediocre research reports. If the ratings on each report were simply summed, a large number of reports of little quality might well outweigh a smaller number of more valuable reports. This is not to presume that this conclusion would be incorrect—but the decision should not be made by accident of rating technique.

In the 1959 Criterion Committee Report, Gamble made the following suggestions for rating aspects of the criterion problem dealing with products:

1. Concentrate work mainly on research scientists and related professionals located in large research laboratories having a wide variety of types of research work.

2. Base the selection of criterion groups primarily on an evaluation of research products or contributions rather than characteristics of individuals.

3. Use "breadth of applicability" as one primary basis for evaluating the level or degree of creativity of contributions.

4. Develop for each of several discernible levels of creativity a general definition applicable across a broad range of types of contributions.

5. Develop a set of specific examples for each of the several levels of creativity. (These sets would be highly specific for a given narrow specialty at the bottom levels and would tend to become broader and even interdisciplinary at the top levels.)

6. Use scientists or related professionals of proven ability and reputation in the appropriate field as judges.

7. In the rating, place heaviest if not exclusive weight on each individual's best contribution, on the assumptions that the ability of an individual is inferred from his work and that his single highest-

level achievement is the best available indicator of his level of ability.

8. Ignore or study separately the problem of research workers who are presumed to have worked for years on problems of such difficulty and complexity that they have not yet been able to produce any concrete contributions.

9. Ignore the problem of the possible future major impact of contributions that are now judged to be of minor importance.

10. Maintain and analyze separately the information collected for each distinct occupational group. (The occupational groupings should be by function rather than by discipline, because both the work done and the related abilities and skills could be masked by using such broad academic disciplines as physics, chemistry, etc.)

11. Record and utilize additional measures of creative ability for their intrinsic value in order to cross-check the assumptions and procedures outlined above.

12. Utilize also what information there is concerning environmental factors, including identification of laboratory and division, lone-wolf versus team-work conditions, availability of support personnel, etc.

As a supplement to the above procedures, it is important to establish the acceptability of any metric of the value of the product, to check that the individuals most concerned with its use are truly in favor of it. This problem might be solved in part by using as judges persons representative of the group to whom the criterion must apply. Another feasible choice of judges would be from those specifically concerned with the values attributed to the products. After judges have sorted products into a series of categories according to quality, they could be requested to estimate the relative value of typical products in each category in the form of a judgment, such as that one product in category $X$ is worth three products in category $Y$. Then, using all possible pairs of categories, we could check to see whether the estimated worth resulting from this step gave values such that each pair, so evaluated, was judged to be equal. This procedure might well be useful in combining a variety of criterion variables.

The problem of weighting criterion variables has been approached from another angle by Sprecher in the 1959 University of Utah creativity report. Sprecher suggested that a judge's overall estimate of the creativity of products (or persons) is a function of two main classes of variables. The first is how the judge sees these products in terms of descriptive variables. The second is essentially an artificial weight ascribing a certain importance to each of these variables. For instance, although two judges might agree that a product had marked originality, their final overall ratings of that product might be different because one judge valued originality highly and the other placed little value on it. Similarly, both might value originality highly, but one, not realizing that a contribution was indeed original, could give it a lower overall rating than the judge who described it—properly—as original. If this is true, and if such weights and descriptions of persons or products can be determined reliably for any individual judge, there arises the prospect of finding criterion combinations unique to a particular supervisor, a particular department, or a particular organizational need.

## CONTROL VARIABLES

The first category of control variables listed—conventional biographical variables—is obvious. Most of the other categories are also straightforward, but two exceptions will be elaborated here, those listed under Section B, concerned with time dimensions, and those under Section F, concerned with opportunity variables.

### Time dimensions

Subpoints under the overall reference to time are fairly obvious; they indicate the possibility that criteria will vary with the stage of the developmental process and suggest use of a rough criterion that can later be refined.

It is also possible, however, to study individuals as they change through time by studying their biographies, as R. B. Cattell reported at the 1959 University of Utah conference. Cattell developed "personality profiles" of eminent individuals of the past and then compared these with "profiles" of research workers now living (R. B. Cattell, 1963). An earlier study of this kind was done by Cox (1926) and reported in Terman's *Genetic Studies of Genius*.

There is definite need for measures of creativity applicable during grade school, high school, and college years. Methods now used to select students for higher education depend primarily on ability to learn and acquire information, not explicitly on creativity as such. Therefore it is possible that many creative individuals, who fail to fit the mold that society attempts to force upon them, are not accepted, and find their potential diverted from socially important tasks.

Studies directed toward finding ways of identifying and measuring creative talent at an early age would have obvious value. Ideally, such studies should follow a grade school group over a period of ten to twenty years, through university and graduate training, and through sufficient professional experience to allow evidence of creativity to accumulate. Such studies should include drop-outs at all stages, as well as those who continue in education and research. A study of this magnitude could be valuable well before its completion; interim results would be very useful, even though final results would not be available for twenty years.

In the meantime, a work-sample measure of creativity might provide the basis for a series of useful studies. It would be helpful, first of all, to know the degree of overlap between work samples and other criteria. If the work sample is found to measure some acceptable criterion variable or is judged suitable in its own right, a series of studies in different age groups might be undertaken to determine whether creative individuals can be identified at earlier ages. In essence, such studies would seek to establish either the equivalence of the work sample as a criterion in various age groups or similarity of factor structure at various ages. If at ages 8, 10, 12, 14, 16, 18, and 20, the same types of tests were found to correlate with the work-sample criterion to a similar degree, or if studies at these different ages, involving similar variables, discovered the same factor structure, it might be reasonable to suppose that the nature of the work-sample criterion had remained unchanged.

## Opportunity variables

The last item in the list of control variables is "opportunity variables." It may be important to control or at least to allow statistically for three somewhat arbitrary categories of opportunity: material resources; the psychological and social environment; and the difficulty and potential of the problem area worked with. Although some individuals contend that the creative person makes his own opportunity, one cannot assume that this is universally the case. Taking opportunity factors into account may be a legitimate way of rating sufficiently high those who work under difficult circumstances, or of qualifying the success of those particularly favored (through no effort of their own) by ample resources, a stimulating environment, or an easy and new set of problems. It is not known in detail how these variables can be measured and utilized, for they have only been suggested and not worked on or developed. A little creative thinking and research in this area, as well as in other areas discussed in this chapter might contribute appropriately to progress in the study of scientific creativity.

# chapter 6

# SOME KNOWNS,
# NEEDS, AND LEADS

*Calvin W. Taylor*

UNIVERSITY OF UTAH

THE AUTHORS feel that creativity, perhaps more than any other human quality, is vital to the shaping of man's future. To recognize the importance of creativity is not in itself sufficient. There is need to focus the scientific method upon it, so that we can accumulate and implement detailed knowledge to aid in the development of man's creative talents.

The authors feel that, despite many questions that are still open at our present state of knowledge, several things can be said with assurance. First, psychologists are convinced that all people are, to some degree, potentially creative, including persons of all ages, all cultures, and all fields of human endeavor. Second, individuals differ in their degree of creative potential for various fields of activity and in the modes of expression of their creativeness.

The problem is to identify and develop creative persons, who are to be sought literally everywhere. We must not impose false restrictions by assuming that only certain kinds of work draw or require creative talent. Nor should we assume that all individuals participating in science or the arts are automatically creative. It is of first importance to recognize and develop those with the highest degree of creative potential. It is important also to increase the number of creative people and to alert the public to the progressive role of creative talent in all fields. Some attention and recognition should be given to individual creativity (which is of value at least to the individual himself), as well as to the highly important creativity that affects society and the world.

Recent studies have indicated beyond a doubt that fruitful research on creativity is possible; but too little has been done. Although much more attention and financial aid have been devoted to creativity research in recent years, further support is imperative. Among the many research needs, uppermost is the need for valid criteria of creativity. Such criteria must be determined if we are to move ahead in the identification of creative individuals, creative research proposals and projects, and creative products. Sound criteria are essential not only to research programs but also to action programs in creativity.

In addition to criterion studies, research should include work both on predictive characteristics and on educational and environmental factors; these factors may modify the relations between predictive characteristics and later creative performance, as measured by the criteria. The individual's response to a particular situation can determine whether his creative potential will be enhanced or suppressed by that situation; to the extent that environmental influences affect creative potential, predictions must be modified. One relevant environmental influence may be the personalities of others in the situation.

It is important also to put into action more programs based on available research findings. For both research work and action programs, teamwork is desirable, so that competent persons in all kinds of activities may work in cooperation with psychologists and other behavioral scientists who are knowledgeable in creativity.

The balance of this chapter will survey some of the scientific progress made to date and the potential for future research.

In order to identify early those who are potentially creative, it is essential to have valid prediction measures. Although definite judgments cannot yet be made concerning all predictor variables, certain personal and situational attributes (outlined in detail in Chapter 2) have been found to be promising predictors of creative performance.

Certain intellectual characteristics, for instance, appear to have some relationship with creative performance; these fall within the categories of memory, cognition, evaluation, convergent production, and divergent production. The divergent-production factors, including fluencies and flexibilities, seem to be most important. The fact that these intellectual aspects of creativity are relatively distinct components indicates the probability of multiple types of creative talent. The generally low correlation of these factors with intelligence test scores suggest that creative talent is not only various, but relatively different from intelligence.

Certain intellectual components, such as awareness of problems, may underlie motivational characteristics. And other motivational factors are important, such as drive, dedication to work, resourcefulness, striving for general principles, desire to bring order out of disorder, and desire for discovery.

Both intellectual and motivational factors are linked with a third set: personality factors. Several personality traits have been found to be valuable indicators of creative potential, among them independence, self-sufficiency, tolerance of ambiguity, femininity of interests, and professional self-confidence. Biographical inventories have been found especially useful as techniques for prediction, since they can provide information about a multitude of personality attributes and relevant life history.

It is important that emphasis be placed on the assessment of a broad range of predictor variables. Predictions that rely solely on a single measuring device, such as a measure of one personality trait or a traditional intelligence test, have comparatively little significance.

Research work to date has yielded a rough classification of prediction devices. These, listed in order of descending efficiency, are the following: biographical items and past achievements; self-ratings and direct expression of goals and aspirations; originality and personality inventories; high-level aptitude and intelligence tests; reports of parental attitudes. Further work is needed to determine the best combination of predictors. The available data on the concurrent validities of certain batteries of scores constitute one immediate starting point for possible future work.

New tests should be devised. A number of mental characteristics have been recognized but cannot now be adequately tested, such as idea manipulation power; nonverbal originality; mental imagery; intuition and preconscious rapport; long-range, sustained, incubation-like thinking; and other measures of the creative process.

Since environmental influences can either enhance or hinder development of those attributes which seem to be predictors of creative performance, measures of relevant environmental factors that have affected each individual could be included in a predictor battery.

In the development of valid measurements, both concurrent-validity studies of tests and the use of test scores as criteria have some value as quick intermediary or exploratory steps. However, there is an urgent need to verify the findings of concurrent-validity studies in predictive longitudinal studies. So far there have been very few studies that test individuals and then follow their histories until later, more ultimate external criteria can be applied.

Other research needs include replication of studies on larger samples, and the exploration of multiple criteria at all age levels. A problem in this connection is that some of the tests designed to measure creativity appear somewhat irrelevant to real-life situations.

Studies need to be made of persons on the job. A wide battery of the most promising predictors should be used on large samples of persons in different organizational settings. These studies would then need to be supplemented with longer-range longitudinal studies. A good coverage of the most pertinent occupations is needed; business, government, and industry would have to cooperate in providing samples of persons and criterion information that would be required for such studies.

In the field of education, which has sound reasons for concern about all aspects of creative talent, there is currently an unprecedented demand for information about creativity. One factor responsible for this demand is the promising and provocative body of knowledge that has already been amassed. Good beginnings have been made in several directions. For instance, there are several training programs in business and industry that incorporate some of the accumulated information. Many schools are also using experimental programs designed on the basis of research findings. In addition, a "literature" is evolving.

Although an encouraging number of projects have received enthusiastic support, there is need for more financial aid for research in creativity in education. The following research projects are both necessary and promising:

1. More definitive determination of the intellectual characteristics of those people with "wasted talent"; the relationship between creativity and mental health

2. Investigation of preverbal and nonverbal manifestations of creative thinking, particularly at ages one to three

3. Determination of the factors responsible for the drop in creativity found to occur at approximately age five; sustained imaginative research, including longitudinal studies, on the problem of the rise and fall in creativity that take place in the critical elementary school years

4. Development of programs designed to nurture creativity during the high school years, the period which has been most neglected to date in creativity research

5. Incorporation of creativity-research findings in the admission practices, the teaching, and the evaluation of student achievement in higher education, at both undergraduate and graduate levels

6. Development of specific suggestions for the design of school experiences that will foster rather than inhibit creative learning at each educational level

7. Determination of instructional ways of interjecting, during "creative processes," comments and demonstrations that have facilitating effects on the creativeness of the process

8. Development of tested materials and procedures that teachers can use to foster creativity

9. An enlargement of the scope of both test tasks and observations used in predicting creativity; some standardization of assessment techniques to facilitate growth of a systematic body of scientific knowledge

10. Exploration of various new frontiers in education that may be important in creativity, such as self-initiated learning, learning on one's own, utilization of responsive environments, revision of readiness concepts, emergence of self-concepts, and recognition of uniqueness

11. Evaluation of the education of teachers, the supervision of student teachers, and the in-service training and incentive systems for the development of creative, stimulating teachers

There is unfortunately very little scientific knowledge concerning the effect of environment and training on creativity. In fact, in most creativity studies to date the effects of environmental variables have been uncontrolled and unknown.

Currently there are many adult training programs designed to prepare the individual both intellectually and emotionally to become more creative. These are necessarily remedial in nature, because they must attempt to overcome earlier deficiencies in education and training. Although these remedial programs are steps in the right direction, great strides in the improvement of creativity will be possible only when there is simultaneous progress in providing a stimulating climate. *Each feature of adult training programs and of the so-called "creative" climate should be evaluated scientifically to determine its soundness.*

It is now known that a creative scientist is the product of a fortunate combination of intellectual characteristics, emotional dispositions, and a favorable climate. Several studies have been made of the intellectual and emotional variables; fewer have been devoted to climate variables. Consequently, there is a real need for research on the environmental conditions that are conducive to high-quality scientific research. There is some belief, though as yet untested, that dividends in creativity can be attained most rapidly through proper change of environmental factors. What the more crucial environmental factors are and whether they can readily be changed to produce an "ideal" climate have yet to be determined.

In order to attempt to provide the best possible work environment for a scientist or a creator in another field, studies must be focused on certain key questions. More must be learned about those aspects of the climate which are truly significant in nurturing creativity. Perhaps we shall discover that most of those crucial aspects are the human factors in the environment.

Many provocative questions for research and for practice are raised in Chapter 4, about the creativeness of the climate at the national level, at the corporate level, at the supervisory level, and at the level of group functioning. It should be determined whether the "ideal" climate for creativeness is the same or similar for all people or whether there are wide individual differences.

Programs must be designed both to change people's attitudes toward and understanding of those who are most creative and also to increase the encouragement and the expectations of the creativity of persons in all disciplines. Finally, *in order truly to test* the findings on environment, some organization should try to embody in its own research climate each of the "positive" factors, in turn, and another organization should attempt to make one single complex change to produce "almost overnight" the climate that, according to the best current advice, is ideal. The authors cannot overstress that *such changes should be a part of an experimental study that is well designed for testing the effects,* if any, *of each change.*

Although the authors realize that there are many important areas for research in creativity, they believe that there is no more urgent need for research than in the difficult and complex area of criteria of creative performance. The success of all creativity research will be determined by the validity of whatever criteria are used, yet studies devoted exclusively to criteria of creativity are very rare. Most investigators are guilty of neglecting the development of the criteria they use. Therefore, suggestions for improvement in this area are of vital importance.

First, it seems necessary to mention that multiple criteria exist. Thus, an investigator who seeks a single criterion may only falsify the true situation. The differences between creativity and productivity must also be recognized. Longitudinal studies to interrelate multiple criteria of creativity at each stage in life should prove to be basic and provocative, especially if the later, more nearly ultimate criteria are included.

What is measured in a criterion can be divided into two broad categories: products and persons. "Products" are not only physical objects but also theories and designs; a product is something that finally exists independent of the person responsible for it. Several aspects of a product must be studied to assess its creativity, and numerous suggestions are listed in the criterion chapter. In general, it can be said that the most creative product is one that generates further creative activity.

Persons, both as represented by their products and as represented by processes, are often measured by psychologists. There are a variety of possible approaches to the study of persons; however, the writers generally contend that products provide a much better basis for measurement for criterion purposes than do persons or psychological processes.

Several aspects of methodology are of central importance in the criterion problem. For example, the source of information, the source of a value judgment, and the qualification of that source are significant. Minimum reliability of measurement techniques is essential, although, given a certain minimum, reliability is less important than validity. Investigations are needed to determine the interrelationships among criteria. These investigations may be in the form of factor analysis or the criterion-equivalence approach. Problems of the combination of various criteria into a single complex criterion are largely unresolved. Scaling and weighting methods must be given explicit recognition, and, as far as possible, various kinds of potential bias should be controlled or dealt with in a suitable manner. Comparative criterion studies between fields, such as art and science, already show promise of being illuminating to both fields.

The possible effects of control variables, such as conventional biographical variables (age, sex, etc.) and those of employer, field, function, and opportunity, need to be studied empirically; techniques are then needed that will properly control those variables found to be related to creative performance, in order to avoid their otherwise troublesome effects.

The authors recognize the need for theory in each of the subtopics of creativity and the need for larger theoretical formulations that attempt to encompass all subtopics simultaneously and systematically.

In conclusion, the authors hope that this interpretive and evaluative review has at least partially fulfilled its purposes, first, of presenting the highlights of the current research knowledge in creativity and, second, of presenting promising research leads and urgent research needs. They recognize that others may find different areas to be more promising or more urgent; nevertheless, they feel that those listed here are clearly worthy of attention. They trust also that this book has provided stimulation and some guidelines for researchers and practitioners interested in the fundamental nature of creativity and its implications for all types of human endeavor in our world.

# BIBLIOGRAPHY

* Entries marked with an asterisk also appear in *Scientific creativity: Its recognition and development,* C. W. Taylor and F. Barron, 1963.

Abramson, J.: Essai d'étalonnage de deux tests d'imagination et d'observation. *J. de Psychologie,* 1927, pp. 370–379.

Adler, A.: *Problems of neuroses.* New York: Cosmopolitan Book Corp., 1930.

Alexander, F.: *Fundamentals of psychoanalysis.* New York: Norton, 1948.

Allen, A. B.: *Imagination and reality in color.* London: Warne, 1939.

Allen, M. S., J. P. Guilford, and P. R. Merrifield: *The evaluation of selected intellectual factors by creative research scientists.* Los Angeles: University of Southern California Press, 1960.

Allport, G. W.: *Personality.* New York: Holt, 1937 (especially pp. 190–207).

American Management Association: *Creativity: Key to continuing progress.* New York: *AMA Mgmt Bull.,* no. 4, 1960.

Anastasi, A., and J. P. Foley, Jr.: A survey of the literature on artistic behaviour in the abnormal, II. Approaches and interrelationships. *Abstr. New York Acad. Sci.,* August, 1941, 42:1–111.

Andersen, I., and R. Munroe: Personality factors involved in student concentration on creative painting and commercial art. *J. Proj. Tech.,* 1948, 12:141–144.

✕Anderson, H. H. (ed.): *Creativity and its cultivation.* New York: Harper, 1959a.

———: Creativity as personality development. In *Creativity and its cultivation,* H. H. Anderson, 1959b.

———: Developing creativity in children. Paper prepared for the 1960 White House Conference on Children and Youth, 1960. (Mimeographed.)

———: Creativity and education. *Association Higher Educ. Coll. Univer. Bull.,* 1961, 13 (14):4 p.

Anderson, J. E.: The nature of abilities. In *Education and talent,* Torrance, 1960, pp. 9–31.

Anderson, K. E. (ed.): *The coming crisis in the selection of students for college entrance.* Washington, D.C.: American Educational Research Association, 1960.

———: *Research on the academically talented student.* Washington, D.C.: National Education Association, 1961.

Andrews, E. G.: The development of imagination in the pre-school child. *Univer. Iowa Stud. Charact.,* 1930, 3 (4).

Andrews, M. F. (ed.): *Creativity and psychological health.* Syracuse, N.Y.: Syracuse University Press, 1961.

Applegate, M.: *Helping children write.* Scranton, Pa.: International Textbook, 1949.

———: *Everybody's business—our children.* Evanston, Ill.: Harper & Row, 1952.

188

Ardleigh, J. D.: How to get profits, not problems from creative people. *Mgmt Methods,* 1959, 17:91–98.

Arnheim, R., W. H. Auden, K. Shapiro, and D. A. Stauffer: *Poets at work.* New York: Harcourt, Brace, 1949.

Arnold, J. E.: Useful creative techniques. In *A source book for creative thinking,* Parnes and Harding, 1962.

Aschner, M. J.: The language of teaching. *Teachers Coll. Rec.,* 1960, 61:242–252.

————: The productive thinking of gifted children in the classroom. Paper presented at Amer. Educ. Res. Assoc. Chicago, February, 1961.

Ash, B., and B. Rapaport: *Creative work in the junior school.* London: Methuen, 1957.

Ashby, W. R., and M. Bassett: The effect of leucotomy on creative ability. *J. Ment. Sci.,* 1949, 95:418–430.

Astin, A. W.: A re-examination of college productivity. *J. Educ. Psychol.,* 1961, 52:173–178.

———— and J. L. Holland: The environmental assessment technique: A way to measure college environments. *J. Educ. Psychol.,* 1961, 52: 308–316.

Balin, R. P.: Encourage creativity. *Industr. Arts Voc. Educ.,* 1960, 49:20–21.

Barkan, M.: *Through art to creativity.* Englewood Cliffs, N.J., Allyn and Bacon, 1960.

Barron, F.: Complexity-simplicity as a personality dimension. *J. Abnorm. Soc. Psychol.,* 1953, 48:163–172.

————: Some personality correlates of independence of judgment. *J. Pers.,* 1953, 21:287–297.

————: Some relationships between originality and style of personality. *Amer. Psychologist,* 1954, 9:326.

————: The disposition toward originality. *J. Abnorm. Soc. Psychol.,* 1955, 51:478–485.

* ————: The disposition toward originality. In *The 1955 University of Utah research conference on the identification of creative scientific talent,* C. W. Taylor, 1956, pp. 156–170.

————: Originality in relation to personality and intellect. *J. Pers.,* 1957, 25:730–742.

* ————: The needs for order and disorder as motives in creative activity. In *The second (1957) University of Utah research conference on the identification of creative scientific talent,* C. W. Taylor, 1958a, pp. 119–128.

————: The psychology of imagination. *Sci. Amer.,* 1958, 199:151–166.

————: Current work at the Institute for Personality Assessment and Research. In *The third (1959) University of Utah research conference on the identification of creative scientific talent,* C. W. Taylor, 1959, pp. 72–76.

————: Creativity: What research says about it. *NEA J.,* March, 1961, 50:17–19.

————: Motives, traits and intellect in the creative writer. *Calif. Mon.*, 1962, 72(5): 11–14.

————, J. P. Guilford, et al.: Interrelations of various measures of creative traits. ONR contract NG-onr-73810.

Bartlett, Sir F.: *Thinking*. New York: Basic Books, 1958a.

————: *Thinking: An experimental and social study*. New York: Basic Books, 1958b.

Batten, Barton, Durstine and Osborn Staff: *Creative thinking engineered for industrial editing*. Buffalo, N.Y., 1955.

Bellows, R.: Procedure for evaluating vocation criteria. *J. Appl. Psychol.*, 1941, 25:499–513.

Benham, E.: The creative activity. *Brit. J. Psychol.*, 1929, 20:59–65.

Benton, M. (comp.): Bibliography on creativity in research and invention in the physical sciences. Washington, D.C.: Library Branch, Technical Information Division, U.S. Naval Research Laboratory, 1961.

Berg, E.: A simple objective technique for measuring flexibility in thinking. *J. Genet. Psychol.*, 1948, 30:15–22.

Berger, R. M., J. P. Guilford, and P. R. Christensen: A factor-analytic study of planning abilities. *Psychol. Monogr.*, 1957, 71(6).

Berlin, L. T. Guthrei, A. Weider, H. Goodel, and H. G. Wolff: Studies in human cerebral function: The effects of lysergic acid on cerebral processes pertinent to creative activity. *J. Nerv. Ment. Dis.*, 1955, 122:487–491.

Biber, B.: Premature structuring as a deterrent to creativity. *Amer. J. Orthopsychiat.*, 1959, 29:280–290.

Binet, A.: *Les idées modernes sur les enfants*. Paris: E. Flamarion, 1909.

Bingham, N. E.: Teaching creatively. *Sci. Educ.*, 1957, 41:271–277.

Birch, H. G., and H. S. Rabinowitz: The negative effect of previous experience on productive thinking. *J. Exp. Psychol.*, 1951, 41:121–125.

Bittel, L. R.: How to make good ideas come easy. *Factory Mgmt*, 1956, 114(3):84–90.

————: *What every supervisor should know*. New York: McGraw-Hill, 1959.

Bjorksten, J.: The limitation of creative years. *Sci. Mon.*, 1946, 62:94.

Blacher, R. S.: The creative drive: A case history. *J. Nerv. Ment. Dis.*, 1954, 120:106–107.

Blakely, R. J.: Is individuality maladjustment? In *Current issues in higher education*, Association for Higher Education. Washington, D.C.: National Education Association. 1957, pp. 12–24.

Blatt, S. J., and M. I. Stein: Some personality, value and cognitive characteristics of the creative person. *Amer. J. Psychol.*, 1957, 12:406 (abst.).

* Bloom, B. S.: Report on creativity research at the University of Chicago. In *The 1955 University of Utah research conference on the identification of creative scientific talent*, C. W. Taylor, 1956, pp. 182–194.

✕ ———: Some effects of cultural, social, and educational conditions on creativity. In *The second (1957) University of Utah research conference on the identification of creative scientific talent*, C. W. Taylor, 1958, pp. 55–65.

Bohnhorst, B. A., and P. J. Hosford: Basing instruction in science on children's questions. *Sci. Educ.*, 1960, 44:146–149.

Bond, J. A.: Analysis of observed traits of teachers rated superior in demonstrating creativeness in teaching. *J. Educ. Res.*, 1959, 53:7–12.

Boraas, J.: *Teaching to think*. New York: Macmillan, 1922.

Boring, E. G.: The problems of originality in science. *Amer. J. Psychol.*, 1927, 4(39):70–90.

Bouthilet, L.: The measurement of intuitive thinking. Unpublished doctoral dissertation, University of Chicago, 1948.

Bramwell, W. G.: Galton's hereditary genius and the three following generations since 1869. *Eugen. Rev.*, 1948, 39:146–153.

Brandwein, P. F.: *The gifted student as future scientist*. New York: Harcourt, Brace, 1955.

✕ Brecher, R. and E.: Creative ability—What is it? Who has it? What makes it flourish or falter? *Parents Mag.*, 1960, 35(11):56–57.

Brimhall, D. R.: Family resemblances among American men of science. *Amer. Naturalist*, 1922, 61:504–547.

Bristol, L. H., Jr.: The application of group thinking techniques to the problems of pharmaceutical education. *Amer. J. Pharm. Educ.*, 1958, 22:143–146.

Brittain, W. L.: Experiments for a possible test to determine some aspects of creativity in the visual arts. *Penn. State Univer. Abstr. Dissertations*, 1952–1953, 15:277–279.

Broadley, M. E.: *Square pegs in square holes*. Garden City, N. Y.: Doubleday, 1943.

Brogden, H. E., and E. K. Taylor: The dollar criterion—applying the cost accounting concept to criterion construction. *Personnel Psychol.*, 1950, 3:133–154.

——— and ———: The theory and classification of criterion bias. *Educ. Psychol. Measmt*, 1952, 16:1–31.

———, ———, and D. E. Baier: Experimental design: Utilization of an unreliable and a biased criterion. *Educ. Psychol. Measmt*, 1953, 13:27–33.

✓ Bromley, D. B.: Some experimental tests of the effect of age on creative intellectual output. *J. Geront.*, 1956, 11:74–84.

Brown, A. E.: Creativity can be stimulated. *Chem. Engrg News*, 1960, 38 (43):102–110.

Brozek, J.: The age problem in research workers: Psychological viewpoint. *Sci. Mon.*, 1951, 72:355–359.

Bruner, J. S.: Learning and thinking. *Harvard Educ. Rev.*, 1959, 29:184–192.

———: Individual and collective problems of the psychology of thinking. In *Fundamentals of psychology: The psychology of thinking*, Harms, 1960a.

———: *The process of education.* Cambridge, Mass.: Harvard, 1960b.

———: After John Dewey, what? *Sat. Rev.*, 1961, 44(24):58–59.

Brush, F. R.: Stimulus uncertainty, response uncertainty, and problem-solving. *Canad. J. Psychol.*, 1956, 10:239–247.

Bryson, L.: Training for creativity. *Sch. Arts*, 1960, 60(1):5–8.

Buel, W. D.: The validity of behavioral rating scale items for the assessment of individual creativity. *J. Appl. Psychol.*, 1960, 34:407–412.

——— and Bachner, V. M.: The assessment of creativity in a research setting. *J. Appl. Psychol.*, 1961, 45:353–358.

Buhl, H. R.: *Understanding the creative engineer.* New York: American Society of Mechanical Engineers, 1961.

Burchard, E. M. L.: The use of projective techniques in the analysis of creativity. *J. Proj. Tech.*, 1952, 16:412–427.

Burkhart, R. C.: Four creativity personality factors in art and teacher education. Central Michigan University, Mt. Pleasant, 1961. (Mimeographed.)

———: *Spontaneous and deliberate ways of learning.* Scranton, Pa.: International Textbook, 1962.

Burks, B. S., D. W. Jense, and L. M. Terman: The promise of youth: Follow-up studies of a thousand gifted children. In *Genetic studies of genius*, Terman, vol. 3, 1930.

Burrows, A. T., et al.: *They all want to write.* Englewood Cliffs, N.J.: Prentice-Hall, 1952.

Burton, W. H., R. B. Kimball, and R. L. Wing: *Education for effective thinking.* New York: Appleton-Century-Crofts, 1960.

Cady, E. L.: *Developing executive capacity.* Englewood Cliffs, N.J.: Prentice-Hall, 1958.

Cannon, W. B.: The role of chance in discovery. *Sci. Mon.*, 1940, 50:204–209.

Carlson, R. K.: Emergence of creative personality. *Childh. Educ.*, 1960, 36:402–404.

———: Stimulating creativity in children and youth. *Elem. Engl.*, 1961, 38:165–169.

Castle, C. S.: A statistical study of eminent women. *Columbia Univer. Contr. Phil. Psychol.*, 1913, 22(1).

Cattell, J. McK.: A statistical study of eminent men. *Popular Sci. Mon.*, 1903, 62:359–377.

———: A statistical study of American men of science: The selection of a group of one thousand scientific men. *Science*, 1906a, n.s., 23:658–665.

————: A statistical study of American men of science, 2: The measurement of scientific merit. *Science*, 1906b, n.s.,24:699–707.

————: Families of American men of science. *Popular Sci. Mon.*, 1915, 86: 504–515.

Cattell, R. B. (ed.): *Guide to mental testing*. London: London University Press, 1948.

————: *Personality and motivation structure and measurement*. Tarrytown-on-Hudson, N.Y.: World, 1957.

* ————: The personality and motivation of the researcher from measurements of contemporaries and from biography. In *The third (1959) University of Utah research conference on the identification of creative scientific talent*, C. W. Taylor, 1959, pp. 77–93.

———— and P. S. de Q. Cabot: A scale for measuring intrafamilial attitudes. In *Guide to mental testing*, R. B. Cattell, 1948.

———— and J. E. Drevdahl: A comparison of the personality profile (16 P.F.) of eminent researchers with that of eminent teachers and administrators and of the general population. *Brit. J. Psychol.*, 1955, 46:248–261.

Chassell, L. M.: Tests for originality. *J. Educ.*, 1916, 4(7):317–328.

* Chorness, M. H.: An interim report on creativity research. In *The 1955 University of Utah research conference on the identification of creative scientific talent*, C. W. Taylor, 1956, pp. 132–155.

———— and D. N. Nottelmann: The predictability of creative expression in teaching. *USAF Personnel Lab. Rep.*, No. 5954–195F, 1956.

———— and ————: The prediction of creativity among Air Force civilian employees. *USAF Personnel Train. Res. Cent. Res. Rep.*, no. AFPTRC-TN57-36, 1957.

Christensen, P. R., J. P. Guilford, and R. C. Wilson: Relations of creative responses to working time and instructions. *J. Exp. Psychol.*, 1957, 53:82–88.

Clague, E.: The age problem in research workers: Sociological viewpoint. *Sci. Mon.*, 1951, 72:359–363.

Clark, E. L.: American men of letters, their nature and nurture. *Stud. History, Economics and Public Law*, 1916, 72(1).

Clark, K. E.: *America's psychologists: A survey of a growing profession*. Washington, D.C.: American Psychological Association, 1957.

Clark, W. H.: A study of some of the factors leading to achievement and creativity with special reference to religious skepticism and belief. *J. Soc. Psychol.*, 1955, 41:57–69.

Cleeton, G. U.: Originality: A summary of experimental literature. *J. Abnorm. Soc. Psychol.*, 1926, 21:304–315.

Clifford, P. I.: Emotional contacts with the external world manifested by a selected group of highly creative chemists and mathematicians. *Percept. Mot. Skills*, 1959, 8:3–26, *Monogr. Suppl.*, no. 1.

Cohen, D. J., W. Whitmyre, and W. W. Funk: The effect of group cohesiveness and training upon creative thinking. *J. Appl. Psychol.*, 1960, 44:319–322.

Cole, C. C., Jr.: *Encouraging scientific talent.* New York: College Entrance Examination Board, 1956.

Cole, N. R.: *The arts in the classroom.* New York: John Day, 1940.

Cole, W., and J. Colmore (eds.): *The poetry-drawing book.* New York: Simon and Schuster, 1960.

Coleman, J. S.: *Social climates in high schools. Cooperative Res. Monogr.*, no. 4, 1961.

Colvin, S. S.: Invention versus form in English composition. *Pedag. Seminary*, 1902, 9:393–421.

———— and I. F. Meyer: Imaginative elements in the written work of school children. *Pedag. Seminary*, 1906, 13:84–93.

Conant, J. B.: The highly creative three per cent of the population. In *Creativity of gifted and talented children.* New York: Teachers College, 1959, pp. 16–19.

Constable, F. C.: *Poverty and hereditary genius: A criticism of Mr. Francis Galton's theory of hereditary genius.* London: Arthur C. Fiffield, 1905.

Cook, P. H.: A look at creativity. *Sch. Sci. Math.*, 1960, 60:417–423.

Cook, W. W., and E. P. Torrance: The educated man is creative. *Minnesota J. Educ.*, 1960, 41(3):17–20.

Cooley, W. W.: Attributes of potential scientists. *Harvard Educ. Rev.*, 1958, 28:1–18.

Coopersmith, S., C. Church, and J. Markowitz: Creativity and social class. Paper presented at East. Psychol. Assoc., April, 1960.

Copland, A.: *Music and imagination.* New York: Mentor Books, 1959.

Cotton, J., and R. E. Stoltz: The general applicability of a scale for rating research productivity. *J. Appl. Psychol.*, 1960, 44:276–277.

Cox, C. M.: The early mental traits of three hundred geniuses. In *Genetic studies of genius*, Terman, vol. 2, 1926.

Crawford, R. P.: *The techniques of creative thinking.* Englewood Cliffs, N.J.: Hawthorn, 1954.

Crutchfield, R. S.: Male superiority in "intuitive" problem solving. *Amer. Psychologist*, 1960, 15:429 (abstr.).

Darrow, H. F., and R. V. Allen: *Independent activities for creative learning.* New York: Teachers College, 1961.

Davis, N.: Creative activities for gifted pupils. *Sch. Rev.*, 1955, 63:85–90.

Dennis, W.: Variations in productivity among creative workers. *Sci. Mon.*, 1955, 80:277–278.

————: Age and achievement: A critique. *J. Geront.*, 1956a, 11:331–333.

————: Age and productivity among scientists. *Science*, 1956b, 123:724–725.

————: The age decrement in outstanding scientific contributions: Fact or artifact? *Amer. Psychologist,* 1958, 13:457–460.

Derthick, L. G.: Both creativity and intelligence are important. *Mich. Educ. J.,* 1960, 38:276–277.

Deutsch and Shea, Inc.: *Company climate and creativity.* New York: Industrial Relations News, 1959.

Dewey, J.: *How we think.* Boston: Heath, 1933.

Dimnet, E.: *The art of thinking.* New York: Simon and Schuster, 1930.

Dougan, C. P., E. Schiff, and L. Welch: Originality ratings of department store display personnel. *J. Appl. Psychol.,* 1949, 33:31–35.

Dougherty, N. W.: Discovering and nurturing originality. *Phi Kappa Phi J.,* 1960, 40(3):10–23.

Drevdahl, J. E.: An exploratory study of creativity in terms of its relationship to various personality and intellectual factors. Unpublished doctoral dissertation, *Dissertation Abstr.,* 1954, 14:1256. University of Nebraska, 1954.

————: Factors of importance for creativity. *J. Clin. Psychol.,* 1956, 12:21–26.

Drews, E. M.: A critical evaluation of approaches to the identification of gifted students. In *Measurement and evaluation in today's schools,* A. Traxler (ed.). Washington, D.C.: American Council on Education, 1961, pp. 47–51.

Dyer, H. S.: Some problems in identifying creative scientific talent at various academic levels. In *The 1955 University of Utah research conference on the identification of creative scientific talent,* C. W. Taylor, 1956, pp. 111–131.

Easton, W. H.: Creative thinking and how to develop it. *Mech. Engrg,* 1946, 68:697–704.

Edgerton, H. A.: Two tests for early identification of scientific ability. *Educ. Psychol. Measmt,* 1959, 19:299–304.

Eiduson, B. T.: Artist and non-artists: A comparative study. *J. Pers.,* 1958, 36:13–28.

Eindhoven, J. E., and W. E. Vinacke: Creative processes in painting. *J. Genet. Psychol.,* 1952, 47:139–164.

Elliott, J. M.: Measuring creative abilities in public relations and in advertising work. In *The fifth (1962) University of Utah research conference report on creative talent,* C. W. Taylor, 1964.

Ellis, H.: *A study of British genius.* London: Hurst and Blackett, 1904.

Erikson, E. H.: Sex differences in the play configurations of American preadolescents. In *Childhood in contemporary cultures,* Mead and Wolfenstein, 1955, pp. 324–341.

Exton, E.: Foster creativity in the schools—a growing challenge. *Amer. Sch. Bd J.,* 1960, 141(6):32–33.

Eyring, H.: Scientific creativity. In *Creativity and its cultivation,* H. H. Anderson, 1959, pp. 1–11.

Ferren, J.: The problem of creative thinking in painting. In *The nature of creative thinking,* Industrial Relations Institute, 1953.

Fiedler, F. E.: Leadership group composition and group creativity. Paper read at APA, 1960. *Amer. Psychologist,* 1960, 15:390 (abstr.).

———, A. R. Bass, and J. M. Fiedler: *The leader's perception of co-workers, group climate, and group creativity: A cross validation.* Urbana, Ill.: Group Effectiveness Research Laboratory, University of Illinois, 1961.

———, P. London, and R. S. Nemo: *Hypnotically induced leader attitudes and group creativity.* Urbana, Ill.: Group Effectiveness Research Laboratory, University of Illinois, 1961.

———, W. Meuwese, and S. Oonk: *Performance on laboratory tasks requiring group creativity: An exploratory study.* Urbana, Ill.: Center for Research in Social Psychology, University of Illinois, 1960.

Fisichelli, V. R., and L. Welch: The ability of college art majors to recombine ideas in creative thinking. *J. Appl. Psychol.,* 1947, 31:278–282.

Flanagan, J. C.: *Critical requirements for research personnel.* Pittsburgh: American Institute for Research, 1949.

* ———: Definition and measurement of ingenuity. In *The second (1957) University of Utah research conference on the identification of creative scientific talent,* C. W. Taylor, 1958, pp. 109–118.

———: The relation of a new ingenuity measure to other variables. In *The third (1959) University of Utah research conference on the identification of creative scientific talent,* C. W. Taylor, 1959, pp. 104–123.

Fletcher, F. M.: Manpower for tomorrow: A challenge. *Personnel Guidance J.,* 1958, 37:32–39.

Flick, P. B.: An intercorrelative study of two creative types: the visual type and the haptic type. Unpublished doctoral dissertation, Pennsylvania State University, 1960.

Forslund, J. E.: An inquiry into the nature of creative teaching. *J. Educ.,* 1961, 143(4):72–80.

Francesco, I. L. de: Creativity in the teaching process. *Penn. Sch. J.,* 1960, 108:247–249.

Frederiksen, N.: *Development of the test "formulating hypotheses": A progress report.* Princeton, N.J.: Educational Testing Service, 1959.

French, J. W.: *The description of aptitude and achievement tests in terms of rotated factors.* Univer. Chicago Psychometr. Monogr., no. 5, 1951.

———: *The description of personality measurements in terms of rotated factors.* Princeton, N.J.: Educational Testing Service, March, 1953.

French, R. L.: Research as a basis for creative teaching. *Educ. Horizons,* 1961, 40:28–34.

Freud, S.: *Three contributions to the theory of sex.* New York: Nervous and Mental Disease Publishing, 1910.

———: *Civilization and its discontents* (trans. J. Riviere). New York: Cope and Smith, 1930.

Fricke, B. G., and A. H. Matlin: The empirical assessment of creative potential. Paper presented at APA, Chicago, September, 1960.

Fromm, E.: Creativity. In *Creativity and its cultivation,* H. H. Anderson, 1959, pp. 44–54.

Fry, C. L.: The religious affiliations of American leaders. *Sci. Mon.,* 1933, 36:241–249.

Gallagher, J. J.: *Analysis of research on the education of gifted children.* Springfield, Ill.: Office of the Superintendent of Public Instruction, 1960.

Galton, F.: *Hereditary genius.* New York: Appleton, 1870.

———: *English men of science, their nature and nurture.* New York: St. Martin's, 1874.

———: *Inquiries into human faculty and its development.* New York: Dutton, 1911.

Gamble, A. O.: An analytical study of the nature of research work in the physical sciences. Unpublished doctoral dissertation, University of California, Berkeley, 1949.

———: Suggestions for future research. In *The third (1959) University of Utah research conference on the identification of creative scientific talent,* C. W. Taylor, 1959, pp. 292–297.

Gaylord, R. H.: *Conceptual consistency and criterion equivalence: A dual approach to criterion analysis.* Personnel Research Branch, Research Note 17, PRB, The Adjutant General's Office, DA, June, 1953.

Georgopoulos, B. L., G. M. Mahoney, and N. W. Jones, Jr.: A path-goal approach to productivity. *J. Appl. Psychol.,* 1957, 41:345–353.

Gerber, B. W.: Creativity: A frame of reference. *N.Y. State Educ.,* 1960, 48:14–15.

Gerry, R., L. DeVeau, and M. Chorness: *A review of some recent research in the field of creativity and the examination of an experimental creativity workshop.* Training Analysis and Development Division, Lackland Air Force Base, Texas, 1957.

Getzels, J. W.: Non-IQ intellectual and other factors in college admission. In *The coming crisis in the selection of students for college entrance,* K. E. Anderson, 1960.

——— and P. W. Jackson: The meaning of "giftedness"—an examination of an expanding concept. *Phi Delta Kappan,* 1958, 40:75–77.

* ——— and ———: The highly intelligent and the highly creative adolescent: A summary of some research findings. In *The third (1959) University of Utah research conference on the identification of creative scientific talent,* C. W. Taylor, 1959, pp. 46–57.

———— and ————: Occupational choice and cognitive functioning: Career aspirations of highly intelligent and highly creative adolescents. *J. Abnorm. Soc. Psychol.,* 1960a, 61:119–123.

———— and ————: The study of giftedness: A multidimensional approach. In *The gifted student, Cooperative Res. Monogr.,* no. 2, 1960b.

———— and ————: Family environment and cognitive style: A study of the sources of highly intelligent and highly creative adolescents. *Amer. Sociol. Rev.,* 1961, 26:351–359.

———— and ————: *Creativity and intelligence.* New York: Wiley, 1962.

Ghiselin, B. (ed.): *The creative process.* New York: Mentor Books, 1955.

* ————: The creative process and its relation to the identification of creative talent. In *The 1955 University of Utah research conference on the identification of creative scientific talent,* C. W. Taylor, 1956, pp. 195–203.

* ————: Ultimate criteria for two levels of creativity. In *The second (1957) University of Utah research conference on the identification of creative scientific talent,* C. W. Taylor, 1959, pp. 141–155.

Gibb, J. R.: The effects of group size and of threat reduction upon creativity in a problem-solving situation. *Amer. Psychologist,* 1951, 6:324 (abstr.).

Gibson, W. C.: Contributions by medical undergraduates to the science of preventive medicine. *Publ. Hlth Rep.,* 1955, 70:935–942.

————: The undergraduate activities of some contributors to neurological science. *Yale J. Biol. Med.,* 1955–1956, 28:273–284.

————: *Young endeavour.* Springfield, Ill.: Charles C Thomas, 1958.

————: Student medical researchers and their contributions. *New England J. Med.,* 1961, 264:802–810.

Gilfillan, S. C.: The prediction of invention. *J. Patent Office Soc.,* September, 1937, 19:623–645.

Glass, S. J.: Creative thinking can be released and applied. *Personnel J.,* 1960, 39:176–177.

Goldner, B. B.: Need ideas? Nurture a creative atmosphere. *Amer. Bus.,* 1958, 28(11):11–14.

* Golovin, N. F.: The creative person in science. In *The third (1959) University of Utah research conference on the identification of creative scientific talent,* C. W. Taylor, 1959, pp. 268–281.

Gordon, K.: Imagination: A psychological study. *J. Genet. Psychol.,* 1935, 12:194–207.

Gordon, W. J. J.: Operational approach to creativity. *Harvard Bus. Rev.,* 1956, 34(6):41–51.

————: *Synectics: The development of creative capacity.* New York: Harper, 1961.

Gough, H. G.: Some theoretical problems in the construction of practical assessment devices for the early identification high level talent. Paper read at Soc. Sci. Res. Committee, Princeton, N.J., April, 1953.

———: Stylistic variations in the self-views and work attitudes of a sample of professional research scientists. Paper read at West. Psychol. Assoc., Monterey, Calif., April, 1958.

——— and D. G. Woodworth: Stylistic variations among professional research scientists. *J. Psychol.*, 1960, 49:87–98.

Green, L. A.: A study of creativity and the self-attitudes and sociability of high school students. *Dissertation Abstr.*, 1957, 17:1807–1808.

Gregory, J. M.: *The seven laws of teaching.* Boston: Pilgrim Press, 1886.

Grener, N., and L. Raths: Thinking in grade three. *Educ. Res. Bull.*, 1945, 24:38–42.

Griffin, D. P.: Movement responses and creativity. *J. Consult. Psychol.*, 1958, 22:134–136.

✗Griffiths, R.: *A study of imagination in early childhood.* London: Routledge, 1945.

Grippen, V. B.: A study of creative artistic imagination in children by the constant procedure. *Psychol. Monogr.*, 1933, 45(1):63–81.

Grozinger, W.: *Scribbling, drawing, painting.* New York: Praeger, 1955.

Gruber, H. E., and M. Weitman: Self-directed study: Experiments in higher education. Boulder, Colo.: University of Colorado Behavior Research Laboratory, 1962.

———, G. Terrell, and M. Wertheimer (eds.): *Contemporary approaches to creative thinking.* New York: Atherton Press, 1962.

Guilford, J. P.: Creativity, *Amer. Psychologist*, 1950, 5:444–454.

———: The relation of intellectual factors to creative thinking and science. In *The 1955 University of Utah research conference on the identification of creative scientific talent*, C. W. Taylor, 1956a, pp. 69–95.

———: Structure of intellect. *Psychol. Bull.*, 1956b, 53:267–293.

———: Creative abilities in the arts. *Psychol. Rev.*, 1957, 64:110–118.

———: Basic traits in intellectual performance. In *The second (1957) University of Utah research conference on the identification of creative scientific talent*, C. W. Taylor, 1958, pp. 66–81.

* ———: Intellectual resources and their values as seen by scientists. In *The third (1959) University of Utah research conference on the identification of creative scientific talent*, C. W. Taylor, 1959a, pp. 128–149.

———: *Personality.* New York: McGraw-Hill, 1959b.

———: Three faces of intellect. *Amer. Psychologist*, 1959c, 14:469–479.

———: Basic conceptual problems of the psychology of thinking. In *Fundamentals of psychology: The psychology of thinking*, Harms, 1960a.

✗———: Frontiers in thinking that teachers should know about. *Reading Teacher*, 1960b, 13:176–182.

———, P. R. Christensen, N. A. Bond, Jr., and M. A. Sutton: A factor-analysis study of human interests. *Psychol. Monogr.*, 1954, 68(4).

———, ———, J. W. Frick, and P. R. Merrifield: *The relations of creative-*

*thinking aptitudes to non-aptitudes personality traits. Univer. Sth. Calif. Psychol. Lab. Rep.*, no. 20, December, 1957.

——, B. Fruchter, and H. P. Kelley: Development and application of tests of intellectual and special aptitudes. *Rev. Educ. Res.*, 1959, 29:26–41.

—— and R. B. Guilford: A prognostic test for students in design. *J. Appl. Psychol.*, 1931, 15:335–345.

—— and P. R. Merrifield: *The structure of intellect model: Its uses and implications.* Los Angeles: University of Southern California Press, 1960.

——, ——, and A. B. Cox: *Creative thinking in children at the junior high school levels.* Los Angeles: Psychological Laboratory, University of Southern California, 1961.

——, R. C. Wilson, and P. R. Christensen: *A factor-analytic study of creative thinking, II: Administration of tests and analysis of results. Univ. Sth. Calif. Psychol. Lab. Rep.*, no. 8, July, 1952.

——, ——, ——, and D. J. Lewis: *A factor-analytic study of creative thinking, I: Hypotheses and descriptions of tests. Univ. Sth. Calif. Psychol. Lab. Rep.*, no. 4, April, 1951.

Guth, W. L.: Discovering and developing creative engineers. *Machine Design*, March, 1959:89–94.

Hadamard, J.: *An essay on the psychology of invention in the mathematical field.* Princeton, N.J.: Princeton, 1945.

Hall, W. B.: The development of a technique for assessing esthetic predispositions and its application to a sample of professional research scientists. Paper read at West. Psychol. Assoc., Monterey, Calif., April, 1958.

Hammer, E. F.: *Creativity.* New York: Random House, 1961.

Harding, R. E. M.: *An anatomy of inspiration.* Cambridge, England: Heffer, 1948.

Hargreaves, H. L.: The "faculty" of imagination. *Brit. J. Psychol.*, 1927, 3, *Monogr. Suppl.*, no. 10.

Harmon, L. R.: Social and technological determiners of creativity. In *The 1955 University of Utah research conference on the identification of creative scientific talent*, C. W. Taylor, 1956, pp. 42–52.

* ——: The development of a criterion of scientific competence. In *The second (1957) University of Utah research conference on the identification of creative scientific talent*, C. W. Taylor, 1958, pp. 82–97.

Harms, E. (ed.): *Fundamentals of psychology: The psychology of thinking.* New York: New York Academy of Science, 1960.

——: A test for types of formal creativity. *Psychol. Bull.*, 1939, 36:526–527.

——: The psychology of formal creativeness, I: Six fundamental types of formal expression. *J. Genet. Psychol.*, 1946, 69:97–120.

Harris, D.: The development and validation of a test of creativity in engineering. *J. Appl. Psychol.*, 1960, 44:254–257.

Harris, R. H.: The development and validation of a test of creative ability. Unpublished doctoral dissertation, Purdue University, 1955.

Harris, R. R., and A. L. Simberg: *AC test of creative ability, examiner's manual.* Flint, Mich.: AC Spark Plug Division, General Motors (no date).

Hart, H. H.: The integrative function of creativity. *Psychiat. Quart.,* 1950, 24:1–16.

Hausman, J. J. (ed.): *Research in art education. Yearb. NAEA,* 1959, 9.

Heath, R. W., M. H. Maier, H. H. Remmers, and D. C. Rodgers: *High school students look at science.* Lafayette, Ind.: Division of Educational Reference, Purdue University, 1957.

Hebb, H. M., and M. J. Martin: Freedom of inquiry—the first requirement. In *Creativity: Key to continuing progress,* American Management Association, 1960, pp. 22–27.

Hebeisen, A. A.: The performance of a group of schizophrenic patients on a test of creative thinking. In *Creativity: Second Minnesota conference on gifted children, Torrance,* 1960, pp. 125–129.

Heibreder, E.: An experimental study of thinking, *Arch. Psychol., N.Y.,* 1924, 11(73).

Hendrix, G.: Learning by discovery. *The Math. Teacher,* May, 1961: 54.

Henrickson, P. R., and E. P. Torrance: School discipline and the creative personality. *East. Art Educ. Res. Bull.,* 1961a, 18(4):36–42.

———— and ————: Some implications for art education from the Minnesota studies of creative thinking. *Stud. Art Educ.,* 1961b, 2:36–44.

Henry, E. M.: Evaluation of children's growth through art experiences. *Art Educ.,* 1953, 6(4):22–23.

Henry, J.: Working paper on creativity. *Harvard Educ. Rev.,* 1957, 27:148–155.

————: The problem of spontaneity, initiative and creativity in suburban classrooms. *Amer. J. Orthopsychiat.,* 1959, 29:266–279.

Herman, D. O.: A factorial study of research potential in chemistry. Unpublished doctoral dissertation, The Ohio State University, 1959.

Hicks, G.: Mail-order creativity. *Sat. Rev.,* 1961, 44(17):35f.

Hiller, R.: Your ideas are important: An experiment in creative writing. In *New educational ideas: Third Minnesota conference on gifted children,* Torrance, 1961, pp. 168–175.

Hills, J. R.: *The relationship between certain factor-analyzed abilities and success in college mathematics. Univer. Sth. Calif. Psychol. Lab. Rep.,* no. 15, 1955.

————: Recent creativity studies at Educational Testing Service. In *The second (1957) University of Utah research conference on the identification of creative scientific talent,* C. W. Taylor, 1958, pp. 181–191.

Hirsch, N. D. M.: *Genius and creative intelligence.* Cambridge, Mass.: Sci-Art Publishers, 1931.

Hix, C. F.: *The creative engineering program: Its purpose and history.* Schenectady, N.Y.: General Electric, 1954.

———, and D. L. Purdy: Creativity can be developed. *Gen. Elec. Rev.,* 1955, 58(3):20–23.

Hobelman, L.: Three creative teachers. *Clearing House,* 1957, 32:161–162.

Hoffman, B.: The tyranny of multiple-choice tests. *Harper's,* March, 1961, 222:37–44.

Hohn, F. E.: Teaching creativity in mathematics. *Arith. Teacher,* 1961, 8:102–111.

Holland, J. L.: Undergraduate origins of American scientists. *Science,* 1957, 126:433–437.

———: Some limitations of teacher ratings as predictors of creativity. *J. Educ. Psychol.,* 1959, 50:219–222.

———: Creative and academic performance among talented adolescents. *J. Educ. Psychol.,* 1961, 52:136–137.

——— and A. W. Astin: The prediction of academic, artistic, scientific and social achievement among undergraduates of superior scholastic aptitude. Evanston, Ill.: National Merit Scholarship Corporation, 1961. (Unpublished manuscript.)

——— and L. Kent: The concentration of scholarship funds and its implications for education. *Coll. & Univer.,* 1960, 35(4):471–483.

Hollister, L. E.: Clinical, biochemical and psychologic effects of psilocybin. *Arch. Int. Pharmacodyn,* 1961:42–52.

Honebrink, R. W.: Stimulating creative thinking among engineers. *Industr. Engrg Chem.,* 1956, 48(8):85A–89A.

Hoppes, W. C.: *The development of written expression among children of elementary school grades.* Chicago: University of Chicago Libraries, 1931.

Hull, C. L.: The mechanism of the assembly of behavior segments in novel combinations suitable for problem solution. *Psychol. Rev.,* 1935, 42:219–245.

Hullfish, H. G., and P. G. Smith: *Reflective thinking: The method of education.* New York: Dodd, Mead, 1961.

Hutchinson, E. D.: Materials for the study of creative thinking. *Psychol. Bull.,* 1931, 28:392–410.

———: *How to think creatively.* Nashville, Tenn.: Abingdon, 1949.

Hutton, E. L., and M. Bassett: The effect of leucotomy on creative personality. *J. Ment. Sci.,* 1948, 94:332–350.

Hyman, R.: *Some experiments in creativity.* New York: General Electric Services, 1960.

———: On prior information and creativity. Paper presented at East. Psychol. Assoc., Philadelphia, April, 1961.

Industrial Relations Institute: *The nature of creative thinking.* New York, 1953.

Israeli, N.: Studies in occupational analysis, II: Originality. *J. Psychol.*, 1946, 22:77–87.

———: Social interaction in creation and criticism in the fine arts. *J. Soc. Psychol.*, 1952, 35:73–89.

Jackson, G. E.: Conformity and creativity in the theological seminary: *Relig. Educ.*, 1960, 55:330–335.

Jackson, P. W., J. W. Getzels, and G. A. Xydis: Psychological health and cognitive functioning in adolescence: A multivariate analysis. *Child Develpm.*, 1960, 31:285–298.

* Jex, F. B.: Negative validities for two different ingenuity tests as criteria for judging the effectiveness of the ingenuity test. In *The third (1959) University of Utah research conference on the identification of creative scientific talent*, C. W. Taylor, 1959, pp. 124–127.

John, E. R., and J. Rinaldi: Contributions to the study of the problem solving process. *Psychol. Monogr.*, 1957, 71(18).

Johnson, D. M.: *The psychology of thought and judgment*. New York: Harper, 1955.

Jones, E.: How to tell your friends from geniuses. *Sat. Rev.*, Aug. 10, 1957, 40:9–10, 39–40.

———: Creativity in the science classroom. *NEA J.*, March, 1961, 50:22–24.

Joyce, K. M.: The cult of originality. *Peabody J. Educ.*, 1960, 37:334–335.

Jung, C. G.: On the relation of analytical psychology to poetic art. In *Contributions to analytical psychology*. New York: Harcourt, Brace. 1928, pp. 225–249.

———: *Psychological types*. New York: Harcourt, Brace, 1946 (esp. chap. 10, general description of types, pp. 412–517).

Kaluger, G., and R. Martin: The loneliness of the gifted child. *Elem. Sch. J.*, 1960, 61:127–132.

* Kaplan, N.: The relation of creativity to sociological variables in research organizations. In *The third (1959) University of Utah research conference on the identification of creative scientific talent*, C. W. Taylor, 1959, pp. 232–249.

———: Some organizational factors affecting creativity. *IRE Trans. Engrg Mgmt*, 1960, EM-7(1):24–30.

Kaya, E. M.: A curricular sequence based on psychological processes rather than subject content. Paper presented at APA, Chicago, September, 1960.

———: New ideas in the dual-progress plan. In *New educational ideas: Third Minnesota conference on gifted children*, Torrance, 1961.

Keiler, M. L.: Creativity: Core of art education. *Educ. Leadership*, 1960, 18:28–32.

Kelley, E. C.: The significance of being unique. In *Our language and our world*, S. I. Hayakawa (ed.). New York: Harper, 1959, pp. 152–171.

Kendrick, V. D.: The influence of repetition on the over-all aesthetic quality and the completion time of a creative art task. Unpublished doctoral dissertation, Pennsylvania State University, 1960.

Kettering, C. F.: The role of invention in industry. *J. Patent Office Soc.*, June, 1932, 14:500–511.

Kettner, N. W., J. P. Guilford, and P. R. Christensen: A factor-analytic study across the domains of reasoning, creativity, and evaluation. *Psychol. Monogr.*, 1959, 73(479).

Kimball, M., Jr.: Imagination. *Sch. Arts,* 1960, 59(9):5–9.

Kincaid, C. E.: The determination and description of various attributes of children. Unpublished doctoral dissertation, Pennsylvania State University, 1960.

Kirchner, W. K.: Is brainstorming really effective? *Office Mgmt Amer. Bus.*, 1960, 21(6):78–80.

Kirkpatrick, E. A.: Individual tests of school children. *Psychol. Rev.*, 1900, 5(7):274.

* Knapp, R. H.: Demographic cultural and personality attributes of scientists. In *The 1955 University of Utah research conference on the identification of creative scientific talent,* C. W. Taylor, 1956, pp. 204–212.

————, and H. B. Goodrich: *Origins of American scientists.* Chicago: University of Chicago Press, 1952.

————, and J. J. Greenbaum: *The younger American scholar, his collegiate origins.* Chicago: University of Chicago Press, 1953.

Kubie, L. S.: *Neurotic distortion of the creative process.* Lawrence, Kans.: University of Kansas Press, 1958.

* Kuhn, T. S.: The essential tension: Tradition and innovation in scientific research. In *The third (1959) University of Utah research conference on the identification of creative scientific talent,* C. W. Taylor, 1959, pp. 162–177.

———— and N. Kaplan: Environmental conditions affecting creativity. In *The third (1959) University of Utah research conference on the identification of creative scientific talent,* C. W. Taylor, 1959, pp. 313–316.

Kupferberg, T., and S. Topp: *Children as authors: Birth bibliography.* New York: Birth Press, 1959.

Kretschmer, E.: *The psychology of men of genius* (trans. R. B. Cattell). New York: Harcourt, Brace, 1931.

Landis, M. A. M.: Creativity—a precious possession. *Childh. Educ.*, 1960, 37:155–156.

Lange-Eichbaum, W.: *The problem of genius* (trans. E. and C. Paul). New York: Macmillan, 1932.

Lansing, K.: The effect of class size and room size upon the creative drawings of fifth grade children. In *Research in Art Education, Yearb. NAEA,* 1959, 9, pp. 70–74.

LaPiere, R.: *The Freudian ethic.* New York: Duell, Sloan & Pearce, 1959.

Leary, T.: Drugs, set and suggestibility. Paper presented at APA, September, 1961.

Lehman, H. C.: *Age and achievement*. Princeton, N.J.: Princeton University Press, 1943.

————: Reply to Dennis' critique of "Age and achievement." *J. Geront.* 1956, 11:333–337.

————: The chemist's most creative years. *Science*, 1958, 127:1213–1222.

————: The age decrement in outstanding scientific creativity. *Amer. Psychologist*, 1960, 15:128–134.

———— and P. A. Witty: Scientific eminence and church membership. *Sci. Mon.*, 1931, 34:544–549.

Leuba, C.: A new look at curiosity and creativity. *J. Higher Educ.*, 1958, 29:132–140.

Levinger, L.: Dramatic play—An intellectual and creative process. In *Imagination in education conference, 1956*. New York: Associates of Bank Street College of Education, 1956.

Levy, C.: The independent mind. *Calif. Mon.*, 1962, 72(5):15–19.

Ligon, E. M.: *The psychology of Christian personality*. New York: Macmillan, 1957.

Likert, R.: *New patterns of management*. New York: McGraw-Hill, 1961.

Lindberg, L.: Democratic processes foster creativity. *Education*, 1958, 79:76–83.

Lindstrom, M.: *Children's art*. Berkeley, Calif.: University of California Press, 1959.

Littwin, M. F.: Experimental investigation of the effect of method of presentation upon the imaginative quality of descriptive writing among elementary-school pupils. *J. Exp. Psychol.*, 1935, 4:44–49.

Lombroso, C.: *The man of genius*. London: Walter Scott, 1891.

Lorbe, I.: The teacher's task in the development of thinking. *Reading Teacher*, 1960, 13:170–175.

Lorge, I., and L. S. Hollingworth: Adult status of highly intelligent children. *J. Genet. Psychol.*, 1936, 49:215–226.

Lowenfeld, V. *Creative and mental growth*. 3d ed., New York: Macmillan, 1957.

————: Current research on creativity. *NEA J.*, 1958, 47:538–540.

————: Creativity and art education. *Sch. Arts*, 1959, 59(2):5–15.

————: What is creative teaching? In *Creativity: Second Minnesota conference on gifted children*, Torrance, 1960, pp. 38–50.

————: Basic aspects of creative teaching. In *Creativity and psychological health*, M. F. Andrews, 1961.

———— and Beittel, K.: Interdisciplinary criteria of creativity in the arts and sciences. In *Research in Art Education, Yearb. NAEA*, 1959, 9, pp. 35–44.

Ludington, C. (ed.): *Creativity and conformity*. Ann Arbor, Mich.: Foundation for Research on Human Behavior, 1958.

McCarty, S. A.: *Children's drawings: A study of interest and abilities*. Baltimore: Williams & Wilkins, 1924.

* McClelland, D. C.: The calculated risk: An aspect of scientific performance. In *The 1955 University of Utah research conference on the identification of creative scientific talent*, C. W. Taylor, 1956, pp. 96–110.

McCloy, W.: Creative imagination in children and adults. *Psychol. Monogr.*, 1939, 51:88–102.

———— and N. C. Maier: Re-creative imagination, *Psychol. Monogr.*, 1939, 51(5): 108–116.

McCray, Curtis, and R. S. Harper: Some relationships of schedules of reinforcement to "creativity." Paper read at APA, Chicago, September, 1960. *Amer. Psychologist*, 1960, 15:400.

McDowell, M. S., and S. R. Howe: Creative use of play materials by preschool children. *Childh. Educ.*, 1941, 17:321–326.

McGuire, C., E. Hindsman, F. J. King, and E. Jennings: Dimensions of talented behavior. *Educ. Psychol. Measmt*, 1961, 21:3–38.

McKeachie, W. J.: The improvement of instruction. *Rev. Educ. Res.*, 1960, 30:351–360.

MacKinnon, D. W.: What do we mean by talent and how do we test for it? In *The search for talent*. New York: College Entrance Examination Board, 1959, pp. 20–29.

————: The highly effective individual. *Teachers Coll. Rec.*, 1960, 61:367–378.

————: Characteristics of the creative person: Implications for the teaching-learning process. In *Current issues in higher education*, Association for Higher Education. Washington, D.C.: National Education Association, 1961, pp. 89–92.

———— (ed.): *The creative person*. Berkeley, Calif.: University of California Press, 1962.

————: The creativity of architects. In *The fifth (1962) University of Utah research conference report on creative talent*, C. W. Taylor, 1964.

McLean, F. C.: The happy accident. *Sci. Mon.*, 1941, 53:61–70.

McMillan, M.: *Education through the imagination*. New York: Appleton, 1924.

McNeil, E. B.: The paradox of education for the gifted. *Improving Coll. Univer. Teaching*, 1960, 8(3):111–115.

* McPherson, J. H.: A proposal for establishing ultimate criteria for measuring creative output. In *The 1955 University of Utah research conference on the identification of creative scientific talent*, C. W. Taylor, 1956, pp. 63–68.

————: Some comments about the relationship between the industrial research laboratory "climate" and the individual scientists. In *The third (1959) University of Utah research conference on the identification of creative scientific talent*, C. W. Taylor, 1958, pp. 94–103.

————: What is creativity? Its nature and implications for management. In *Creativity: Key to continuing progress*, American Management Association, 1960, pp. 9–14.

Maier, N. R. F., and L. R. Hoffman: Quality of first and second solutions in group problem solving. *J. Appl. Psychol.*, 1960, 44:278–283.

———— and A. R. Solem: The contribution of a discussion leader to the quality of group thinking. *Human Relat.*, 1952, 5:277–288.

Maizell, R. E.: *The most creative chemist reads more: Industr. Engrg Chem.*, 1958, 50:64A–65A.

Mallinson, G. G.: Creativity in science and mathematics. *Educ. Leadership*, 1960, 18(1):24–27.

Maltzman, I.: On the training of originality. *Psychol. Rev.*, 1960, 67:229–242.

————, W. Boratz, and L. Breger: A procedure for increasing word association originality and its transfer effects. *J. Exp. Psychol.*, 1958, 56:392–398.

————, L. O. Brooks, W. Bogartz, and S. S. Summers: The facilitation of problem solving by prior exposure to uncommon responses. *J. Exp. Psychol.*, 1959, 56:399–406.

————, E. Eisman, and L. O. Brooks: Some relationships between methods of instruction, personality variables and problem-solving behavior. *J. Educ. Psychol.*, 1956, 47, 71–78.

————, ————, ————, and W. M. Smith: Task instructions for anagrams following different task instructions and training. *J. Exp. Psychol.*, 1956, 51(6):418–420.

Mandell, M. M., and S. Adams: Measuring originality in the physical sciences. *Educ. Psychol. Measmt*, 1948, 8:575–582.

Manufacturing Group 25, Harvard Graduate School of Business Administration: *Individual creativity and the corporation* (copyright by S. Boutourline and Paul Rosenberg, 1959). Boston: Manufacturing Group 25 and The Institute of Contemporary Art, 1958.

Markey, F. V.: *Imaginative behavior in pre-school children*. New York: Bureau of Publications, Teachers College, 1935.

Marks, M. R.: Problem-solving as function of situation. *J. Exp. Psychol.*, 1951, 41:74–80.

Marshall, M.: Helping children to write better themes. *Peabody J. Educ.*, 1960, 38:96–99.

Maschino, A.: *Factors related to success in technical jobs*. Psychology Department, Midland Division, Midland, Mich.: Dow Chemical Co., 1959.

Maslow, A. H.: *Motivation and personality*. New York: Harper, 1954.

———: Self-actualizing people: A study of psychological health. In *The self: Explorations in personal growth*, C. E. Moustakas (ed.). New York: Harper, 1956, pp. 160–194.

———: Emotional blocks to creativity. Paper presented at Creative Engineering Seminars of the U.S. Army Engineers, Ft. Belvoir, Va., April, 1957.

———: Emotional blocks to creativity. *Humanist*, 1958, 18:325–332.

———: Creativity in self-actualizing people. In *Creativity and its cultivation*, H. H. Anderson, 1959a, pp. 83–95.

———: Creativity in self-actualizing people. *J. Appl. Psychol.*, 1959b, 43:189–194.

———: Toward a humanistic psychology. In *Our language and our world*, S. I. Hayakawa (ed.). New York: Harper, 1959c, pp. 180–201.

Mattil, E. L.: A study to determine the relationship between the creative products of children, age 11 to 14, and their adjustment. *Penn. State Univer., Abstr. dissertations*, 1954, 16:327–332.

Maw, W., and E. W. Maw: The relationship between curiosity and scores on a test of general information. *J. Assoc. Res. Growth Relationships*, 1960, 2:27–34.

——— and ———: Establishing criterion groups for evaluating measure of curiosity. *J. Exp. Educ.*, 1961a, 29:299–305.

——— and ———: Nonhomeostatic experiences as stimuli of children with high curiosity. *Calif. J. Educ. Res.*, 1961b, 12(2):57–61.

Mawardi, B. H.: Thought sequences in creative problem solving. Paper presented at APA, Chicago, September, 1960. *Amer. Psychologist*, 1960, 15:429.

May, R.: The nature of creativity. In *Creativity and its cultivation*, H. H. Anderson, 1959, pp. 58–63.

Mayer, M.: *The schools*. New York: Harper, 1961.

Mead, M.: Why is education obsolete? *Harvard Bus. Rev.*, 1958, 36(6):23–27.

———: Bringing up children in the space age. *Air Force*, 1959, 42(2):71–73.

——— and R. Métraux: Image of the scientist among high-school students. *Science*, 1952, 126:384–390.

——— and M. Wolfenstein (eds.): *Childhood in contemporary cultures*. Chicago: University of Chicago Press, 1955.

Meadow, A., and S. J. Parnes: Evaluation of training in creative problem solving. *J. Appl. Psychol.*, 1959, 43:189–194.

———, ———, and H. Reese: Influence of brainstorming instructions and problem sequence on a creative problem solving test. *J. Appl. Psychol.*, 1959, 43:413–416.

Mearns, H.: *The creative adult*. Garden City, N.Y.: Doubleday, 1941.

————: *Creative power.* New York: Dover, 1958.

Mednick, S. A.: Development of admission criteria for colleges and universities that will not eliminate such applicants as the bright nonconformist, the underchallenged, and the individual with highly specialized ability. In *Current issues in higher education*, Association for Higher Education. Washington, D.C.: National Education Association, 1961, pp. 87–88.

Meehl, P. E.: *Clinical vs. statistical prediction.* Minneapolis: University of Minnesota Press, 1954.

Meer, B., and M. I. Stein: Measures of intelligence and creativity. *J. Psychol.*, 1955, 39:117–126. *Psychol. Abstr.*, 1955, 29:9102.

Meier, N. C.: An instrument for the study of creative artistic intelligence. *Psychol. Monogr.*, 1936, 48:164–172.

————: Factors in artistic aptitude: Final summary of a ten-year study of a special ability. *Psychol. Monogr.*, 1939, 51(5):140–159.

————: Reconstructive imagination. *Psychol. Monogr.*, 1939b, 51:117–126.

Meinz, A. P.: General creativity of elementary education majors as influenced by courses in industrial arts and art education. Unpublished doctoral dissertation, Pennsylvania State University, 1960.

Mettler, F. A. and W. Overholser: Evolution of change in patients after psychosurgery. In *Proc. Second Res. Conf. Psychosurg., Pub. Hlth Serv. Publ.* no. 156, 1953.

Meyers, C. E.: The role of educational measurement in stimulating or discouraging attention to creative thinking in the curriculum. Paper presented at APA, Chicago, September, 1960.

Middendorf, W. H., and G. T. Brown, Jr.: Orderly creative inventing. *Elec. Engrg*, 1957, 76:866–869.

Miel, A. (ed.): *Creativity in teaching: Invitations and instances.* San Francisco: Wadsworth, 1961.

Miller, I. E.: *The psychology of thinking.* New York: Macmillan, 1960.

Milton, G. A.: The effects of sex-role identification upon problem-solving skill. *J. Abnorm. Soc. Psychol.*, 1957, 55:208–212.

Mock, R. A.: Effective design of industrial exploratory research. Midland, Mich.: Dow Chemical Co., 1960. (Mimeographed.)

Mogar, M.: Children's casual reasoning about natural phenomena. *Child Develpm.*, 1960, 31:59–65.

Mooney, R. L.: Groundwork for creative research. *Amer. Psychologist*, 1954, 9:544-548.

————: A conceptual model for integrating four approaches to the identification of creative talent. In *Scientific creativity: Its recognition and development*, C. W. Taylor and F. Barron, 1963, pp. 331–340.

Moore, O. K.: Orthographic symbols and the pre-school child—a new approach. *New educational ideas: Second Minnesota conference on gifted children*, Torrance, 1961.

Morgan, E. S.: What every Yale freshman should know. *Sat. Rev.*, 1960, 43(4):13–14.

Mork, G. M. A.: A science lesson on rocket satellites. *Univer. Kansas Bull. Educ.*, 1959, 13, 86–91.

Mosing, L. W.: Development of a multi-media creativity test. Unpublished doctoral dissertation, Purdue University, 1958. *Dissertation Abstr.*, 1959, 19:2137.

Mullins, C. J.: *The prediction of creativity in a sample of research scientists. USAF Personnel Lab. Rep.*, no. AD 211039. Lackland Air Force Base, Texas, 1959.

Munari, B.: *Who's there? Open the door!* Cleveland: World Publishing, 1957.

———: *The elephant's wish.* Cleveland: World Publishing, 1959.

Murphy, G.: Creativeness. In *Personality: A biosocial approach to origins and structure*, G. Murphy. New York: Harper, 1947, pp. 452–475.

———: *Human potentialities.* New York: Basic Books, 1958.

Murray, H. A.: Vicissitudes of creativity. In *Creativity and its cultivation*, H. H. Anderson, 1959, pp. 96–118.

Myden, W. D.: An interpretation and evaluation of certain personality characteristics involved in creative production: An investigation and evaluation of personality structure and characteristics of creative individual in the context of psychoanalytic theory and ego psychology. *Dissertation Abstr.*, 1957: 897–898.

Myers, R. E., and E. P. Torrance: Can teachers encourage creative thinking? *Educ. Leadership,* December, 1961a, 19:156–159.

——— and ———: *Invitations to thinking and doing* (Workbook of exercises). Minneapolis: Perceptive Publishing, 1961b.

——— and ———: *Teacher's manual for "Invitations to thinking and doing."* Minneapolis: Perceptive Publishing, 1961c.

National Council of Teachers of English: *Creative ways in teaching the language arts* (portfolio). Champaign, Ill., 1954.

Nelles, M.: Deliberate creativeness in science and engineering. *Chem. Engrg News,* 1953, 31(15):1520–1523.

New York City Board of Education: Developing children's power of self-expression through writing. *Curr. Bull.,* 1952–53, no. 2.

Newell, A., J. C. Shaw, and H. A. Simon: Elements of a theory of human problem-solving. *Psychol. Rev.,* 1958a, 65:151–166.

———, ———, and ———: The processes of creative thinking. In *Contemporary approaches to creative thinking*, H. E. Gruber, G. Terrell, and M. Wertheimer (eds.), 1962.

Nicholson, P. J., III: An experimental investigation of the effects of training upon creativity. Unpublished doctoral dissertation, University of Houston, 1959.

Nishibori, M., and K. Shibuya: A study of the validity of the Scholastic Aptitude Tests as compared with the validity of the achievement tests in school subjects as a means of selection for higher education. *Res. Bull. Nat. Inst. Educ. Res., Tokyo,* March, 1961, 2:26–32.

Northrop, F. S. C.: Philosophy's statement of the problem of creativity. In *The nature of creative thinking,* Industrial Relations Institute, 1953.

Northway, M. L., and M. McC. Rooks: Creativity and sociometric status in children. *Sociometry,* 1956, 18:450–457.

O'Brien, M., R. A. Elder, P. Putnam, and M. R. Sewell: Developing creativity in children's use of imagination: Nursery ages two and three. *Union Coll. Stud. Charact. Res.,* 1954, 15:33–42.

Ojemann, R. H.: Are creativity and mental health compatible? In *Creativity and psychological health,* M. F. Andrews, 1961.

Ornstein, J. A.: The nature of creativity. *Sch. Arts,* 1959, 59:18.

———: New recruits for science. *Parents' Mag.,* 1961, 36(42):101–103.

Orowan, E.: Our universities and scientific creativity. *Bull. Atomic Scientists,* 1959, 15:236–239.

Osborn, A. F.: *Your creative power.* New York: Scribner, 1948.

———: *Applied imagination.* New York: Scribner, 1957.

Owens, W. A., C. F. Schumacher, and J. B. Clark: The measurement of creativity in machine design. *J. Appl. Psychol.,* 1957, 41:297–302.

———, ———, and ———: The measurement of creativity in machine design. In *The second (1957) University of Utah research conference on the identification of creative scientific talent,* C. W. Taylor, 1958, pp. 129–140.

Pace, C. R., and Stern, G. G.: An approach to the measurement of psychological characteristics of college environment. *J. Educ. Psychol.,* 1958, 49:269–277.

Pappas, G.: An analysis of the process of beginning and developing works of art. *Dissertation Abstr.,* 1957, 17:2882–2883.

Parnes, S. J.: *Creative retailing.* Harrisburg, Pa.: Department of Public Instruction, 1957.

——— and H. F. Harding: *A source book for creative thinking.* New York: Scribner, 1962.

* ——— and A. Meadow: Development of individual creative talent. *In The third (1959) University of Utah research conference on the identification of creative scientific talent,* C. W. Taylor, 1959a, pp. 187–201.

——— and ———: Effects of "brainstorming" instructions on creative problem solving by trained and untrained subjects. *J. Educ. Psychol.,* 1959, 50:171–176.

——— and ———: Evaluation of persistence of effects produced by a creative problem-solving course. *Psychol. Rep.,* 1960, 7:357–361.

Patri, A.: *The questioning child.* New York: Appleton, 1931.

Patrick, C.: Creative thought in poets. *Arch. Psychol.,* 1935, 26:1–74.

————: Creative thought in artists. *J. Psychol.*, 1937, 4:35–73.

————: Scientific thought. *J. Psychol.*, 1938, 5, 55–83.

————: Whole and part relationship in creative thought. *Amer. J. Psychol.*, January, 1941: 128–131.

————: How creative thought is related to thinking. *Amer. Psychologist*, 1949, 4: 266 (abstr.).

————: *What is creative thinking?* New York: Philosophical Library, 1955.

Pearson, D. S.: *Creativeness for engineers.* University Park: Pennsylvania State University Press, 1958.

Peck, R. F.: What makes a man creative? *Personnel*, 1958, 35(2):18–23.

Peel, E. A.: Experimental examination of some of Piaget's schemata concerning children's perception and thinking and discussion of their educational significance. *Brit. J. Educ. Psychol.*, 1959, 29:98–103.

————: *The pupil's thinking.* London: Oldbourne, 1960.

Peet, H. E.: *The creative individual: A study of new perspectives in education.* New York: Ronald, 1960.

* Pelz, D. C.: Relationships between measures of scientific performance and other variables. In *The 1955 University of Utah research conference on the identification of creative scientific talent*, C. W. Taylor, 1956, pp. 53–61.

Pepinsky, P. N.: *Originality in group production, I: Productive independence in three natural situations.* Columbus, Ohio: Research Foundation, The Ohio State University, 1959.

————: The social dialectic of productive nonconformity. Paper presented at APA, Chicago, September, 1960. *Amer. Psychologist*, 1960a, 15:390 (abstr.).

————: Study of productive nonconformity. *Gifted Child Quart.*, winter, 1960b, 4:81–85.

Petersen, O. L., and J. T. Robinson: Creativity: Some aspects and implications. *Sci. Educ.*, 1959, 43:420–426.

Piaget, J.: *The psychology of intelligence.* London: Routledge, 1951.

————: *The construction of reality in the child.* New York: Basic Books, 1954.

Piers, E. V., J. M. Daniels, and J. F. Quackenbush: The identification of creativity in adolescents. *J. Educ. Psychol.*, 1960, 51:346–351.

Platt, W., and R. A. Baker: The relation of the scientific hunch to research. *J. Chem. Educ.*, 1931:969–2002.

Platz, A., and E. Blakelock: Productivity of American psychologists. *Amer. Psychologist*, 1960, 15:310–312.

Poincaré, H.: Mathematical creation. In *The foundations of science.* New York: Science Press, 1913, pp. 393–394.

President's Commission on National Goals: *Goals for Americans.* Englewood Cliffs, N.J.: Prentice-Hall, 1960.

Pulsifer, S. N.: *Minute magic*. Boston: Chapman & Grimes, 1960.

Pye, D.: Program for upgrading creativeness in research. Pittsburg, Calif.: Dow Chemical Co., 1960. (Mimeographed.)

Rank, O.: *Art and artists* (trans. C. F. Atkinson). New York: Knopf, 1932.

Raskin, E.: A comparison of scientific and literary ability: A bibliography study of eminent scientists and men of letters of the 19th century. *J. Abnorm. Soc. Psychol.*, 1936, 31:20–35.

Raudsepp, E.: The industrial climate for creavity: An opinion study of 105 experts. *Mgmt Rev.*, 1958, 47(9):4–8.

————: Supervisor determines productivity of creative people. *Amer. Bus.* 1960, 30(4):30–32.

————: Why engineers work. *Machine Design*, 1960, 32(3):100–113.

Read, Sir H.: *The significance of children's art*. Vancouver: University of British Columbia Press, 1957.

Reed, C. H.: Developing creative thinking in arithmetic. *Arith. Teacher*, February, 1957, 4:10–12.

Reid, A.: *Ounce, dice, trice*. Boston: Little, Brown, 1958.

————: *Supposing*. Boston: Little, Brown, 1960.

Reid, J. B., F. J. King, and P. Wickwire: Cognitive and other personality characteristics of creative children. *Psychol. Rep.*, 1959, 5:729–738.

Reitman, F.: The "creative spell" of schizophrenics after leucotomy. *J. Ment. Sci.*, 1947, 93:55–61.

Remmers, H. H.: Factors in the early motivation of scientists. In *Strengthening science education for youth and industry*. New York: New York University Press, 1957, pp. 79–90.

Repucci, L. C.: *Definitions and criteria of creativity*. Midland, Mich.: Psychology Department, Dow Chemical Co., 1960 (Mimeographed.)

Rhodes, J. M.: The dynamics of creativity: An interpretation of the literature on creativity with a proposed procedure for objective research. Unpublished doctoral dissertation, University of Arizona. *Dissertation Abstr.*, 1957, 17:96.

Ribot, T.: The nature of creative imagination. *Int. Mon.*, 1900, 1:648–675, and 1900, 2:1–25.

————: *Essay on the creative imagination*. London: Routledge, 1906.

Riesman, D.: "Tootle": A modern cautionary tale. In *Childhood in contemporary cultures*, Mead and Wolfenstein, pp. 236–242.

Rivlin, L. G.: Creativity and the self-attitudes and sociability of high school students. *J. Educ. Psychol.*, 1959, 50:147–152.

Robertson, J. P. S.: Creativity in a middle-aged psychotic: A clinical case report and discussion. *J. Clin. Exp. Psychopathol.*, 1951, 12:222–223.

Roe, A.: A Rorschach study of a group of scientists and technicians. *J. Consult. Psychol.*, 1946a, 10:317–327.

————: Artists and their work. *J. Pers.*, 1946b, 15:1–40.

————: Analysis of group Rorschachs of biologists. *J. Proj. Tech.*, 1949, 13:25–43e.

————: A psychological study of eminent biologists. *Psychol. Monogr.*, 1951a, 65(14).

————: A psychological study of physical scientists. *Genet. Psychol. Monogr.*, May, 1951b, 43:121–239.

————: Analysis of group Rorschachs of psychologists and anthropologists. *J. Proj. Tech.*, 1952a, 16:212–224.

————: *The making of a scientist.* New York: Dodd, Mead, 1952b.

————: A psychological study of eminent psychologists and anthropologists, and a comparison with biological and physical scientists. *Psychol. Monogr.*, 1953, 67(2).

*————: Personal problems and science. In *The third (1959) University of Utah research conference on the identification of creative scientific talent*, C. W. Taylor, 1959a, pp. 202–212.

————: *Science begins at home.* New York: Thomas Alva Edison Foundation, 1959b.

————: Crucial life experiences in the development of scientists. In *Talent and education*, Torrance, 1960, pp. 66–77.

Rogers, C. R.: Toward a theory of creativity. *ETC*, 1954, 11:249–260. Also in *Creativity and its cultivation*, H. H. Anderson, 1959, pp. 69–82.

Rosen, J. C.: The Barron-Welsch Art Scale as a predictor of originality and level of ability among artists. *J. Appl. Psychol.*, 1955, 39:366–367.

Rosenbloom, P. C.: Creativity in mathematics. In *Creativity: Second Minnesota conference on gifted children*, Torrance, 1959, pp. 108–112.

Rossman, J.: *The psychology of the inventor: A study of the patentee.* New York (and rev. ed., Washington, D.C.): Inventors Publishing, 1931.

————: A study of the childhood, education, and age of 710 inventors. *J. Patent Office Soc.*, 1935, 17:411–421.

Rubin, L. J. (ed.): *Nurturing classroom creativity.* Ventura, Calif.: Ventura County Secondary Schools, 1960.

Runner, J. R.: For creative people, creative supervision. *Printers' Ink*, Jan. 25, 1957, 258:27–28.

Runner, K.: Some common patterns. *Adult Leadership*, December, 1954, 3:15–17.

Russell, D. H.: *Children's thinking.* Boston: Ginn, 1956.

Sanders, D. C.: *Elementary education and the academically talented pupil.* Washington, D.C.: National Education Association, 1961.

Sanderson, R. A.: Psychological disturbance and artistic creation. *J. Nerv. Ment. Dis.*, 1953, 117:310–322.

* Saunders, D. R.: Some measures related to success in placement in basic engineering research and development. In *The 1955 University of Utah*

*research conference on the identification of creative scientific talent,* C. W. Taylor, 1956, pp. 23–41.

Schaeffer, E. S., and Bell, R. Q.: Development of a parental attitude research instrument. *Child Developm.,* 1958, 29:339–361.

Schafer, R.: Regression in the service of the ego: The relevance of a psychoanalytic concept for personality assessment. In *Assessment of human motives,* G. Lindzey (ed.). New York: Rinehart, 1958, pp. 119–148.

Scheinfeld, A.: Musical talent. *You and heredity.* New York: Garden City, 1939, pp. 234–288.

Schimek, J. G.: Creative originality: Its evaluation by the use of free-expression tests. Unpublished doctoral dissertation, University of California, Berkeley, 1954.

Schofield, R. W.: A creative climate. *Educ. Leadership,* 1960, 18(1):5–6.

Schultz, W. N.: 25 techniques to help you learn to be more creative. *Sales Mgmt,* July, 1957, 79:34–35.

Seelhorst, R. C.: The relationship between human values, aesthetic performance, aesthetic sensitivity, and sensitivity to problems. Unpublished doctoral dissertation, Pennsylvania State University, 1960.

Shane, H. G., and W. A. Yauch: *Creative school administration.* New York: Holt, 1954.

Shannon, J. R.: Traits of research workers. *J. Educ. Res.,* 1947, 40:513–521.

Sharp, S. E.: Individual psychology. *Amer. J. Psychol.,* 1899, 5(10):371–373.

Shaycroft, M. F., and J. W. Altman: *A procedure for evaluating graduate research on the basis of the thesis.* Pittsburgh, Pa.: American Institute for Research, 1955.

Shockley, W.: On the statistics of individual variations in productivity in research laboratories. *Proc. IRE,* 1957, 45:279–290.

Shulman, H. L.: Creativity and engineering education. *J. Engrg Educ.,* 1956, 47:336–340.

Simpson, R. M.: Creative imagination. *Amer. J. Psychol.,* 1922, 33:234–243.

Singer, J. L.: Imagination and waiting ability in young children. *Personality,* 1961, 29:396–413.

Smith, B.: The engineer as an inventor: A statistical study based on "Who's who in engineering." *Mech. Engrg,* 1934, 56:263–265.

Smith, W. J., L. E. Albright, J. R. Glennon, and W. Owens: The predictor of research competence and creativity from personal history, *J. Appl. Psychol.,* 1961, 45:59–62.

Smith, W. R.: Favorable and unfavorable working conditions reported by scientists at two research centers. In *The third (1959) University of Utah research conference on the identification of creative scientific talent,* C. W. Taylor, 1959, pp. 250–267.

Snyder, R.: *The authentic life: Its theory and practice.* Philadelphia: Friends General Conference, 1959.

Sorokin, P.: A "concept test," and energy of spontaneity-creativity. *Sociometry*, 1949, 12:215–224.

Spearman, C. E.: *Creative mind*. New York: Cambridge, 1930.

* Sprecher, T. B.: A proposal for identifying the meaning of creativity. In *The third (1959) University of Utah research conference on the identification of creative scientific talent*, C. W. Taylor, 1959a, pp. 29–45.

————: A study of engineers' criteria for creativity. *J. Appl. Psychol.*, 1959b, 43:141–148.

Springbett, B. M.: An approach to the measurement of creative thinking. *Canad. J. Psychol.*, 1957, 11:9–20.

————, J. G. Dark, and J. Clarke: An approach to the measurement of creative thinking. *Canad. J. Psychol.*, 1957, 11:9–20.

Stanley, J. C., and P. Thomasson: Peer-rated creativity of prominent psychometricians, *Psychol. Newsltr*, 1957, 4:1–6.

Stanton, H. M.: The inheritance of specific musical capacities. *Psychol. Monogr.*, 1922, 31(1):157–204.

Stauffer, R. G.: Productive reading-thinking at the first grade level. *Reading Teacher*, 1960, 13:183–187.

Stein, M. I.: Creativity and culture. *J. Psychol.*, 1953, 36:311–322.

* ————: A transactional approach to creativity. In *The 1955 University of Utah research conference on the identification of creative scientific talent*, C. W. Taylor, 1956, pp. 171–181.

————: Creativity and/or success: A study in value conflict. In *The second (1957) University of Utah research conference on the identification of creative scientific talent*, C. W. Taylor, 1958, pp. 201–232.

————: Problems involved in predictors of creativity. In *The third (1959) University of Utah research conference on the identification of creative scientific talent*, C. W. Taylor, 1959a, pp. 178–186.

————: Toward developing more imaginative creativity in students. In *The two ends of the log*, R. M. Cooper (ed.). Minneapolis: University of Minnesota Press, 1959b, pp. 69–75.

———— and S. J. Heinze: *Creativity and the individual*. New York: Free Press of Glencoe, 1960.

———— and B. Meer: Perceptual organization in a study of creativity. *J. Psychol.*, 1954, 37:39–43.

Stephenson, W.: *Testing school children*. New York: Longmans, 1949.

Stoddard, G. D.: Creativity in education. In *Creativity and its cultivation*, H. H. Anderson, 1959.

Stoltz, R. E.: Development of a criterion of research productivity. *J. Appl. Psychol.*, 1958, 42:308–310.

————: Factors in supervisors' perceptions of physical science research personnel. *J. Appl. Psychol.*, 1959a, 43:256–258.

————: Subordinates' perceptions of the productive engineer. *J. Appl. Psychol.,* 1959b, 43:306–310.

Strang, R.: Developing creative powers of gifted children. In *Creativity of gifted and talented children.* New York: Teachers College, 1959, pp. 20–31.

Stratton, G. M.: *Man, creator or destroyer.* London: G. Allen, 1952.

Strickland, R. G.: Children, reading and creativity. *Elem. Engl.,* 1957, 34: 234–241.

Strong, L.: Creativity in industry: The care and feeding of new ideas. *Mgmt Rev.,* 1957, 46(3):56–72.

Suchman, J. R.: Inquiry training: Teaching children the skills and strategies of productive thinking in science. Paper read at APA, Chicago, September, 1960a.

————: Inquiry training in the elementary schools. *Sci. Teacher,* 1960b, 27(7):42–47.

————: Inquiry training: Building skills for autonomous discovery. Urbana, Ill.: College of Education, University of Illinois, 1961. (Mimeographed.)

Swartz, D.: Developing creative imagination. *High Points,* 1932, 14:43–46.

Taaffe, G.: *The relation of experimental tests of reasoning and creative thinking to research performance.* ONR contract NR-150-044. Los Angeles, Department of Psychology, University of Southern California, 1953.

Tangerman, E. J.: Creativity: Facts behind fads. *Product Engrg,* 1959, 30(34): 20–23.

Taton, R.: *Reason and change in scientific discovery.* New York: Philosophical Library, 1957.

Tauber, E. S., and M. R. Green: *Prelogical experience.* New York: Basic Books, 1959.

Taylor, C. W. (ed.): *The 1955 University of Utah research conference on the identification of creative scientific talent.* Salt Lake City: University of Utah Press, 1956a.

* ————: Some possible relations between expression abilities and creative abilities. In *The 1955 University of Utah research conference on the identification of creative scientific talent,* C. W. Taylor, 1956, pp. 213–218.

———— (ed.): *The second (1957) University of Utah research conference on the identification of creative scientific talent.* Salt Lake City: University of Utah Press, 1958a.

————: Some variables functioning in productivity and creativity. In *The second (1957) University of Utah research conference on the identification of creative scientific talent,* C. W. Taylor, 1958b, pp. 3–19.

———— (ed.): *The third (1959) University of Utah research conference on the identification of creative scientific talent.* Salt Lake City: University of Utah Press, 1959.

————: The creative individual: A new portrait in giftedness. *Educ. Leadership,* 1960, 18(1):7–12.

————: Some educational implications of creativity research findings. *Sch. Sci. Math.,* December, 1961a, 62(8):593–606.

————: Finding the creative. *Sci. Teacher,* December, 1961b:6–13.

————: Research findings on creative characteristics. *Natl. NAEA Stud. Art Educ.,* 1961c, 3(1):9–17.

————: A tentative description of the creative individual. In *Human variability and learning,* Waetjen, 1961d, pp. 62–79.

————: The criterion-oriented approach to the development of creativity tests. In *ETS West. Invitational Testing Conf.* Los Angeles (May, 1962a), pp. 32–45.

————: Effects of instructional media on creativity: A look at possible positive and negative effects. *Educ. Leadership,* April, 1962b, 19:453–458. See also *Audiovisual Instruction,* June, 1962b, 7(6):376–377.

————: Has America neglected her creative minority? *Utah Alumnus,* February, 1962c: 11–15.

————: The status of research knowledge in creativity and some educational challenges. Paper presented at ASCD (NEA), Las Vegas, March, 1962d.

————: Who are the exceptionally creative? *Except. Child.,* April, 1962e, 28(8):421–431.

———— (ed.): *The fifth (1962) University of Utah research conference report on creative talent.* New York: Wiley, 1964. (In press)

———— and F. Barron (eds.): *Scientific creativity: Its recognition and development.* New York: Wiley, 1963.

————, G. M. Cooley, and E. Nielsen: *Identifying high school students with characteristics needed in research work.* NSF grant, University of Utah, 1963. Rep. No. NSF-G17543. (Mimeographed.)

————, B. Ghiselin, and J. Wolfer: Bridging the gap between basic research and educational practice. *NEA J.,* January, 1962, 51:23–25.

————, B. Ghiselin, J. Wolfer, L. Loy, and L. Bourne: A theory of education based upon psychological and other basic research findings. Unpublished manuscript, University of Utah, 1963.

———— and J. Holland: Development and application of tests of creativity *Rev. Educ. Res.,* February, 1962, 32:91–102.

————, W. R. Smith, and B. Ghiselin: A study of the multiple contributions of scientists at one research organization, *IRE Trans. Engrg Mgmt,* December, 1961, 8:194–200.

————, ————, and ————: The creative and other contributions of one sample of research scientists. In *Scientific creativity: Its recognition and development,* C. W. Taylor and F. Barron, 1963, pp. 53–76.

————, ————, ————, and R. Ellison: *Explorations in the measurement and prediction of contributions of one sample of scientists. USAF Per-*

*sonnel Lab. Rep.*, no. ASD-TR-61-96. Lackland Air Force Base, Texas, 1961.

————, ————, ————, B. V. Sheets, and J. R. Cochran: *Identification of communication abilities in military situations. USAF Personnel Lab. Tech. Rep.* No. WADC-TR-58-92. Wright Air Development Center, Lackland Air Force Base, Texas, 1958.

* Taylor, D. W.: Variables related to creativity and productivity among men in two research laboratories. In *The second (1957) University of Utah research conference on the identification of creative scientific talent*, C. W. Taylor, 1958, pp. 20–54.

————: Thinking and creativity. In *Fundamentals of psychology: The psychology of thinking*, Harms, 1960.

————, P. C. Berry, and C. H. Block: Does group participation when using brainstorming facilitate or inhibit creative thinking? *Yale Univer. Industr. Admin. Psychol. Tech. Rep.*, 1957. Also, *Admin. Sci. Quart.*, 1958, 3:23–47.

———— and C. H. Block: Should group or individual work come first on problems requiring creative thinking when equal time is devoted to each? *Yale Univer. Industr. Admin. Psychol. Tech. Rep.*, 1957.

———— and W. L. Faust: Twenty questions: Efficiency in problem solving as a function of size of group. *J. Exp. Psychol.*, 1952, 44:360–368.

Taylor, I. A.: The nature of creative process. In *Creativity*, P. Smith (ed.). New York: Hastings House, 1959, pp. 51–82.

Taylor, M. J.: Conformity and creativity in the local church. *Relig. Educ.*, 1960, 55:336–340.

Terman, L. M. (ed.): *Genetic studies of genius*. Stanford, Calif.: Stanford University Press, vol. 1, 1925a; vol. 2, 1926; vol. 3, 1930; vol. 4, 1957a.

————: Mental and physical traits of a thousand gifted children. In *Genetic studies of genius*, Terman, vol. 1, 1925b.

————: Scientists and nonscientists in a group of 800 gifted men. *Psychol. Monogr.*, 1954, 68:44.

———— and M. H. Oden: *The gifted child grows up*. In *Genetic studies of genius*, Terman, vol. 4, 1957b.

Thistlethwaite, D. L.: The conservation of intellectual talent. *Science*, 1958, 128:822–826.

* ————: The college environment as a determinant of research potentiality. In *The third (1959) University of Utah research conference on the identification of creative scientific talent*, C. W. Taylor, 1959a, pp. 213–231.

————: College environment and the development of talent. *Science*, 1959b, 130:71–76.

————: Effects of social recognition upon the educational motivation of talented students. *J. Educ. Psychol.*, 1959c, 50:111–116.

————: Merit scholarships and the higher education of gifted students. *J. Higher Educ.*, 1959d, 30:295–304.

Thompson, J. J.: People are for talking: Some suggestions for creative oral language activities. In *Yearb. Claremont Coll. Reading Conf.*, 1957, 22, pp. 75–86.

Thorndike, R. L.: The psychology of invention in a very simple case. *Psychol. Rev.*, 1949, 56:192–199.

Thurstone, L. L.: Creative talent. *Univer. Chicago Psychometr. Lab. Rep.*, no. 61, 1950, p. 10.

————: Creative talent. In *Applications of psychology*, Thurstone (ed.). New York: Harper, 1952a, pp. 18–37.

————: The scientific study of inventive talent. *Univer. Chicago Psychometr. Lab. Rep.*, no. 81, 1952b, p. 6.

————: A psychologist discusses the mechanisms of thinking. In *The nature of creative thinking*, Industrial Relations Institute, 1953.

Tisdall, W. J.: *The efficacy of a special class program on the productive thinking abilities of educable mentally retarded children.* Urbana, Ill.: Institute for Research on Exceptional Children, University of Illinois, 1962.

Torrance, E. P.: Current research on the nature of creative talent. *J. Counsel. Psychol.*, 1959a, 6:309–316.

* ————: Explorations in creative thinking in the early school years: A progress report. In *The third (1959) University of Utah research conference on the identification of creative talent*, C. W. Taylor, 1959b, pp. 58–71.

————: *Rewarding creative thinking: A manual for elementary teachers.* Minneapolis: University of Minnesota Bureau of Educational Research, 1959c. (Mimeographed, out of print.)

————: Creative thinking through the language arts. *Educ. Leadership*, 1960a, 18(1):13–18. Reprinted in *OECTA Rev.*, 1960a, 11(2):12–15.

———— (ed.): *Creativity: Second Minnesota conference on gifted children.* Minneapolis: Center for Continuation Study, University of Minnesota, 1960b.

———— (ed.): *Education and talent.* Minneapolis: University of Minnesota Press, 1960c.

————: Explorations in creative thinking. *Education*, 1960d, 81:216–220.

————: Recent research concerning gifted children. In *Yearb. AACTE*, 1960e, 13, pp. 64–72.

————: Can grouping control social stress in creative activities? *Elem. Sch. J.*, 1961a, 62:139–145.

————: The creative teacher and the school team. *Professional Growth for Teachers*, April, 1961b.

————: The creative teacher and the school team: Problems and pleasures for the principal. *Professional Growth for Principals*, April, 1961c, p. 2.

————: The creatively gifted are cause for concern. *Gifted Child Quart.*, 1961d, 5:79–87.

————: Curriculum frontiers for the elementary gifted pupil—flying monkeys and silent lions. *Except. Child*, 1961e, 28(3):119–127.

————: Factors affecting creative thinking in children: An interim research report. *Merrill-Palmer Quart.*, 1961f, 7:171–180.

————: Give the "devil" his dues. *Gifted Child Quart.*, 1961g, 5:115–119.

———— (ed.): *New educational ideas: Third Minnesota conference on gifted children*. Minneapolis: Center for Continuation Study, University of Minnesota, 1961h.

————: Priming creative thinking in the primary grades. *Elem. Sch. J.*, 1961i, 62:34–41.

————: Problems of highly creative children. *Gifted Child Quart.*, 1961k, 5(2):31–34. Reprinted in *Educ. Dig.*, November, 1961j, 27:40–42.

————: Team leadership through creative administration. *Professional Growth for Administrators*, April, 1961k, pp. 1–2.

————: *Guiding creative talent*. Englewood Cliffs, N.J.: Prentice-Hall, 1962a.

————: Developing creative thinking through school experiences. In *A source book for creative thinking*, Parnes and Harding, 1962b, pp. 31–47.

———— and J. A. Harmon: Effects of memory, evaluative, and creative reading sets on test performance. *J. Educ. Psychol.*, 1961, 52:207–214.

———— and V. J. Punsalan: *Creativity: A new dimension of intelligence* (*CAPCI Bibliography*, no. 9). Washington, D.C.: Association for Supervision and Curriculum, 1961.

Toynbee, A.: Has America neglected its creative minority? *Calif. Mon.*, February, 1962, 72:7–10. See also *Utah Alumnus*, February, 1962: 11–15.

True, G.: *Creativity as a function of idea fluency, practicability and specific training*. Iowa City: State University of Iowa Press, 1956.

Trump, J. L.: *Images of the future*. Washington, D.C.: National Association of Secondary School Principals, 1959.

Tsanoff, R. A.: *The ways of genius*. New York: Harper, 1949.

Tumin, M.: Obstacles to creativity. *ETC*, 1954, 11:261–271.

Tuska, C. D.: *Inventors and inventions*. New York: McGraw-Hill, 1957.

Union College Character Education Project: *Developing creativity in children's use of imagination*. Schenectady, N.Y., 1954. (*See* M. A. O'Brien, R. A. Elder, P. Putnam, and M. R. Sewell.)

University of California, Liberal Arts Department: *Proceedings of University of California* conference on "the creative person." Berkeley, Calif., 1961.

Upjohn, W. J.: The organization of creative talent. In *Creativity*, P. Smith (ed.). New York: Hastings House, 1959, pp. 173–178.

Van Zelst, R. H., and W. A. Kerr: Some correlates of technical and scientific productivity. *J. Abnorm. Soc. Psychol.*, 1951, 46:470–475.

———— and ————: A further note on some correlates of scientific and technical productivity. *J. Abnorm. Soc. Psychol.*, 1952, 47:127–129.

———— and ————: Personality self-assessment of scientific and technical personnel, *J. Appl. Psychol.*, 1954, 38:145–157.

Veatch, J.: The structure of creativity. *J. Educ. Sociol.*, 1953, 27:102–107.

Vernon, M. D.: The development of imaginative construction in children. *Brit. J. Psychol.*, 1948, 39:102–111.

Vernon, P. E.: *The structure of human abilities.* New York: Wiley, 1950.

Vinacke, W. E.: Creative thinking. In *The psychology of thinking.* New York: McGraw-Hill, 1952, pp. 238–261.

Visher, S. S.: *Scientists starred 1903–1943 in "American men of science": A study of collegiate and doctoral training, birthplace, distribution, backgrounds and developmental influences.* Baltimore: Johns Hopkins, 1947.

————: Sources of great men. *Eugen. Quart.*, 1955, 2:103–109.

Von Fange, E. K.: *The creative process in engineering.* Schenectady, N.Y.: General Electric, 1954.

————: *Professional creativity.* Englewood Cliffs, N.J.: Prentice-Hall, 1959.

Waetjen, W. B. (ed.): *Human variability and learning.* Washington, D.C.: Association for Supervision and Curriculum Development, 1961.

Walcott, F. G.: The climate for creative learning. *Univer. Mich. Sch. Educ. Bull.*, 1959, 31:33–36.

Walker, D. E.: Consistent characteristics in the behavior of creative mathematicians and chemists. *Amer. Psychol.*, 1952, 7:371.

Wallace, H. R.: Creative thinking: A factor in sale productivity. *Voc. Guidance Quart.*, 1961:223–226.

Wallas, G.: *The art of thought.* New York: Harcourt, Brace, 1926.

Wallen, N. E., and G. M. Stevenson: Stability and correlates of judged creativity in fifth grade writings. *J. Educ. Psychol.*, 1960, 51:273–276.

Wallen, R. W.: Unlocking human creativity. *Machine Design*, 1958, 30(6): 132–138.

Warren, J. R., and P. A. Heist. Personality attributes of gifted college students, *Science*, 1960, 132:330–337.

Weinlander, A. A.: *Your child in a scientific world.* Garden City, N.Y.: Doubleday, 1959.

Weisberg, P. S., and K. J. Springer: Environmental factors influencing creative function in gifted children. Cincinnati: Department of Psychiatry, Cincinnati General Hospital, 1961. (Mimeographed.)

Weisskopf-Joelson, E. A.: Some comments concerning the role of education in the creation of creation. *J. Educ. Psychol.*, 1951, 42:185–189.

———— and T. S. Eliseo: An experimental study of the effectiveness of brainstorming. *J. Appl. Psychol.*, 1961, 45:45–49.

Weitman, M., and H. E. Gruber: Experiments in self-directed study: Effects of immediate achievement, permanence of achievement and educational values. Paper presented at West. Psychol. Assoc., San Jose, Calif., April, 1960.

Welch, L.: Recombination of ideas in creative thinking. *J. Appl. Psychol.* 1946, 30:638–643.

Wertheimer, M.: *Productive thinking.* New York: Harper, 1945.

Wherry, R. J.: Criteria and validity. In *Handb. Appl. Psychol.,* vol. 1, D. H. Fryer and E. R. Henry (eds.). New York: Rinehart, 1950, pp. 170–177.

White, R. K.: Note on the psychopathology of genius. *J. Soc. Psychol.,* 1930, 1:311–315.

————: The versatility of genius. *J. Soc. Psychol.,* 1931, 2:460–489.

Whiting, C. S.: *Creative thinking.* New York: Reinhold, 1958.

Wild, M. K.: Creative writing and achievement in solving developmental tasks in the elementary school. *Dissertation Abstr.,* 1957:2888–2889.

Williams, F. E.: *Foundations of creative problem solving.* Ann Arbor, Mich.: Edwards, 1960.

Willman, R. H.: An experimental investigation of the creative process in music. *Psychol. Monogr.,* 1944, 57(1):76.

Wilson, R. C.: A factor-analytic study of creative thinking. Unpublished doctoral dissertation, University of Southern California, 1953.

————: Research aspects of the program for the gifted children in the Portland, Oregon Public Schools. Paper presented at AAAS, Berkeley, Calif., December, 1954.

————: The program for gifted children in the Portland, Oregon, Schools. In *The 1955 University of Utah research conference on the identification of creative scientific talent,* C. W. Taylor, 1956, pp. 14–22.

————: Creativity. In *Education for the gifted, Yearb. Nat. Soc. Stud. Educ.,* 1958, 57, pp. 108–126.

————: Adaptation of the school to the needs of the creative child. In *Creativity: Second Minnesota conference on gifted children,* Torrance, 1959, pp. 54–66.

————: Developing creativity in children. *Education,* 1960, 81:19–23.

————, J. P. Guilford, and P. R. Christensen: The measurement of individual difference in originality. *Psychol. Bull.,* 1953, 50(5):362–370.

————, ————, ————, and D. J. Lewis: A factor analytic study of creative thinking abilities. *Psychometrika,* 1954, 19:297–311.

Wilson, R. N.: Poetic creativity, process and personality. *Psychiatry,* 1954, 17:163–176.

Wilt, M. E.: *Creativity in the elementary school.* New York: Appleton-Century-Crofts, 1959.

Winch, W. H.: Substance memory and productive imagination in school children. *Brit. J. Psychol.,* 1911, 4:95–125.

Wolfenstein, M.: French parents take their children to the park. In *Childhood in contemporary cultures,* Mead and Wolfenstein, 1955, pp. 99–117.

Wolfle, D.: Diversity of talent. *Amer. Psychologist,* 1960, 15:535–545.

Woods, M. S.: Learning through creative dramatics. *Educ. Leadership,* 1960, 18(1):19–24.

Woodworth, D. G.: A factorial study of trait-rankings used in an assessment of professional research scientists. Paper read at West Psychol. Assoc., Monterey, Calif., April, 1958.

Wrenn, B. and K.: *Fun for everybody: Songs for children.* Cincinnati, Ohio: Willis Music Co., 1949.

Yamamoto, K.: Creativity and sociometric choice among adolescents. Unpublished masters research paper, University of Minnesota, 1960a.

———: Further analysis of ask- and guess-test results. *Res. Memo* BER-60-11. Minneapolis: Bureau of Educational Research, University of Minnesota, 1960b.

———: The role of creative thinking and intelligence in high school achievement. *Res. Memo* BER-60-10. Minneapolis: Bureau of Educational Research, University of Minnesota, 1960c.

———: Creativity and intellect: Review of current research and projection. Paper presented at Minnesota Psychol. Assoc., Minneapolis, April, 1961.

Young, J. F.: Developing creative engineers. *Mech. Engrg,* 1945, 67(2):843–846.

Young, J. W.: *A technique for producing ideas.* Chicago: Advertising Publications, 1949.

Ziegfield, E.: *Art for the academically talented student in the secondary school.* Washington, D.C.: National Education Association, 1961.

Ziller, R. C., R. D. Behringer, and J. D. Goodchilds: Group creativity under conditions of success or failure and variations in group stability. Paper read at APA, Chicago, September, 1960. *Amer. Psychol.,* 1960, 15:429 (abstr.).

Zirbes, L.: The contribution of creative education to human development and fulfillment. In *Aesthetic form and education,* M. F. Andrews (ed.). Syracuse: Syracuse University Press, 1958, pp. 38–49.

———: *Spurs to creative teaching.* New York: Putnam, 1959.

Zwicky, F.: *Morphological astronomy.* Berlin: Springer Verlag, 1957.

# INDEX